Christmas 2000

Dear Jeff,

Here is something to help you as you learn all that Bible history and hope it helps all those facts come alive. For those late night studying, the bookmark to remind you that you are not walking the path of ministry alone. You have friends in high places looking out for you and watching over you and always ready to help you with the cross you may carry if you only ask in His Name.

Love and Prayers,
Claire (the other voice behind the CBT)

CONCISE
BIBLE
ATLAS

CONCISE BIBLE ATLAS

A Geographical Survey of Bible History

J. CARL LANEY

Hendrickson Publishers, Inc.
P.O. Box 3473
Peabody, Massachusetts 01961-3473

Printed in the United States of America
ISBN 1-56563-366-0

First Printing—March 1998

To **Jim Monson**
Whose teaching of historical geography
kindled my love for the Land of the Bible

Contents

List of Maps

Introduction
Why Historical Geography?

G*eography*—the colorful and multi-dimensional stage upon which all of history's lessons are unfolded! The word itself is derived from the Greek *ge* ("earth") and *grapho* ("write") and literally means "earth description." The ancient Greeks coined the term and were also the first to develop geography as a scientific discipline. But geography is so much more than a collection of measurements and tabulations of interest to only the academician.

Geography can be broadly defined as "the science that describes the surface of the earth and its associated phenomena, including its climates, peoples, animals, and products." These factors are vital elements in our planet's development and in many ways determine the destiny of civilizations—their economic base, political confrontations, military campaigns, travel routings, location of cities, and designation of national borders.

Although highly significant in the area's historical development, much of the geography of the Bible lands is unfamiliar to modern readers of Scripture. Most Christians today live in a culture and geographical setting far removed from that in which the biblical events occurred. Yet, ignorance of the physical setting of the saving events of one's faith is a distinct and underrated liability in biblical and theological studies.

This book explores the fascinating biblical lands and their remarkable history. The basic approach will be to trace the biblical chronology and examine broad historical periods and their major events in the context of their geographical settings. Although our study will include all the biblical history and locations, the special focus will be on the land of "Israel," or "Palestine," as it is also called.

The Significance of Biblical Geography

For those who have never traveled to the Holy Land or used a biblical atlas, the geography of the lands of the Scriptures may seem to have little relevance to either Christianity or the other major faith systems that have developed in that area of the world. There are at least four reasons why the study of biblical geography is both important and satisfying.

First, a basic knowledge of the physical and climatic features of the land is necessary for a proper intellectual understanding of the Bible's narrative. Scripture is not merely a treatise on ethics or theology, although it does outline the development of the Judeo-Christian tradition. Rather, it is the historical record of how God involved himself with his people at particular times and places. G. Ernest Wright has remarked, "Geography, history, and religion are so inextricably bound together in it [the Bible] that the religious message cannot be truly understood without attention to the setting and conditions of the revelation" (*Westminster Bible Atlas*, p. 5).

A familiarity with geographical circumstances will enable the student, or even the cursory reader, to more accurately scrutinize and interpret the biblical events. For example, when reading 1 Samuel 17, one might wonder why the Israelite and Philistine armies were at a standoff, why the Philistines did not simply advance across the Ela Valley to engage the outnumbered and underequipped Israelites. Why did the two forces face each other across the valley for forty days? But a survey of the Ela Valley reveals that it is divided by a deep ravine that the Philistine war chariots could not cross. And, since the ridge on each side was easily defended, making it impossible for either army to attack on foot, it was not until the Philistine champion, Goliath, challenged the Israelite warriors to a contest that the deadlock was broken. Many clarifications of this sort result from a study of geographical conditions.

Second, geography—by providing a rich and decorative backdrop for the dramatic events of biblical history—heightens the sensory and emotional impact of the narrative. Studying the text without a basic knowledge of its physical setting is like watching a play without scenery. The interrelationships in any series of events cannot be fully comprehended apart from a consideration of where they took place. This is especially applicable to studying the Bible, a setting where land features are so varied and yet so vital in determining the script and human reactions in this stranger-than-fiction saga. In short, geographical data helps us to relate in depth to this fascinating cast of characters as living, breathing fellow humans.

How can one fully appreciate Israel's sufferings during the wilderness wanderings without giving attention to the barren and desolate conditions of the Sinai? How can the incident of Gideon and the fleece be meaningful unless we know about the heavy dew that characterizes the Valley of Jezreel? How was David so successful in eluding Saul by hiding in the Wilderness of Judah? Again, an understanding of geography illuminates the setting and suggests answers to such questions.

Picture the scene and mentally join the actors! Within the confines of a land approximately fifty miles wide (east to west) and a hundred and fifty miles long (north to south), there is an almost infinite variety of settings. From the slopes of 9,100-foot Mount Hermon to the shores of the Dead Sea (1,300 feet below sea level), one moves through lush Galilean greenery to the salt-encrusted fringes of the Judean wilderness. Numerous hills, valleys, rivers, and streams dot the landscape. Few of these features are without biblical or historical significance. The Bible lands are especially notable for their unusually distinctive topographical features. For example, the longest and deepest rift on the earth's surface runs through the Jordan Valley and Dead Sea and then continues through the Gulf of Eilat into Africa.

Without a knowledge of the unique geography of the Bible lands, readers of Scripture tend to project their own settings into the text, yet these lands are far too unusual to be subject to such generalizations. For example, before studying Israel's geography, I had thought of the "mountains of Judah" in terms of my own experience with the Oregon Cascades. Such comparisons are faulty and hinder one's proper understanding of the biblical texts.

Third, familiarity with biblical geography is important for one's theological view. The mighty works of God in history serve as the very foundation of our faith. Through the historical deliverance of Israel from Egypt, God revealed himself to his people as Deliverer. In the same way, the resurrection of Jesus exemplified the saving power of God and became the central element of the gospel proclamation. We have already shown that history and geography are interwoven. As C. H. Dodd affirms in *History and the Gospel*, "Some religions can be indifferent to historical fact, and move entirely upon the plane of timeless truth. Christianity cannot."

Christianity must ever be aware of history, because it rests on the affirmation of a series of actual events. Doing theology without regard for the very real setting of those events can lead to an over-spiritualization of the text, which is equivalent to denying essential elements of the faith. To neglect either history or its geographical setting is to omit important aspects of divine revelation, a position that can lead only to an inadequate view of God.

Fourth, the study of biblical geography has an important relevance to the teaching of the Scriptures. An effective Bible teacher uses the geography of Bible lands as a framework for presenting historical information. Many travelers in those lands have acknowledged that the Bible truly came alive in that geographical environment. Viewing pictures of biblical sites and identifying them on maps—both ancient and contemporary—provides the same kind of experience. Associating events with their locations furnishes a natural background for the historical narrative and imparts a memorable sense of reality to the Bible as nothing else will do. As geographer James Fleming has said, "An up-to-date atlas—maybe more than one—is a tool no serious student of the Bible can be without."

Identifying Biblical Sites

There still remains considerable debate over the location of some of the important biblical sites. Is Cana of Galilee—the setting of the water-into-wine miracle—to be identified with Kefr Kenna or Khirbet Kana? One site boasts an ancient church and displays purported remains of the stone vessels used by Jesus to change the water to wine at the wedding feast. How reliable is Kefr Kenna's claim to be the authentic site of this miracle? How about biblical Emmaus? Is it to be located at Amwas? On which side of the Jordan is the site of Bethsaida?

Although such questions may not matter to the average reader, they require that biblical geographers think carefully about their procedures for identifying a site. Although it is not within the scope of this text to present a detailed analysis of the arguments involving disputed sites, some basic ground rules must be established. The late American archaeologist William Foxwell Albright suggested that a geographer must consider five aspects of a topographical problem. A brief mention of those points will prepare us for future discussion of certain debated sites.

1. *Critical study of the written sources in which the ancient place-name appears.* All written manuscripts in which the name occurs must be evaluated with a view to establishing the most reliable reading found in the ancient texts.

2. *Approximate location of the site from related documentary indications.* The geographer must analyze accounts of journeys, military campaigns, and city lists to select the most likely location for an ancient site. Military defenses, communication routes, water supply, and agricultural factors are among the factors that must be considered in the identification process.

3. *Linguistic analysis of place-names and their cross-cultural transmission.* This process begins by comparing an ancient place-name with its modern counterpart(s). Even though the ancient name is preserved among local residents up to the present, there is a need for caution. Not every name preserved from earlier times has remained attached to its original site.

4. *Archaeological indications.* If a site can be generally located in a certain district, careful examination of all possible sites in the entire area may yield the correct identification. This is done by comparing the available written sources with the documented periods of occupation, as determined by geographical survey and/or archaeological excavation. The site in question must meet the expected requirements from the standpoint of its size and nature of settlement.

5. *Evidence of tradition.* Unwritten legends and traditions are sometimes helpful in pinpointing a biblical site. However, this approach must be used with great care, since many traditions are relatively recent, dating from the Crusades (A.D. 1099–1291) or even later—far removed in time from the actual series of events linked to the site.

Establishing a Biblical Chronology

Simply stated, history is a systematic record of past events. Chronology serves as the backbone of history, in that it establishes the order and dates for the events. Chronology is essential for any thorough study of history, and biblical history allows for no deviation from that rule.

A foundation for biblical chronology has been established by comparing events recorded in Scripture with ancient Assyrian annals. These records list the names of certain rulers and principal astronomical events of the year, such as the eclipse of June 15, 763 B.C. Examples of important dates established through such lists are the Battle of Qarqar (853 B.C.), the tribute of Jehu to Shalmaneser III (841 B.C.), the western campaign of Tiglath-pileser III (743 B.C.), the conquest of Samaria (722 B.C.), and the attack on Jerusalem by Sennacherib (701 B.C.). Although a rough chronology of other biblical events can be established as we work backward or forward from these commonly recognized dates, such study is not without its difficulties.

A major problem in establishing a biblical chronology involves harmonizing the purported "biblical dates" with the archaeological evidence. If excavation determines that a certain site was not occupied at the time of its supposed association with a specified biblical event, it has been generally assumed that the Scripture is in error and that the dates attached to certain events be adjusted accordingly. Although there is certainly room to refine our understanding of the biblical dating system, another possible explanation to be considered is that the archaeological data are either incomplete or have been misinterpreted. Perhaps the site in question is not the one to which the Bible refers! A cautious approach necessitates exploring numerous alternatives before rejecting or modifying the biblical information.

Some of the problem areas discussed by those who have devoted themselves to the study of biblical chronology include the birth of Abraham, the exodus, the conquest of Canaan, the duration of the period of the judges, the division of the monarchy, the date of Ezra's return to Jerusalem, and the year of Christ's crucifixion. It is not within the scope of this survey to tackle these problems in depth. The chronology presented in these pages is based on thorough study of the biblical record, with equal attention given to other ancient texts and pertinent archaeological findings. (For further study on the subject, a good reference is Jack Finegan's *Handbook of Biblical Chronology* [Princeton University Press, 1964]).

The chronological table below represents a general consensus on the key dates and events of the biblical period.

B.C.
2166 Birth of Abraham
1876 Jacob's entrance into Egypt
      430-year Egyptian sojourn
1526 Moses born in Egypt
1446 Exodus of Israel from Egypt
1406 Conquest of Canaan by Joshua
      Period of the judges (325 years)
1168 Major invasion of "the sea people" (Philistines)
1050 Saul anointed king
1010 David rises to kingship
 966 Building of Solomon's temple
 931 Division of the kingdom
          Kingdom of Israel in the north (10 tribes)
          Kingdom of Judah in the south (2 tribes)
 733 Capture of Galilee by Tiglath-pileser
 722 Capture of Samaria by Sargon II

605   Deportation of Daniel by Nebuchadnezzar
597   Deportation of 10,000 Judeans by Nebuchadnezzar
586   Destruction of Jerusalem by Babylonians and exile to Babylon
539   Fall of Babylon to Cyrus
538   Decree of Cyrus to rebuild the Jerusalem temple
537   Return by Sheshbazzar to rebuild the temple
458   Return by Ezra to establish worship in the temple
444   Return by Nehemiah to rebuild the walls of Jerusalem
332   Alexander the Great's conquest of Persia
301   Ptolemies rule Palestine from Egypt
198   Seleucids rule Palestine from Syria
167   The Maccabean revolt
164   Jerusalem temple cleansed by the Maccabees
 63   Pompey conquers Jerusalem; beginning of Roman rule
 37   King Herod established as ruler of Judea
5/4   Birth of Christ

A.D.

 33   Crucifixion of Christ
 66   First Jewish revolt
 68   Execution of the apostle Paul
 70   Destruction of Jerusalem by Titus
131   Second Jewish revolt, led by Bar Kokhba
135   Jerusalem rebuilt Roman-style by Emperor Hadrian

The time has now come to begin exploring the lands of the Bible—the places and the people woven into the rich tapestry of human history in a broad region of the ancient world.

1

The Primeval Period
Creation to 2166 B.C.

Civilization had its birth and childhood in the eastern Mediterranean region known as the Fertile Crescent. This broad land area stretches north from the Persian Gulf along the Tigris and Euphrates Rivers to the mountains of eastern Turkey and then extends southward along the eastern Mediterranean seacoast into the delta and Nile Valley of Egypt.

Most of the region is quite fertile, being watered by the great rivers of Mesopotamia and Egypt and the moisture-laden winds of the Mediterranean. The modern countries of Iraq, Syria, Lebanon, Israel, Jordan, and Egypt are the primary beneficiaries of this agriculturally productive terrain. It is to the eastern half of the crescent that the beginnings of biblical history may be traced.

Early Biblical History in Mesopotamia

The primeval history recorded in Genesis includes creation (1–2), the fall (3:1–6:4), the flood (6:5–8:14), and the new beginning by Noah's family (8:15–11:27).

Since there was no eyewitness at the creation of the physical universe, we must rely on God to tell us how it took place. Such an account is provided in the first two chapters of Genesis, although debate rages

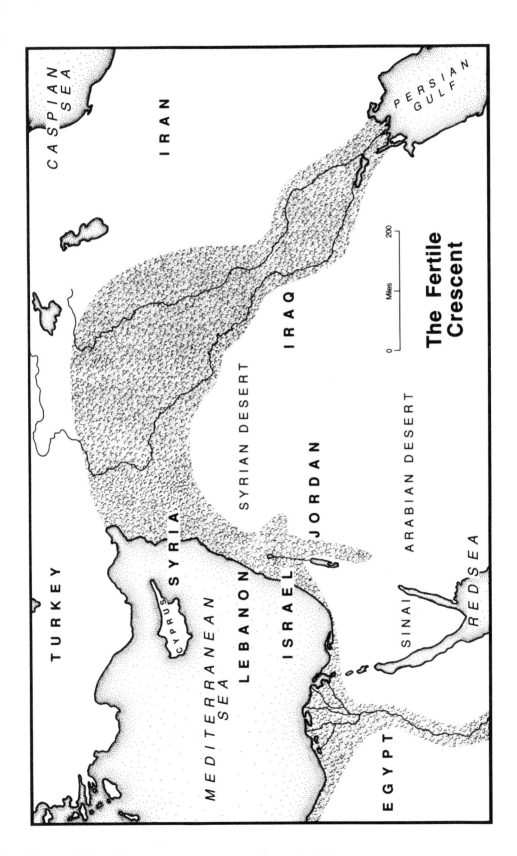

The Fertile
Crescent

among biblical scholars and scientists as to whether this account is to be interpreted literally or figuratively. It would not advance the purpose of this study to enter into that discussion, but the biblical text would clearly affirm that creation was no accident. Creation was a supernatural event that took place as a result of God's spoken word. The expression "without form and void" (Gen. 1:2) is the literary key for the creation account which documents that God both formed and filled the heavens and the earth (Gen. 1:3–31).

God provided the first couple with an ideal environment—a lovely garden "in Eden, in the east" (Gen. 2:8). The term *Eden* is probably not a proper name, but is derived from the Sumerian word for "plain" or "steppe." It would be futile to try to pinpoint the garden's location, but it appears to be to the east of Palestine, probably in Mesopotamia. This is suggested by the reference to the river that flowed from the garden and divided into four streams, including the Tigris and the Euphrates (Gen. 2:10–14).

Many scholars have been impressed by the similarities between the biblical account of creation and the Babylonian version, Enuma Elish, composed about 1800 B.C. Both accounts have a similar order of events and make frequent use of the number seven. Yet the differences are significant. Genesis has a monotheistic view of God, whereas the Babylonian account is clearly polytheistic and seems confused and contradictory in comparison with the beauty and simplicity of the biblical record. In Enuma Elish, matter is eternal—Tiamat's corpse is made into the firmament from which the earth is fashioned. The biblical record views matter as created—separate from the Creator. Perhaps both narratives drew from a common, older source, which would account for the similarities and allow for the differences that reflect opposing world views.

The fall of man (Gen. 3) resulted in the corruption of the human family. God eventually judged man's ever-increasing wickedness by a worldwide deluge from which Noah, his family and the animals appointed to their care were the sole escapees. They took refuge in Noah's ark, which was more like a barge than a ship. It was approximately 450 feet long, 75 feet broad, and 45 feet high, large enough to contain 522 modern railroad boxcars. Since two of each of the air-breathing creatures in the world today could be comfortably carried in a mere 150 boxcars, it would appear that there was no shortage of space on the ark. As the waters receded, the ark settled on the high "mountains of Ararat" in the Armenian region of eastern Turkey. Although Scripture identifies only the region, not the precise peak, Mount Ararat (16,916 feet) has been traditionally viewed as the resting place of Noah's ark.

There is no end to the debate among scholars as to whether the flood

Noah's Ark

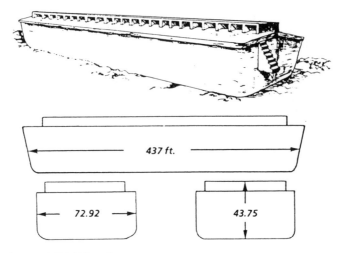

437 ft.

72.92

43.75

Volume: 1,396,000 cu. ft.
Gross tonnage: 13,960 tn.

was universal or local. While a global deluge is beyond the comprehension of rational, modern man, that appears to be the viewpoint expressed in the biblical text. The waters covered all the mountains of the earth (Gen. 7:19–20) and resulted in the destruction of all living creatures (v. 21). The duration (371 days) suggests that it was something other than a local, seasonal flood.

Accounts of a universal flood are found in the legends of almost every culture on earth. The most famous of these accounts is the Babylonian version in the Epic of Gilgamesh. It tells of a man called Uta-napishtim and his wife, who built a boat and became the sole survivors of a universal flood. Likewise, the Hopi Indians in the American Southwest and the Incas in the Peruvian Andes have legends of a great flood that covered the tops of the mountains and destroyed virtually all life on earth.

There is even scientific evidence for such a far-reaching flood. Examination of cores of sediment from the Gulf of Mexico indicate a dramatic change in salinity about 11,600 years ago. At this time, during the last Ice Age, the North American ice cap began rapidly melting, releasing a huge amount of ice-melt water down the Mississippi River into the Gulf of Mexico and causing coastal flooding around the world. A massive tidal wave, created by the rush of water into the gulf, circled the globe, destroying settlements and forcing inland migrations. Was this the biblical flood? While this documentation does not match exactly with the Genesis account, it illustrates that there is an increasingly positive attitude in the scientific community toward the possibility of such a universal deluge as is recorded in Scripture.

After the flood, God instructed Noah and his family to "be fruitful and multiply, and fill the earth" (Gen. 9:1). The human family experienced a new beginning. Noah's descendants are recorded in the "table of nations" (Gen. 10). Chronologically this record follows the Tower of Babel incident (Gen. 11: 1–9) which reveals why the people were scattered. Genesis 10 catalogs *where* Noah's descendants were dispersed.

Noah had three sons—Japheth, Ham, and Shem. The sons of Japheth became the northern nations—the Indo-Europeans. The sons of Ham became the southern nations—the Africans. And the sons of Shem became the central nations—the Semitic peoples. Shem, "the father of all the children of Eber" (Gen. 10:21) is thought to be the chief forefather of the Hebrew people. Abraham, the commonly acknowledged father of the Hebrew nation is a descendant of Shem through Eber (Gen. 11:10–26).

Careful study of biblical chronology indicates that the birth of Abraham can be dated about 2166 B.C. It is not possible to provide precise dating for biblical events prior to Abraham. Although the genealogies in Genesis 5 and 11 have been used by some in attempting to date earlier events, it is quite evident that the genealogies contain gaps (cf. Gen. 11:13, Luke 3:36). The purpose of a genealogy is to trace a family line back to a chief progenitor, not to establish a precisely dated historical record. Abraham is the earliest biblical figure to whom a date may be applied with any accuracy.

Abraham was a Semite living in Mesopotamia. Little more is known of his background. He was called Abram ("exalted father") until God changed his name to Abraham or "father of a multitude" (Gen. 17:5).

Joshua 24:2 reports that Terah, Abraham's father, "served other gods." The primary deity worshiped at Ur was the moon god, Sin (the equivalent of the Sumerian Nanna).

While Abram/Abraham was living in Ur, the ancient capital of the Sumerian kingdom, he was called to leave his homeland and travel to a place God had yet to reveal (Gen. 12:1). This was the future patriarch's first step away from people and situations that might hinder his obedience to God—a step of faith into the unknown.

The Land of Mesopotamia

The name *Mesopotamia* is the transliteration of two Greek words meaning "between [the] rivers." The rivers referred to are the Tigris

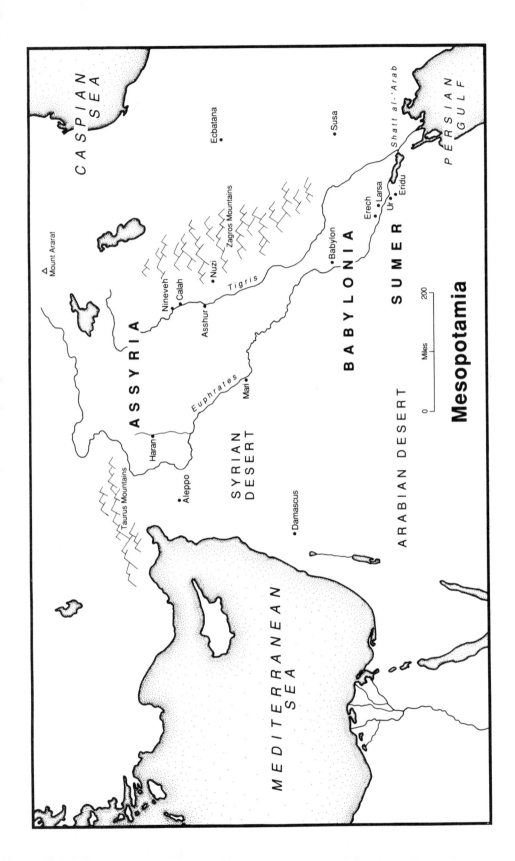

and the Euphrates. The term corresponds to the one used in the Hebrew Scriptures, Aram-naharaim, "Aram of the two rivers" (Gen. 24:10; Deut. 23:4; Judg. 3:8).

Mesopotamia is situated within present-day Iraq and the term is used to refer to the alluvial plain between and on either side of the Tigris and Euphrates. This region forms something of a rectangle, tilting northeast and measuring about 600 miles long and 200 miles wide. Although bordered by the Taurus Mountains on the north and the Zagros Mountains on the east, the elevation of most of Mesopotamia is less than 600 feet above sea level.

Rivers of Mesopotamia

The Tigris and Euphrates rivers are the central physical features of the area. They made irrigation possible and encouraged a stable agricultural economy in Mesopotamia. Both the Tigris (to the east) and the Euphrates (to the west) originate in the mountains of Ararat in today's Turkey. They flow southeast, swinging within about twenty miles of each other near Baghdad and then uniting into one river, the Shatt al-'Arab, about a hundred miles north of where they empty into the Perisan Gulf. As previously noted, the Tigris and Euphrates were two of the four streams that branched from the river flowing from the Garden of Eden (Gen. 2:10–14).

The northern stretches of the two rivers cut deeply into permanent beds of rock and have remained unchanged since early times. However, the riverbeds in the alluvial plain have frequently been altered by flooding. This has left some settlements isolated and necessitated their relocation. Tells ("mounds") marking the sites of the ancient Sumerian cities of southern Mesopotamia have little relationship to the present river channels.

One of the most striking features of the Tigris and Euphrates is the heavy content of silt they carry. Little of this sediment reaches the Persian Gulf; it is generally deposited on the vast alluvial plain of which Mesopotamia is composed.

The Tigris River arises on the southern slopes of the Taurus Mountains and the western slopes of the Zagros. The river is actually fed by streams flowing from the Zagros Mountains all along its 1,180-mile journey to the Persian Gulf. Because of its proximity to the Zagros Mountains on the east, the Tigris is generally swifter and carries more water than the Euphrates. Calculations have shown that the Tigris sometimes removes as much as three million tons of eroded soil from the mountain highlands in a single day. In ancient times, the upper part of the river could be navigated by rafts, and the lower part by small boats. The ancient capitals of the Assyrians—Nineveh, Calah, and Asshur—are three of the major cities situated along the banks of the Tigris. Like the Euphrates, the lower Tigris has changed course several times during its history, necessitating the relocation of many settlements once dotting its banks.

The Euphrates is referred to in Scripture as "the River" (Josh. 24:3) and serves as one of the boundaries of the Promised Land (Gen. 15:18). It arises on the slopes of the Taurus Mountains and flows 1,700 miles to the Persian Gulf. On the way, it swings west to within 90 miles of the Mediterranean Sea. Navigation on the Euphrates was difficult, due to its many rapids, but this river was more valuable for irrigation than the Tigris because the floods were not as devastating.

The Euphrates served as the main travel route between the Mesopotamian cities and the Mediterranean region. The ancient people of this region sought to establish trade with more prosperous Egypt to the south. Major cities along the banks of the Euphrates include Ur, Erech, and Babylon.

Climate of Mesopotamia

An understanding of the climate of Mesopotamia helps one to appreciate the importance of the two rivers. In the alluvial plain, July and August temperatures reach 120°F. (108° in the shade!). Archaeological excavations are limited to the winter months, when the weather is cooler. Since Mesopotamia gets no more than about four to eight inches of rainfall annually, the great fertility of this region is dependent upon the seasonal flooding of the rivers. Yet the water must be properly distributed. Excessive runoff from melting snow brings floods, which can destroy the dikes and canals. A low river, on the other hand, means drought and famine.

Both rivers have two flood periods. The first, from November until March, is due to rain in the mountains. The main flood period is in April and May and results from the runoff of the winter snowpack. The volume drops off rapidly in June, leaving a layer of moist silt for summer crops. Even in ancient times, the flooding was controlled through a vast system of dikes and canals. Such projects required cooperation among people, so they worked together to survive and eventually gathered into communities and formed governments. It is believed that inhospitable climate and geography more than any other factors encouraged the rise of civilization in Mesopotamia.

One of the major problems for Mesopotamian agriculture has been the salinization of the soil. The irrigation water from the rivers is slightly saline. When evaporation takes place under the hot summer sun, the minerals and salts are drawn to the surface of the ground. Salt is also forced to the surface by rising groundwater. Since there is little rain to wash and cleanse the soil, the salts and minerals remain. The cumulative effect over the centuries has been significant.

The Mesopotamian farmer estimates the value of land by its salt content. He knows that even .5 percent of salt means no wheat. With 1 percent, there will be no barley; with 2 percent of salt even the date palms stop bearing fruit. The salinization of the soil is probably the major factor contributing to the decline of civilization in southern Mesopotamia and the cultural shift to the north.

Economy of Mesopotamia

Although Mesopotamia has no significant deposits of minerals, stone, or timber, the region is a consistent food producer. Agricultural products have been traded through the centuries for items the Mesopotamians did not have the raw materials to produce.

The rich alluvial soil deposited by the flooding Tigris and Euphrates provides a solid basis for agriculture. The alluvium averages sixteen to twenty-three feet in depth and is up to thirty-six feet deep in some places. Mesopotamia has been primarily a pastoral and agricultural society where its people raise camels, sheep,and goats and grow wheat, barley, and dates. It is reported that eighteen million date trees (of which there are over three hundred different varieties) line the riverbanks of the region.

Clay was ancient Mesopotamia's most important resource for construction. Buildings were made of baked clay bricks, and clay was also used for pottery and writing tablets. Wool and flax provided material for clothing. River boats and rafts were made from the giant reeds that grow in swampy regions.

Regions of Mesopotamia

From the viewpoint of biblical history, Mesopotamia had two geographical centers—Assyria and Babylonia. The ancient Assyrians, who reached their peak of power during the eighth and early-seventh centuries B.C., occupied the region north of the "waist" (where the rivers nearly join) to the Taurus Mountains. The Babylonians occupied the area between the "waist" and the Persian Gulf. They reached their zenith in the late-seventh century B.C. and continued as a powerful influence in the ancient Near East until Cyrus' conquest of Babylon in 539 B.C. Both of these ancient powers were invaders and oppressors of Israel.

Assyria, in the northern region of Mesopotamia, is at a higher elevation than Babylonia to the south. The land is hilly and even mountainous along its northern and eastern borders. These mountains gave the people of the north greater access to timber and stone. There, too, the rainfall was sufficient for farming without irrigation.

Assyria was first governed by independent kings, of which little is known. Her rulers often vied for control over Mesopotamia with the rulers of Babylonia, with Assyria eventually becoming the more dominant of the two ancient power centers. The Assyrians periodically expanded their borders to the west, depending on the strength of those living in those outlying regions.

Assyria rose to its greatest period of strength and expansion in the ninth through seventh centuries B.C. During most of this period, the capital was at Asshur. Ashurnasirpal II (883–859 B.C.) moved the capital to Calah. Sennacherib (705–681 B.C.) established Nineveh as the capital, and it remained so until its fall in 612 B.C.

It was Tiglath-pileser III (745–727 B.C.) who was able to enlarge the borders of Assyria, establishing an empire that encompassed most of the Fertile Crescent from the Persian Gulf to Palestine. His successors advanced the borders of Assyria north into the mountains of Armenia and south into Egypt. It was during the reign of Tiglath-pileser that the Assyrians carried out their devastating campaign into Philistia and Galilee (734–733 B.C.). Shalmaneser V (726–722 B.C.) led a campaign against the kingdom of Israel, and the city of Samaria fell to Sargon II (722–705 B.C.) in 722 B.C. The Assyrians continued to menace the southern kingdom of Judah until being overthrown by the Babylonians at the end of the seventh century B.C.

The region of Babylonia consists mainly of the alluvial deposits of the two rivers. It is a flat terrain and swampy in the south, where the rivers unite as they near the Persian Gulf. The earliest civilization in this region was that of Sumer, centering in the vicinity of Ur, Erech, Larsa, and Eridu. The first of these Sumerian city-states were established between 2800 B.C. and 2360 B.C. as a result of the need to cooperate in maintaining a system of dams and canals to make use of the water from the Tigris and Euphrates.

The Sumerians continued to prosper until 1894 B.C., when the First Dynasty of Babylon was established. Babylon soon became a prosperous capital and trading center. The city walls were restored and enlarged. Hammurabi (1792–1750 B.C.) set up a copy of his now-famous law code. Babylon continued to prosper under a succession of kings, ruling southern Mesopotamia until its capture by the Hittites around 1600 B.C. The region eventually fell under the shadow of the advancing Assyrian Empire.

Babylon remained an Assyrian vassal until 626 B.C., when Nabopolassar led the people in overthrowing their rulers. The combined armies of Babylon and the Medes conquered Nineveh in 612 B.C.

and captured Haran, the last Assyrian stronghold, in 610 B.C. Babylonia remained the dominant power in Mesopotamia for the next seventy years, until the city of Babylon was captured by Cyrus the Mede (539 B.C.), founder of the Persian Empire.

Principal Ancient Cities of Mesopotamia

The Fertile Crescent is noted for having some of the oldest cities of ancient civilization. Several have biblical significance, which merits their consideration here.

Ur

Ur, the capital of ancient Sumer, and the reputed early home of Abram/Abraham, was located in southern Mesopotamia on the west bank of the Euphrates River, about halfway between Babylon and the Persian Gulf. The biblical designation "Ur of the Chaldees" represents the attempt of a scribe to locate Ur in southern Mesopotamia after the site had become abandoned. This region was referred to as "Kaldu" in the Assyrian annals. When Nabopolassar, a native Chaldean governor, came to the Babylonian throne in 626 B.C., he inaugurated a dynasty that made the name famous. The term *Chaldea* is used in the Bible as a virtual synonym for "Babylonia."

Ur was a prosperous trading and commercial center as it was strategically situated on the main trade route from the Persian Gulf to the eastern Mediterranean region. This route ran north along the Euphrates and connected with other routes going south and west. Ships from the Persian Gulf brought gold, alabaster, copper, ivory, and hardwoods into the ports at Ur. Merchandise from Egypt, Ethiopia, and India reached the trading houses of Ur in the time of Abraham.

Ur was also an important religious center. The patron deity of the city was Nanna, the moon god. Until the sixth century B.C., Ur boasted the most important temple area in Mesopotamia, the great ziggurat. According to Mesopotamian mythology, the gods dwelt in the mountains in the north. Since there were no mountains in the alluvial plain, the ziggurats were built to give the gods a place to dwell. The three-staged pyramid tower at Ur was built by Ur-Nammu (2113–2096 B.C.) and remodeled by Nabonidus (556–539 B.C.). The mud-brick structure measured 200-by-150 feet and was 70 feet in elevation. The terraces of the pyramid were planted with trees. A one-room temple graced the top of the pyramid, enabling the moon god to dwell in a "mountain" shrine.

The city of Ur is also noted for its legal and literary achievements. Ur-Nammu, the first Sumerian ruler of the Third Dynasty of Ur is

This figure of a goat eating leaves is from Ur, ca. 2500 B.C., about five hundred years earlier than the time of Abraham. *Courtesy, Philadelphia Museum of Art.*

known for his famous law code, which antedates by over three hundred years that of Hammurabi. The Ur-Nammu law code (2050 B.C.) deals with such matters as weights and measures, the protection of orphans and widows, and problems associated with the oppression of the poor. Ur was no insignificant place. It stood at the apex of early Mesopotamian culture. Yet this was the city that Abraham left at God's command "not knowing where he was to go" (Heb. 11:8).

Babylon

Ancient Babylon was located on the east bank of the Euphrates River, about 150 miles northwest of Ur and 50 miles south of modern Baghdad. According to Scripture, the city was founded by a descendant of Noah named Nimrod who was "a mighty hunter before the Lord" (Gen. 10:8–10). The original name of the city was Babili, meaning "gate of god," but the name that appears in most versions of the Bible is Babel, which sounds like the Hebrew word for "confused" and symbolizes the confusion of tongues and dispersion of people from the city (Gen. 11:1–6). "Babylon" is the Greek form of that name.

Babylon rose to its classic greatness during the First Dynasty, especially in the reign of Hammurabi. For five generations, great temples were built, irrigation channels excavated, and literature and the arts flourished. After a period of decline and invasion by other peoples, the city experienced a revival in the thirteenth century B.C. but was continually beaten down by the rival Assyrians. After several centuries, during the reign of Nebuchadnezzar II (605–562 B.C.), Babylon rose again to heights of glory and became the most important city of Mesopotamia and the hub of the new Babylonian Empire. Nebuchadnezzar built thirteen miles of walls around the city, reportedly 250 to 300 feet high and 80 feet thick! The "hanging gardens" of Babylon were one of the seven wonders of the ancient world. The famous Ishtar Gate, decorated with enameled bricks, gave access to the "processional way" leading to the most sacred part of the city, where stood the temple of the city-god Marduk (the "Esagila"). Daniel ministered in Nebuchadnezzar's Babylon during his captivity, and Jehoiachin, king of Judah, lived out his exile there after the conquest of Jerusalem (2 Kings 25:27–30).

Babylon fell to Cyrus the Great in 539 B.C. Herodotus records that the Euphrates, which ran through the city, was diverted to allow the Persian invaders to enter the city by night through the river channel.

Ruins of the Ishtar Gate in Babylon.

"King" Belshazzar co-regent with his father Nabonidus, was killed (Dan. 5:30), and Darius the Mede was appointed ruler by Cyrus. Babylon was relatively prosperous under Persian rule, although there were periodic revolts, all suppressed. The city declined after its conquest by Alexander the Great, who died there in 323 B.C., but a small community continued until at least A.D. 100.

Nineveh

The site of Nineveh lies 250 miles north of Baghdad on the east bank of the Tigris River, opposite modern-day Mosul. The city was situated at the main crossing of the Tigris in the northern plain, the center of a rich agricultural region. Ancient Nineveh was often a royal residence for Assyrian rulers and was finally established as the capital of Assyria by Sennacherib (705–681 B.C.). Esarhaddon and Ashurbanipal adorned the capital with magnificent palaces.

The Lord's judgment on Nineveh was averted by repentance in response to the preaching of Jonah, but about a century later, judgment fell on what Nahum called the "bloody city." According to the chronicle of Babylonian King Nabopolassar, the united forces of the Chaldeans and Medeans destroyed Nineveh in 612 B.C., a fate predicted by Nahum and described in vivid detail (Nahum 2:3–13). Nineveh was so devastated that Xenophon did not recognize it as the site of a once-great city when he passed by in 401 B.C.

The walls of the ancient site have a circumference of over seven miles. Five gates of the ancient city have been excavated. At the citadel of Nineveh, archaeologists have discovered a royal library containing more than 16,000 clay tablets and fragments, representing an estimated 10,000 texts. The throne room of Sennacherib's palace has been excavated, exposing bas-reliefs depicting the king's conquests. Many of these were moved to the British Museum and the Louvre in the nineteenth century, but some remain at the site. One of the most famous of these reliefs depicts Sennacherib's siege of Lachish.

Haran

Haran is located about 600 miles northwest of Babylon and 150 miles from the northeast corner of the Mediterranean Sea. It lies on the Balikh River, a tributary of the Euphrates. Since the word means "route" or "journey," some of the earliest forms of the city's name appear in the plural or with a sign depicting a crossroad. Haran was on the main route from Nineveh to the Euphrates and Aleppo, another important commercial center. Trading routes extended from Haran like spokes on a wheel—south to Babylonia, east to Assyria, north to Anatolia, west to Asia, and southwest to Syria and Palestine.

Sinuhe (1960 B.C.), an ancient Egyptian official, described the area as a "good land with figs and grapes, and more wine than water. Plentiful was its honey, and abundant its olives. There was barley there and no limit to its cattle."

The moon god, Nanna, was worshiped at Haran. It has been suggested that the citizens of Haran learned of Nanna through travelers from Ur. Perhaps the presence of this religion in Haran explains the sojourn there of Abraham's father, Terah (Gen. 11:31). Abraham stayed at Haran until Terah's death and was seventy-five years old when God called him to leave Haran (Gen. 12:1–4). Abraham took over the leadership of the family and moved on to Canaan, thereby initiating what is commonly designated as the patriarchal period of Old Testament chronology.

2

The Patriarchal Period
2166 to 1876 B.C.

The land of the Israelites, or "Canaan," is commonly designated as the Promised Land (Deut. 9:28) because of the prominence of the region in the promises given by God to his chosen people. This land, situated along the eastern shore of the Mediterranean Sea, contains some of the most sacred, strategic, and bloodiest territory on earth. It was a God-appointed place, selected "to make his name dwell there" (Deut. 12:11). It was here that the divine Son of God was to present himself and sacrifice his own life for the world's redemption.

The Coming of the Patriarchs

Abraham (we will use his later name) was seventy-five years old when God called him to leave Haran and journey on to Canaan (Gen. 12:4). The Bible tells us nothing about his itinerary, but a knowledge of the cultural and geographic background can lead us to some valid assumptions. As a trader and stockman, Abraham would know the routes available and their conditions in the various seasons. He would probably have left Haran in the spring of the year (c. 2090 B.C.), when the pastures lying ahead would still be green from the winter rains. We can surmise that he traveled south from Haran to the

Euphrates and then directly west to Aleppo, from where he journeyed south to Damascus, an oasis richly supplied with water from the Anti-Lebanon mountains. Damascus, an important commercial center, was situated at the crossroads of the two main international highways of the ancient Near East: (1) the Via Maris ("way of the sea," Isa. 9:1), swinging west through present-day Israel to Egypt; and (2) "the King's Highway," leading south through Transjordan to Arabia and the northeast arm of the Red Sea.

Abraham chose the Via Maris and traveled south with his family and livestock to Canaan, "the land of promise" (Heb. 11:9). At Shechem, situated about thirty-five miles north of Jerusalem between Mount Ebal and Mount Gerizim, Abraham built an altar to the Lord. There God confirmed his promise to give Abraham's descendants the land of Canaan (Gen. 12:7). Abraham journeyed farther south, stopping between Bethel and Ai to build another altar, and then continued on to the southern region of the territory, the Negev, which became an important center for the patriarchs.

Abraham soon found himself in the midst of a famine and sought refuge in Egypt. This situation was not infrequent in Palestine, which has a marginal climate and where agriculture was then totally dependent on rainfall. In Egypt, the Nile River, originating in the well-watered mountains of Africa, provided a more certain supply of water for crops and cattle. The inhabitants of the land of Canaan, including Jacob and his family, often sought refuge in Egypt during times of famine (Gen. 46:6). After an embarrassing incident involving Sarah (Gen. 12:13–20), Abraham was expelled from Egypt by the pharaoh and returned north through the Negev to the hill country.

After separating from Lot, Abraham settled at "the oaks of Mamre," which later became known as Hebron (Gen. 13:18). There, too, Abraham built an altar to the Lord. His kinsman Lot's choice of the "well-watered" valley of the Jordan is a bit problematic in light of the present conditions of this region. But the biblical text acknowledges that this region was like "the garden of the LORD . . . before the LORD destroyed Sodom and Gomorrah" (Gen. 13:10). It appears that some major geographical changes took place as a result of God's judgment on those evil cities.

That Abraham was not just a desert shepherd is illustrated by his rescue of Lot and his family from the four Mesopotamian kings (Gen. 14). It is in connection with this incident that Abraham is for the first time referred to as "the Hebrew" (Gen. 14:13). Abraham and his 318 trained men overtook the plunderers in Upper Galilee, defeated them, and pursued them north of Damascus. On his return from victory, he was greeted by Melchizedek, the king-priest of "Salem" (vv. 18–20).

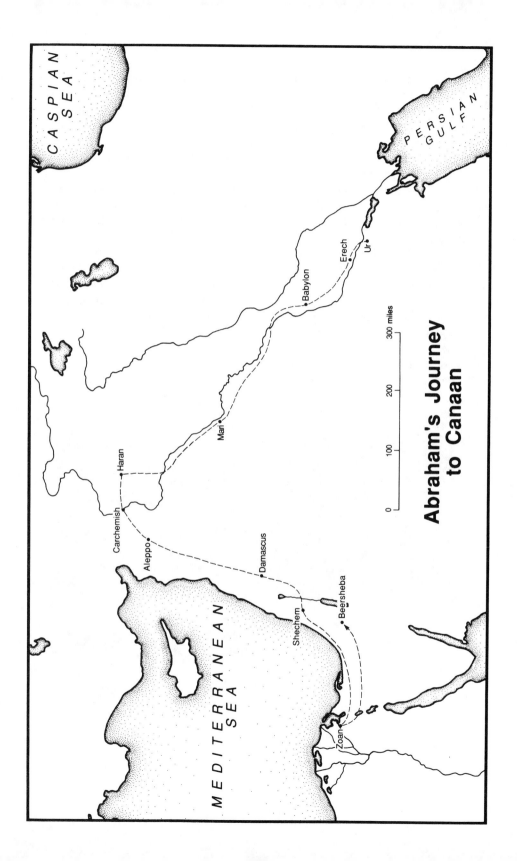

Abraham's Journey to Canaan

This is the earliest biblical reference to Jerusalem, a Jebusite fortress city at this time. It was probably on the mountain just north of this Salem that Abraham later offered God his son Isaac as a sacrifice (Gen. 22:2; cf. 1 Chron. 21:28; 2 Chron. 3:1).

Genesis 20 records that after the destruction of Sodom and Gomorrah Abraham once again journeyed into the Negev. He sojourned for a time at Gerar, where he repeated his earlier offense of passing off Sarah as his sister. Abimelech, the Philistine king of Gerar, took Sarah into his palace, as had the Egyptian pharaoh about twenty-five years earlier. In truth, though Sarah was Abraham's half-sister (Gen. 20:12), she was fully his wife!

Peaceful relations between Abraham and Abimelech were established at a well located in the center of the Negev (Gen. 21:22–34). The place was called Beersheba, meaning "well of swearing" (Gen. 21:31; 26:33). There Abraham planted a tamarisk tree and worshiped God.

The references to the Philistines in connection with the wanderings of Abraham have been viewed by many as chronologically inaccurate, since the main invasion of these "sea people" did not occur until around 1168 B.C. However, archaeological evidence supports the view that there were Philistines in Israel in the patriarchal era. It has been

Traditional site of Abraham's Well at Beersheba. *Eugene Henderson and Batsell Barrett Baxter.*

suggested that they came with a desire to export grain to their rocky, homeland islands in the Aegean.

Although Abraham had sojourned in the hill country and the Negev for about sixty years, he did not own any land at the time of Sarah's death. Hence, he had to negotiate with Ephron the Hittite for the purchase of a burial cave in a field at Machpelah near Mamre (Gen. 23:17). Ancient tradition places this cave under the Haram el-Khalil at Hebron (the walls of that structure were built in the time of King Herod). The Cave of Machpelah became the burial place for Abraham, Isaac, Rebekah, Leah, and Jacob.

The Land of Israel

The land of Israel is located on a land bridge between Asia, Africa, and Europe. All travelers, caravaners, and ancient armies had to pass through this region in order to move north or south. Communication and traffic between Egypt and Mesopotamia also needed to traverse Israel. Although it was not as richly endowed with resources as the Nile Valley to the south or the Tigris-Euphrates Valley to the northeast, no land in the Fertile Crescent was more strategic. No major cultural development in the ancient Near East came about without the land of Israel playing some part. Israel was, and still is, the geographical key to the Middle East countries of Turkey, Syria, Lebanon, Jordan, and Egypt—and indirectly affects Iran, Iraq, and Saudi Arabia as well.

This area is often referred to by the term *Palestine*, derived from the word *Philistine*—referring to the "sea people" who migrated from Asia Minor and the Aegean islands around the middle of the twelfth century B.C. Having been repulsed from the Egyptian delta, these Indo-Europeans settled on the eastern Mediterranean coast. The land they occupied (Philistia) was commonly known as Palestine. Recent conflict between modern Israelis and certain political activists deemed "Palestinian" has given this geographical word a strongly political flavor. Hence, we will generally avoid the use of this term. Should it occasionally appear, its use is strictly a geographical reference, a synonym for "the land of Israel."

Borders of Israel

The land mass of Israel is situated between the Mediterranean Sea on the west and the Transjordan Desert to the east. The Mediterranean lies between the continents of Europe and Africa. It is 2,196 miles in length (from Gibraltar to the coast of Lebanon) and varies between about 100 and 600 miles in width. The maximum depth is 2.7 miles. Sardinia, Sicily, Corsica, Crete, and Cyprus are the five largest islands.

Israel: The Land Bridge Between Continents

Because of its size, the Old Testament often refers to the Mediterranean as "the Great Sea" (Num. 34:7, Josh. 9:1). It is also called "the Western Sea" because of its proximity to the land of Israel (Deut. 11:24; 34:2). Not only does the Mediterranean serve as a significant border, it has a major effect on Israel's climate, as we shall later see.

The Transjordan desert lies east of the Great Rift Valley and the Transjordan hills. It is a vast wilderness and was occupied only by nomadic tribes during the biblical period. The region extends east between three and seven hundred miles to Mesopotamia and the Persian Gulf respectively. It is known as the Syrian Desert in the north and the Arabian Desert in the south. This desert region is noted for its extreme temperatures and arid conditions. The Syrian Desert receives between four and eight inches of rainfall a year; the Arabian Desert receives less than four inches annually. Like the Mediterranean Sea, the Transjordan desert has had a very significant effect on Israel's climate.

The Lebanon Mountains (10,000 feet) and Mount Hermon (9,100 feet) serve as a natural border to Israel's north. The southern border of the land is the Wadi el-'Arish, referred to in Scripture as the "brook of Egypt" (Josh. 15:4). This riverbed *(wadi)* is dry except during the rainy season, when its flow unites with other wadis to drain the northern half of the Sinai Peninsula. The Wadi el-'Arish empties into the Mediterranean about halfway between Egypt's Port Said and Israel's Tel Aviv.

In contrast to its great importance in biblical and religious history, the land area of Israel is relatively small, being approximately the size of New Hampshire or Vermont. This land area, as defined by its natural geographical borders, measures about two-hundred miles from north to south. The expression "from Dan to Beersheba" is used in Scripture to describe the entire land with reference to those occupied extremities (Judg. 20:1), a distance of about a hundred and fifty miles. The area extends to the west as the Mediterranean coastline swings toward the Nile delta. In northern Galilee, the width of Israel measures about thirty-five miles (from the Mediterranean to the Great Rift Valley), about fifty-five miles at the latitude of the Jordan's entrance into the Dead Sea, and about eighty-five miles from the Mediterranean coast at Rafah to the Great Rift south of the Dead Sea.

Regions of Israel

Israel is a land of many contrasts, and geographical variety is probably its most significant characteristic. The land can be divided longitudinally into four distinct geographical regions: the *coastal plain*, the *hill country*, the *Great Rift Valley*, and the *Transjordan highlands*. Each one of these regions will be considered in greater detail later on, but an initial orientation will help prepare for further study.

Israel's coastal plain is a band of sandy and alluvial soil bordering the Mediterranean Sea. The region begins at the Ladder of Tyre (Rosh Ha-Niqra), where the mountains of Lebanon jut into the sea, and extends south 165 miles to the Wadi el-'Arish. The region is only about three miles wide in the north but broadens as it swings westward to about twenty-five miles. The coastline of Israel is unbroken except by the projection of Mount Carmel into the sea. Unlike the Phoenician lands to the north, Israel's coastline is generally unmarked by inlets or bays. This probably explains why the ancient Israelites were never a seafaring people. The coastal plain falls into four natural divisions. From north to south these are the Plain of Asher, the Coasts of Dor, the Plain of Sharon, and the Plain of Philistia.

The hill country is a mountainous region running north and south and extending from upper Galilee to the Negev. Its topography is dominated by a great limestone arch, rising out of the coastal plain on the west and then bending down toward the Great Rift Valley. This area is broken in the north by the Jezreel (Esdraelon) Valley, which extends along the northern backbone of Mount Carmel in a southeasterly direction toward the Jordan Valley. The hilly region is divided into four major sectors: upper and lower Galilee, the hill country of Ephraim (Samaria), and the hill country of Judah. The highest elevations are in upper Galilee, where the mountains rise to nearly 4,000 feet above sea level. The highest point south of the Esdraelon is three miles north of Hebron, where the elevation reaches 3,373 feet. The hill country was forested in antiquity, but most of the trees were cut down as settlements arose.

To the east of the hill country lies a fissure in the earth's crust, the Great Rift Valley, which is part of a major fault system extending south from the Lebanon Mountains, through the Red Sea, and on into eastern Africa. The Rift in Israel starts at 1,800 feet above sea level and drops to 1,300 feet below sea level at the latitude of the Dead Sea. It averages about ten miles in width throughout the land of Israel. The Rift Valley and the bodies of water that fill it (the Jordan, Sea of Galilee, Dead Sea) provided a natural barrier between settlers east and west of the Jordan. From north to south, Israel's Rift Valley is divided into five regions: the Huleh Valley, the Sea of Galilee, the Jordan Valley, the Dead Sea, and the Arabah.

The fourth major geographical region to be considered is the Transjordan highlands, a high plateau, rising to nearly 4,000 feet. These highlands descend steeply on the west to the Great Rift. Toward the east, the region slopes gradually into the Syrian-Arabian Desert. This region is noted for its chilling winds in the winter and its burning winds (siroccos) in the spring and fall. Most of the rainfall in the highlands flows into the Rift Valley. This runoff accumulates in four rivers that divide the region laterally. From north to south, they are the Yarmuk, Jabbok, Arnon, and Zered.

Climate of Israel

Israel lies between a great sea and a vast desert, and these two geographical features provide the primary climatic influences on the territory. Winds sweeping off the Mediterranean bring moist, cool air to the land. Winds from the desert to the east bring arid air and scorching heat. Because of its proximity to the sea, much of Israel is blessed with sufficient rainfall for profitable agriculture. But proximity to the desert means that the rainfall is sometimes marginal and drought may occur. God placed his people Israel on a land where he could bless their obedience by sending plenty of rain (Deut. 28:12)—or he could disci-

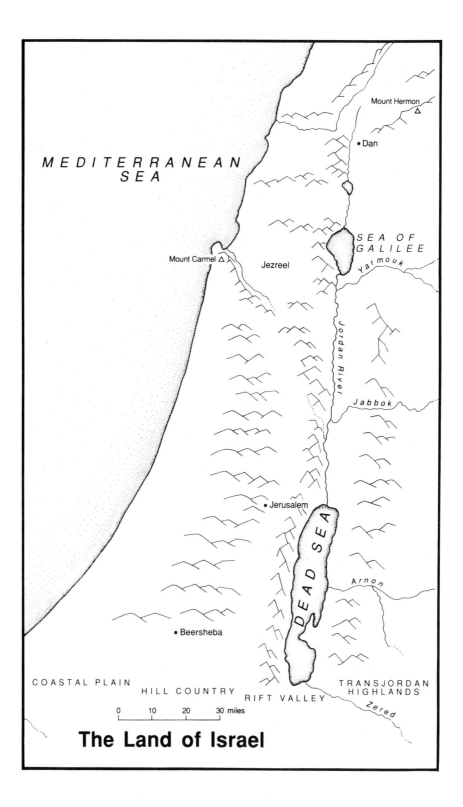

MEDITERRANEAN
SEA

Mount Hermon
△

• Dan

SEA OF
GALILEE

Mount Carmel △

Jezreel

Yarmouk

Jordan River

Jabbok

• Jerusalem

DEAD SEA

Arnon

• Beersheba

COASTAL PLAIN

HILL COUNTRY

RIFT VALLEY

TRANSJORDAN
HIGHLANDS

Zered

0   10   20   30 miles

The Land of Israel

pline their disobedience by allowing the desert to have the greater influence when he withheld the rain (v. 24).

The climate in any particular region of Israel is primarily determined by two factors: distance from the sea and elevation. Close to the Mediterranean, the land is significantly influenced by the moist sea air. Further inland, the climate is subject to the influence of the hot, arid desert. As a result, the western portions of Israel have more moderate temperatures and higher annual rainfall than the eastern sectors, which have hotter summers, colder winters, and less precipitation.

Two simple guidelines can be followed to estimate the approximate rainfall anywhere in Israel. Rainfall increases to the north, to the west, and as you ascend the mountains (25 to 45 inches annually). Rainfall decreases to the south, to the east, and as you descend to lower elevations (2 to 25 inches annually). As one might expect, the climate is milder and damper along the coast and on the western slopes of the hill country, whereas it is more extreme and arid along the eastern slopes of the hill country toward the Rift. And there is more rainfall in Galilee than in Judah.

Temperature levels in Israel also depend on elevation and distance from the sea. Since temperatures tend to decrease with an increase in elevation, it is cooler in the mountains. And the farther the region is from the Mediterranean, the less the cooling effect of sea breezes. This accounts for higher temperatures in such places as the Jordan Valley. Another significant climatic feature is that the temperature range tends to increase with a decrease in rainfall. This results in greater temperature extremes in the desert and Negev. Summer temperatures in the hill country range from 65 to 85° F.; in the Rift Valley, the range is between 80 and 105° F. Winter temperatures in the mountains range from 45 to 50° F.; in the Rift Valley, the temperatures range between 50° and a comfortable 70° F.

The wind is also a significant factor in Israel's climate. Usually the wind blows inland from the Mediterranean. This sea breeze is a result of convection; as the land area warms under the hot sun, the warm air rises and the cool air over the Mediterranean flows inland to take its place. The sea-to-land breeze is felt along the coast by midmorning and in the mountains by noon. By early afternoon, the even-stronger breeze reaches the Rift Valley. This breeze brings cooling relief to those who live under Israel's hot sun.

Another wind that has a very significant effect on Israel's climate comes out of the desert to the east, a "scorching wind" (James 1:11, NAS) that sucks the moisture right out of the ground, plants, and inhabitants. This hot, dry desert wind, called the sirocco, usually blows during the transitional seasons at the beginning and end of summer.

The siroccos produce the highest temperatures of the year and are especially destructive to spring vegetation. The beautiful wild flowers of Israel can wither overnight under the hot blast of the sirocco (cf. Isa. 40:6–8).

Economy of Israel

The economy of ancient Israel focused on food production. The Cenomanian limestone that dominates the hill country not only made an excellent building material, but also weathers into a fertile, red-brown soil—the famous *terra rossa* of the Mediterranean region. This soil is potentially very productive but is today often rocky and patchy due to centuries of neglect. Terracing has been used in ancient and modern times to guard against erosion and preserve the soil. The three most important agricultural products are mentioned repeatedly in Scripture—oil, grain, and grapes (Deut. 7:13; Neh. 5:11; Ps. 104:15). Olive trees grew throughout the hill country, and their bounty was pressed into oil for cooking, for burning in lamps, and for medicinal use (1 Kings 17:12; Matt. 25:3–4; Isa. 1:6; Mark 6:13). Grain, including wheat and barley, was used for bread. The coastal plain, the hill country of Ephraim, and the valleys of Galilee were especially valuable as grain producers. The hill country between Bethlehem and Hebron was noted for its excellent vineyards, and the grapes were used to produce wine, vinegar, and raisins.

Today many of the hills in Israel are barren and rocky, except where reforestation has been introduced. In ancient times there seems to have been no lack of trees, but the forests were destroyed by war (Deut. 20:19–20) and in clearing land for agriculture (Josh. 17:15). Timber for major building projects came from the famed cedars of Lebanon (I Kings 5:6). Most of the building in ancient Israel was done with stone and mud brick. The aforementioned Cenomanian limestone was one of Israel's most important natural resources, since it breaks along even lines and is easily shaped.

Pastoral pursuits have also played an important part in Israel's culture and economy. Sheep and goats were raised for their wool, hair, skins, milk, and meat. It should be noted, however, that meat was not a normal part of the average Israelite's daily diet. Meat was usually only served in connection with a sacrifice, a festival, or honoring a special guest.

The Negev of the Patriarchs

While the patriarchs of Israel usually sojourned throughout the hill country, we frequently find them camped in the Negev, a name that means "dry land" or "south country." This region is situated directly

Sheep, an important factor in Israel's ecomony. *John McRay.*

south of the hill country of Judah and was inherited by the tribes of Simeon (Josh. 19:1–9) and Judah (Josh. 15:20–31). The region is shaped something like a butterfly, with its "body" situated at Beersheba, the center of the biblical Negev, and its "wings" stretched out to the basins on either side. Because of its position between the highlands to the north and south, the Negev has a rich alluvial soil, which collects in the form of a fine-blown sand.

The land area occupied by the Negev extends about fifteen miles north and south of Beersheba and about forty miles from east to west. The Negev is essentially a fertile alluvial basin surrounded on all sides, except for the west, by mountains. This basin is drained to the west by two streams—the Nahal Beersheba and Nahal Besor—which eventually join and empty into the Mediterranean. They are "seasonal" in that they are filled only after heavy rain (Ps. 126:4).

A camel in the Negev. *JCL*

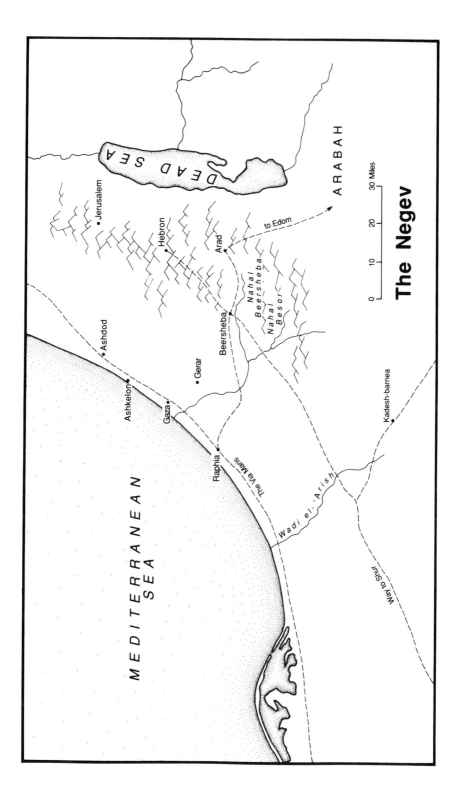

The Negev

MEDITERRANEAN SEA

DEAD SEA

ARABAH

•Jerusalem

Hebron•

Arad•

to Edom

•Ashdod

Beersheba•

•Gerar

Nahal Beersheba

Nahal Besor

Ashkelon•

Gaza•

Raphia

The Via Maris

Wadi el-'Arish

•Kadesh-barnea

Way to Shur

0   10   20   30 Miles

The sparse rainfall in the Negev (two to eight inches annually) makes water conservation a very important aspect of the area's economy. Droughts are frequent. Settlements have usually existed along the wadis (seasonal streams), where water could be collected during the rainy season to be stored for later use. The Nabateans flourished in this desert region due to their careful water conservation. Because of its limited rainfall, the economy of the Negev has focused more on pastoral than agricultural activity. Residents of this region raised sheep and goats, and donkeys and camels were bred and used in the caravan traffic.

The wind in the Negev is stronger because of the sharper difference between the sea and land temperatures. The mean temperature at Beersheba in August is 79° F., but the daytime temperature is somewhere in the 90's. The chilly night temperature lowers the average considerably. The mean temperature in January is 53° F.

The Negev was crossed by several minor travel routes. Although not a great commercial center, Beersheba served as the junction from which these roads branched out in all directions. A road to the west of Beersheba joined the Via Maris at Raphia (Rafah), the border town between Israel and Egypt today. To the east, "the way of Edom" (2 Kings 3:20, NAS) passed through Arad to the Arabah. The hill-country road ascended north from Beersheba to Hebron, and a less frequently traveled route extended south to join "the way to Shur" (Gen. 16:7) east of Kadesh-barnea.

Places of the Patriarchs

It is a misnomer to refer to the "cities" of the patriarchs, since many of these named places did not exist as cities until a later period. We will

Both Jews and Moslems worship at this traditional site of the Cave of Machpelah, the burial place of the patriarchs. *Israel Office of Information.*

consider several of the more important camps where the patriarchs dwelled or tented.

Hebron

Hebron is one of the most ancient cities of Judah. Its early name was Kiriath-arba, "the town of four," suggesting perhaps that four small communities, including Mamre, were united into one. Although Numbers 13:22 mentions that Hebron was built seven years before Zoan (Tanis) (founded about 1720 B.C. in Egypt), other biblical data and archaeological evidence suggest a much greater antiquity. Excavations on the slope of Gebel er-Rumeida indicate occupation as early as 3300 B.C. The beautiful wall that surrounds the Cave of Machpelah belongs to the time of Herod. The enclosed area measures 160 by 90 feet. The walls, eight feet thick, are made up of finely hewn stones as large as 22 by 5 by 5 feet. Hebron was taken by Caleb, one of the original spies sent out by Moses, (Num. 3–14; Josh. 15:13) and served as David's capital during the first seven and a half years of his reign (2 Sam. 5:5).

Mamre

Mamre was one of the four confederated communities located near Hebron. The site has been identified with Ramat al-Khalil, a little over a mile north of Hebron. There King Herod built a wall enclosing an area of 150 by 200 feet. Inside this perimeter, excavators discovered a sacred well in which money and figurines of worshipers were found. The Roman emperor Hadrian later dedicated this site to the worship of Hermes (Mercury). Constantine removed Hadrian's pagan altar and erected a church on the site purportedly the location of an altar erected by Abraham (Gen. 13:18).

Beersheba

Beersheba ("well of swearing," Gen. 21:31; 26:33) is located about twenty-five miles south of Hebron in the center of the biblical Negev. The ancient site is located several miles east of the modern city, at the juncture of two seasonal streams, the Wadi Beersheba and the Wadi Hebron. Both Abraham and Isaac concluded covenants there with "Abimelech," probably a dynastic title (Gen. 21:22–32; 26:23–33). Jacob later offered sacrifices there before journeying to Egypt with his family (Gen. 46:1). During a later period, Samuel's sons were established as judges in Beersheba (1 Sam. 8:2).

The city is mentioned with Dan, Bethel, and Gilgal as a religious center (Amos 5:5; 8:14), and the sweeping reformations of Josiah (639–608 B.C.) extended as far south as Beersheba (2 Kings 23:8). Although it was once destroyed, probably by the Assyrian Sennacherib in 701 B.C., Beersheba was resettled by the Jews after the Babylonian captivity (Neh. 11:27). The city appears to have been absorbed in Idumea during the intertestamental period, but the expression "from Dan to Beersheba" (Judg. 20:1, 1 Sam. 3:20; 2 Sam. 3:10) reflects the site's importance as an early religious and administrative center.

Excavations by Tel Aviv University have uncovered the two-and-a-half-acre city of the Israelite period. Adjacent to the city gate were three storehouses, each about fifty feet long, in which archaeologists have found numerous storage jars for grain, wine, and oil. A most interesting discovery at Beersheba was that of a horned altar dating to the eighth century B.C. It stands about sixty-three inches, approximately the same height as the altar at Arad, although a foot higher than the altars at the tabernacle and temple (cf. Exod. 27:1; 2 Chron. 6:13).

Arad

Although mentioned only four times in the Bible (Num. 21:1; 33:40; Josh. 12:14; and Judg. 1:16), Arad was an important city in the biblical period. It was both a fortress and an administrative center. Although destroyed six times during the period of the monarchy, the importance of the site is evidenced by the fact that it was always quickly rebuilt.

The most remarkable discovery at Arad is the only Israelite temple yet discovered in an archaeological excavation. The orientation and plan appear to follow that of Solomon's temple. It had one main room and a holy of holies, which contained a high place and a standing stone. Flanking the entrance were two incense altars. In the outer court was an altar for burnt offerings built of earth and unhewn stone. This worship center, like that at Beersheba, was in competition with the orthodox and legitimate temple in Jerusalem.

Gerar

Gerar was prominent in the early history of the patriarchs. There Abraham and Isaac enjoyed the hospitality of its king, Abimelech (Gen. 20:1–18; 26:1–11). Although the identification of the site has been debated, most modern archaeologists favor the site of Tell Abu Hureira located about fifteen miles northwest of Beersheba. Excavations have determined this site to have been inhabited continually from Chalcolithic times to the Iron Age. A most interesting discovery there was several smelting furnaces, illustrating the Philistine iron industry (cf. 1 Sam. 13:19–21).

3

The Egyptian Sojourn
1876 to 1446 B.C.

Egypt—the land of the Nile, the pyramids, and the pharaohs! Next to Palestine, more biblical history elapsed in Egypt than in any other region. Unlike Israel, Egypt was not dependent for her survival upon the uncertainties of seasonal rainfall. Egypt had a gift from the gods—the river Nile—which unceasingly provided water even in times of drought. It was in this land that the nation of Israel experienced its infancy and adolescence (Hos. 11:1). Jacob entered Egypt in 1876 B.C. with a family of seventy. Moses left four centuries later with a nation of two million.

The Israelites in Egypt

Moses records that the people of Israel lived in Egypt a total of 430 years (Exod. 12:40). Although this is a lengthy period, we know little of their activities in Egypt except at the beginning and end of this sojourn.

Famine in Israel had led Abraham to find temporary refuge in Egypt, a land whose agriculture was not dependent on the fluctuating Mediterranean rainfall (Gen. 12:10). In 1876 B.C., Jacob was forced by similar circumstances to follow in his grandfather's footsteps. Yet the Lord encouraged Jacob concerning the ultimate outcome of this migration to Egypt when he declared, "I am God, the God of your father; do not be afraid to go down to Egypt, for I will there make of you a great nation" (Gen. 46:3). However, since the land of Israel, not Egypt, had been promised to the chosen people, God added these words, "I will go down with you to Egypt, and I will also bring you up again. . ." (v. 4).

When Jacob arrived in Egypt with his family and flocks, there was a tearful but joyous reunion with his beloved son Joseph, who had been elevated to the position of "prime minister" of Egypt after being sold into slavery by his jealous brothers. Under the sovereignty of God, Joseph was in a position to help his family and preserve their lives during the coming years of famine (Gen. 45:5–7).

Due to his position in the pharaoh's court, Joseph was able to secure permission for Jacob and his family to reside in the land of Goshen in the northeast region of the Nile delta. This area was regarded as "the best of the land" (Gen. 47:11) because the delta region received more rainfall than any other part of Egypt. There the rich soil produced an abundance of grass and was an ideal location for the Israelites to raise their livestock. Although the Egyptians tended to avoid this region because it was usually the first to be attacked by invading armies swooping down from the north, God was with his people and protected them from harm. As a result, they prospered, acquired property, and became quite numerous (Gen. 47:27).

Joseph died around 1805 B.C., during the reign of Pharaoh Amenemhet III. For the next two hundred years, the Israelites lived in relative peace and prosperity in Egypt. They received favorable treatment under the Hyksos ("foreign rulers") who controlled Egypt from 1730 to 1580 B.C., for the Hyksos were also of Semitic origin. There then arose an Egyptian ruler, Ahmose I (1580–1548 B.C.), who liberated his people from Hyksos rule and founded the eighteenth dynasty. He is probably identifiable as the pharaoh who "did not know Joseph" (Exod. 1:8).

The new pharaoh quickly appointed taskmasters over the Israelites and enslaved them to build storage cities, including Pithom and Raamses (Exod. 1:11). Why was this oppression imposed on the Israelites? First, we can assume that the new Egyptian ruler had neither historical knowledge of Joseph nor respect for his accomplishments. Ahmose may also have been prejudiced against all Semitics because of the Hyksos domination that had so recently passed. Second, the Israelites were seen to be "too many and too mighty" (Exod. 1:9) and imposed something of a threat against the new regime. Third, the pharaoh feared that the Hebrews might join with the Hyksos and rebel against Egyptian rule (v. 10).

Two oppressive measures were instituted against the Israelites in order to undermine their strength and hinder their growth as a people. First, hard labor was imposed on them (Exod. 1:12–14). Second, male children were taken from their Israelite parents and put to death (Exod. 1:15–22). These were difficult days for the people of Israel. Yet, as they cried out to God from their bondage and misery, he began to raise up a deliverer—Moses.

Due to the faith and courageous ingenuity of Moses' godly parents, his life was spared after he was hidden and then providentially discovered and adopted by the pharaoh's daughter, probably Hatshepsut. Moses was raised in the royal court of Egypt and received the very finest education and training available in his day (Acts 7:22). He probably lived at Thebes, the capital of Egypt at this time. There he tasted of the splendor, luxury, and riches of the Egyptian royal court.

But Moses knew his Hebrew heritage, and when he grew to manhood he made a decision that required courage and self-sacrifice. He turned from the passing pleasures of Egypt to identify himself with his kinsmen (Heb. 11:24–26). Turning down the opportunities his privileged position afforded, Moses chose instead to aid his own people in their plight of bondage. While this decision was commendable, his immediate action was not. Assuming the role of a deliverer, he killed an Egyptian taskmaster who was beating a Hebrew slave. Fearing discovery, he was forced to flee the country.

Moses spent the next forty years as a shepherd for Jethro in the land of Midian, east of the Sinai Peninsula. During this time, he acquired a wife, Zipporah (one of Jethro's daughters), and two sons, Gershom and Eliezer. After meeting God at Mount Sinai (Horeb), where he saw the miraculous burning bush, Moses returned to Egypt with a divine call to lead his people out of bondage.

Ten plagues of judgment (Exod. 7:14—12:30) fell upon Pharaoh and the Egyptians before Moses and the people of Israel were given permission to depart from the land. These plagues were designed to demonstrate to Egypt and all the earth the greatness and sovereignty of God (Exod. 9:16; 10:2). The Israelites were protected from the last plague— death of the firstborn—by the sacrifice of a lamb. In executing judgment, God promised to "pass over" the houses where the Hebrews had applied blood to the doorpost and lintel (Exod. 12:1–14). This deliverance is still commemorated annually through the celebration of the Feast of Passover. With great power and mighty judgments, God brought his people out of Egypt. After over four hundred years as displaced persons, they were on their way back to the Promised Land.

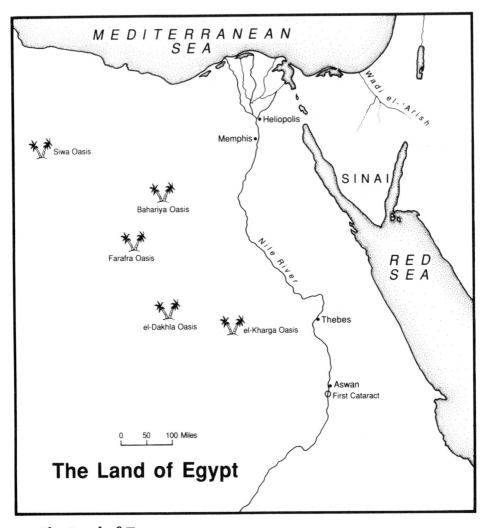

The Land of Egypt

The Land of Egypt

The name *Egypt* is probably derived from a designation for Memphis, "the house of the spirit of Ptah" (Ha-ku-Ptah) through the Greek form *Aigyptos*. The ancient Egyptians had several terms for their homeland. They often referred to Egypt as "the black land," as opposed to the desert, "the red land." Because of the distinctive geographical settings and histories, they identified "two lands," Upper and Lower Egypt. The Hebrew name for Egypt, *Misrayim*, is a dual form and probably refers to these two distinct regions.

Modern Egypt, the United Arab Republic, is roughly a square situated in the northeast corner of Africa. It is bounded on the north by the Mediterranean Sea, on the west by Libya, on the south by Sudan, and on the east by the Red Sea and the State of Israel. The boundaries of ancient Egypt are somewhat harder to define. The southern frontier, traditionally at the first cataract of the Nile, extended further south during periods of great strength. The most populated region of Egypt was along the Nile River, but the western boundary encompassed a line of desert oases running from Siwa in the north to el-Kharga in the south. These parallel the Nile, lying approximately 130 miles to the west. The eastern boundary of Egypt in the biblical period was "the brook of Egypt" known today as the Wadi el'Arish, which cuts across the northern Sinai Peninsula in a southeasterly direction. The pharaohs recognized the strategic importance of Israel as a land bridge between the continents and often sought to extend their borders beyond the Wadi el-'Arish to control this region.

The Nile River

Egypt is actually a river oasis in the desert. For life-giving water, Egypt depends wholly upon the Nile. The importance of the Nile to Egypt's existence is reflected by the words of Herodotus, the fifth century b.c. Greek historian: "Egypt is the gift of the Nile." The ancient Egyptians deified the river, calling it by the name of the god Hapi, represented by a male-female figure—a well-fed man with large breasts. Hapi symbolized the power and inherent forces of the Nile. The Nile would rise because Hapi willed it and would fall if Hapi was displeased. In honor of the Nile god, the ancient Egyptians would sing, "Hail to you, Hapi . . . . When he floods, earth rejoices!" The Nile was also simply called "the river" and is thus referred to in the Hebrew Scriptures (Gen. 41:1–3).

The Nile is the world's longest river—twice as long as the Mississippi. It flows 4,145 miles, from the equator through the parched desertlands of North Africa to the Mediterranean Sea. It was not until the nineteenth century a.d. that explorers established that the Nile has two sources. The White Nile rises from the 8,500-foot mountains of Rwanda and Burundi, just south of the equator. The torrential rains from these mountains fill lakes Victoria, Albert, and Edward. The White Nile passes through gigantic Lake Victoria, the jungles of Uganda, and plunges down mighty Murchison Falls before meandering through the marshy Sudd and emerging into the Sudan desert. The Blue Nile rises from the 6,000-foot highlands of Ethiopia. It passes through Lake Tana, cascades over Tessisat Falls, and plunges through a 4,000-foot gorge before gliding into the sand-duned desert of Sudan.

The Nile's two branches join just north of Khartoum, Sudan's cap-

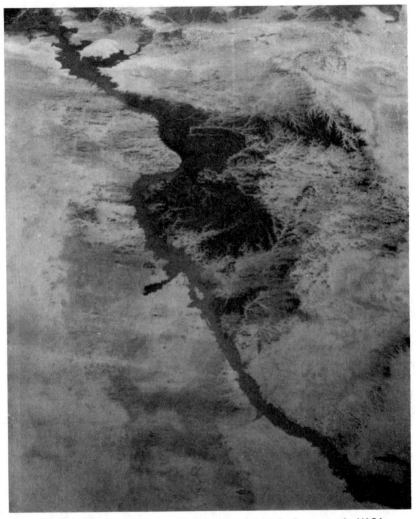

View of the Nile River and Lake Nasser from the Apollo 7 spacecraft. *NASA.*

ital. The river still has 1,850 miles to flow before reaching the Mediter-ranean. As it continues its journey, the Nile passes over six cataracts—stretches of rapids where the river crosses ledges of hard granite. At each of the cataracts, the riverbed drops an average of sixty feet. The Nile passes over its last cataract just beyond the Aswan Dam, which holds back the waters of 310-mile Lake Nasser. Here the river is about half a mile wide. The Nile flows on at about three knots (barely walking speed) to Cairo, where the river is more than a mile wide. Beyond Cairo, the Nile splits into a multitude of canals and waterways that

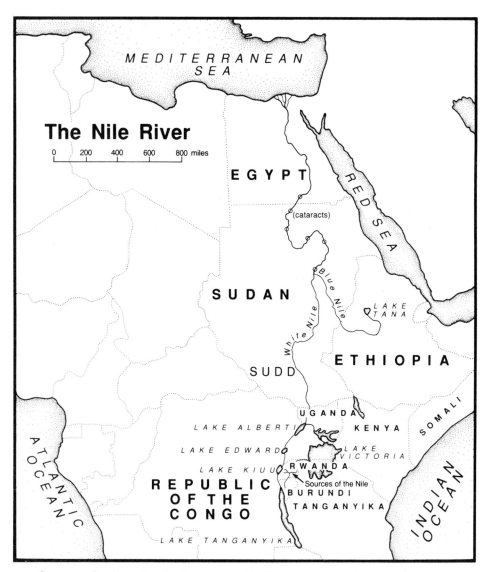

The Nile River

0   200   400   600   800 miles

MEDITERRANEAN SEA

EGYPT

RED SEA

(cataracts)

SUDAN

Blue Nile

White Nile

LAKE TANA

SUDD

ETHIOPIA

UGANDA

KENYA

SOMALI

LAKE ALBERT

LAKE EDWARD

LAKE VICTORIA

ATLANTIC OCEAN

LAKE KIUU

RWANDA

Sources of the Nile

REPUBLIC OF THE CONGO

BURUNDI

TANGANYIKA

INDIAN OCEAN

LAKE TANGANYIKA

flow another hundred miles to the Mediterranean, irrigating the green triangle of delta along the way.

Unlike many rivers, which fluctuate considerably in response to random rainfall, the Nile is noted for its reliable flood pattern. The ancient Egyptians invented a 365-day calendar so that they could anticipate the annual inundation. Before the erection of modern dams and flood-control devices, the river would begin to rise in July, reaching its peak in October, when it covered most of the land in the Nile

Valley and delta. The Nile would then recede until March, when spring planting would take place.

The flooding of the Nile was all-important to Egypt's economic prosperity. The annual inundation softened the ground, watered the soil, and deposited a new layer of rich alluvial soil, excavated by the Nile from the rich African highlands. A "good" flooding meant abundant crops and prosperity; a low Nile meant a poor harvest and hunger. Of course, an excessive Nile brought about the destruction of dikes and mud-brick houses, although such extremes were rare. Egypt was regarded as a haven from famine because of the reliable waters of the Nile (Gen. 12:10; 42:1). The economy of Egypt could prosper independent of the Mediterranean rainfall that was so vital to the prosperity of Palestine (Deut. 11:10).

The Nile was essential to more than Egypt's agriculture, for the people depended upon it as their main highway between Upper Egypt and the delta. Barges floated on the Nile, bearing such products as the fine, quarried granite used for Egypt's temples and statuary. Other Nile boats, taking advantage of the gentle breeze blowing through the valley, hauled commodities from the delta to ancient Thebes (Luxor).

The Nile Valley extends from the first cataract at Aswan to the base of the delta (at the site of Memphis)—a distance of about six hundred miles. The valley is bordered by cliffs that rise from the flood plain. The distance between these cliffs varies from ten to thirty miles in the stretch between Aswan and Cairo. The cultivated area of the Nile Valley is about six to ten miles wide, narrowing to one or two miles at Aswan. Only this valley and the delta are suitable for agriculture. This area amounts to about 6 or 7 percent of Egypt's land mass. The rest is desert.

Climate of Egypt

Egypt is situated in the North African desert between twenty-two and thirty-two degrees latitude. Consequently, Egypt is known for its hot sun, with little cloud cover to protect the inhabitants from its burning rays. In such close communion with this mighty force, it is not surprising that Re (Ra), the sun god, was worshiped by the ancient Egyptians. The usefulness of the sun is still acknowledged in the making of sun-dried mud-bricks—a basic building material for both ancient and modern Egyptians. In a land of little rain, mud-bricks can last a lifetime.

Egypt's rainfall is negligible. The delta receives a little rain during the winter months; Alexandria on the Mediterranean coast receives about seven inches annually; and Cairo receives about one inch a year. Even the lovely date palms in the vicinity of Memphis are a dirty, dusty green because cleansing rain is so infrequent. Aswan, 120 miles south of ancient Thebes, receives virtually no rain. Almost every drop of water used by the Egyptian people comes from the Nile.

The same sea-to-land breeze observed in Israel appears along the Mediterranean coast of Egypt. This breeze continues up the Nile Valley, filling the sails of the small boats transporting goods and people on the river. In the desert, dust storms *(khamsin)* may occur from March to June. These *khamsin* are the result of tropical air from the south moving northward (caused by an extension of a low-pressure system in Sudan). The phenomenon is accompanied by a sharp increase in temperature and a drop in relative humidity, and the dust-laden winds can reach gale force.

Regions of Egypt

Because of the sharp contrasts between the regions, the ancient inhabitants recognized Egypt as two lands—Upper and Lower Egypt. Upper Egypt, symbolized by the lotus blossom, extends about six hundred miles, from the first cataract at Aswan to Memphis, the ancient capital at the beginning of the delta. The valley on each side of the river has been cultivated since ancient times, and a line of towns was strung out along the river, the most significant being Thebes (modern Luxor).

Lower Egypt, symbolized by the papyrus plant, is essentially the Nile delta—a large triangle extending 125 miles north, from Memphis to the Mediterranean Sea. The delta is about 155 miles wide at its northern extremity along the coast. This region is very flat, green, and generously watered. Modern satellite photos frequently show cotton-ball-like puffs that indicate cloud cover over the delta, while the more arid regions are clearly visible. The delta probably contained considerable marshlands in ancient times, due to the deposits of alluvium that blocked the ancient waterways emptying into the Mediterranean.

Although not a separate region of Egypt, Goshen is important in connection with the Israelite sojourn. It was here that Jacob's family settled and multiplied (Gen. 47:27). Goshen, also known as "the land of Rameses" (Gen. 47:11), is located in the eastern delta area of Lower Egypt. It includes the Wadi Tumilat, a fertile region connecting the Nile River to the Bitter Lakes. Because of its rainfall and easy access to irrigation from the Nile, Goshen was indeed "the best of the land" of Egypt (Gen. 47:6, 11). Why, then, was it not being occupied by Egyptians? While Goshen is blessed with some of the most fertile land in Egypt, it is also the most susceptible to attack and was the first area to be captured and subjugated by invading armies from the north. The more cautious Egyptians built their major cities further inland at Memphis or as far up the Nile Valley as Thebes. Yet, under the protec-

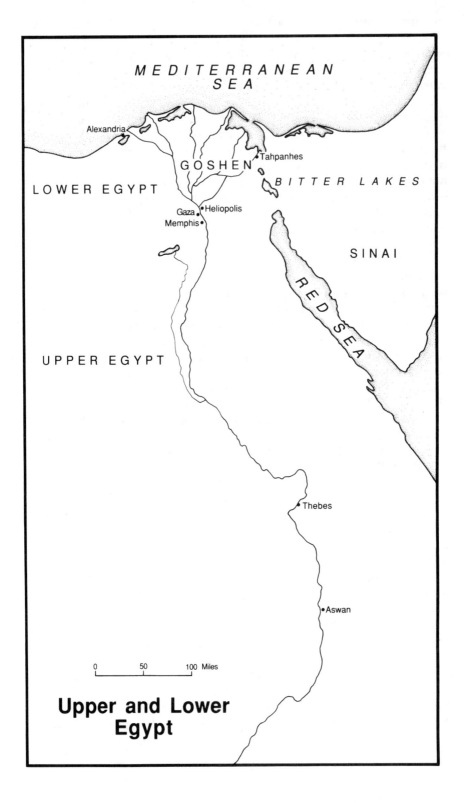

MEDITERRANEAN
SEA

Alexandria

Tahpanhes

GOSHEN

LOWER EGYPT

BITTER LAKES

Gaza • Heliopolis
Memphis •

SINAI

RED SEA

UPPER EGYPT

Thebes

Aswan

0   50   100 Miles

**Upper and Lower
Egypt**

tive hand of God, Israel flourished in Goshen, and the nation grew in number and strength.

Desert claims the land to the east and west of the Nile Valley and characterizes approximately 93 percent of modern Egypt's territory. The eastern desert, between the Nile and the Red Sea, is characterized by broken terrain and is dissected extensively by wadis and granite mountains. This long, narrow spine of mountains parallels the Red Sea in a southeasterly direction. They reach elevations of 6,600 feet in the extreme south. The eastern desert was known for its mineral wealth in ancient times and was mined for gold and alabaster. Although the mountains are not lacking in springs and can be crossed in several places, there is little incentive to do so because of the barrenness of the Red Sea's coast.

The western desert is actually an eastern extension of the vast Sahara. Its generally flat surface is broken by rocks and dunes of drifted sand. A series of oases supplied by artesian wells parallels the Nile Valley and allows for some cultivation and habitation. Nomadic Bedouins travel among these oases, drawing fresh water for their camels and harvesting delicious dates.

Economy and Culture of Egypt

Ancient Egypt was sufficiently isolated by the surrounding deserts to allow its people to develop their own distinctive culture, as evidenced by Egyptian writing, religion, and architecture. But there was also the opportunity for cross-fertilization with other cultures as the Egyptians engaged in trade to the east through northern Sinai and by means of the Mediterranean Sea.

The economy along the Nile River was primarily agricultural, and there were crops of wheat, barley, flax (for linen), castor oil, sesame (for oil) and saffron (for flavoring), lettuce—and the celebrated cucumbers, melons, leeks, onions, and garlic remembered by the Israelites during their wilderness wanderings (Num. 11:5). Fish from the Nile was undoubtedly an important item in the Egyptians' diet. In the desert and more marginal areas, the ancient Egyptians raised camels, cattle, sheep, and goats. Horses were introduced by the Hyksos and became valuable for export (1 Kings 10:28). Gold and silver were mined in the mountains to the east. Sandstone and limestone, quarried from the hills on either side of the Nile, furnished stone for the pyramids and temples. Granite was transported from Aswan for obelisks, statues, and sarcophagi. At Serabit el-Khadim, an Egyptian copper and turquoise mining center in Sinai, some of the earliest alphabetic inscriptions have been discovered, providing a link between Egyptian hieroglyphics and modern alphabets.

The great Via Maris linked Egypt with trade centers in Damascus and Mesopotamia, and Egyptian ships ventured from Egypt to Crete and Phoenicia, and traders traveled into Africa seeking incense, myrrh, gum, and ivory for Egyptian markets. (Egypt was later the chief granary for the Roman Empire. In the first century A.D., Paul took an Alexandrian grain ship from Myra to Miletus [Acts 27:6] and from Miletus to Rome [Acts 28:11]).

The Egyptians were clean-shaven, in contrast to the Asians and Hebrews. They generally wore white linen skirts and leather sandals. It is reported that beer was their favorite beverage! The pharaohs lived a life of luxury, as can be demonstrated by the rich treasures found in the tomb of the otherwise rather insignificant ruler, Tutankhamen (1350 B.C.).

Art and literature flourished in the days of the pharaohs. Much of the preserved art of Egypt has been discovered in royal tombs, since it was believed that the artifacts left there or represented in paintings could be used by the deceased in the afterlife. Egyptian literature includes myths and legends, treaties, historical texts and records, rituals and incantations, hymns, prayers, and wisdom materials. The wisdom instruction of Amen-em-opet has remarkable similarities to the biblical Proverbs (especially Prov. 22:17—24:22).

The ancient Egyptians tended to worship local deities rather than some more encompassing figure of national or cosmic scope. Their gods personified the powers of nature (fertility) and natural phenomena (the Nile). Various plants and animals were thought to be the manifestations of certain deities. Some spirits were friendly and life-giving, such as the domesticated cow; others were menacing, such as the crocodile and cobra. The Apis bull of Ptah was worshiped at Memphis. Horus, the hawk, and the sun god, Re (Ra), had more than local appeal as "sky gods," and Re was also depicted as hawk-headed. The sun god's main worship center was at Heliopolis (biblical On). Osiris, the god of the netherworld and afterlife, became associated with the dead kings. The pharaoh himself was thought to represent the gods and to move freely in their world. Pharaoh's tomb was regarded as his eternal dwelling. Belief in the afterlife was a leading feature of Egyptian religion. Since one's body was considered the material abode for the soul, efforts were made to preserve its physical form through mummification after death.

The History of Egypt

In the third century B.C., an Egyptian priest named Manetho categorized the long line of Egyptian kings into thirty dynasties or families. Modern historians have grouped these dynasties into seven larger units that correspond to the main divisions of Egypt's history. The three greatest periods of Egyptian history are identified as the Old, Middle, and New Kingdoms. These were preceded by the Early Dynastic Period and followed by the Late Dynastic era. Between the major kingdom ages were two transitional periods of lesser significance, the First and Second Intermediate Periods.

The *Early Dynastic Period* (3200–2780 B.C.) comprises the first two dynasties. Egyptian chronology begins with the union of Upper and Lower Egypt under King Menes (apparently identified with King Narmer), who conquered the delta and established a new capital at Memphis. Hieroglyphic writing first appeared during this era.

The *Old Kingdom* (2780–2280 B.C.) comprises roughly the third through the sixth dynasties. It was during this glorious age that Egypt's most enduring monuments were erected—the pyramids. Pharaoh Djoser (Zoser), founder of the third dynasty, built the first pyramid at Sakkara. Its distinctive appearance has earned it the name "step pyramid." The stone structure was 200 feet high and stood in a vast enclosure nearly 600 yards long and over 300 yards wide. Associated with the pyramid were a number of special buildings, including a mortuary temple. The fourth dynasty (2680–2560) is one of the significant eras in Egyptian history. It was during this period that the Great Pyramids of Cheops (Khufu), Chephren (Khafre), and Mycerinus (Menkure) were built at Giza, eight miles southwest of modern Cairo. To the east of his pyramid, Chephren had the Great Sphinx carved out of solid limestone.

The *First Intermediate Period* (2280–2052 B.C.)—the seventh through tenth dynasties—was a time of decline. The reigns of the pharaohs of the seventh and eighth dynasties were brief and not known for any major undertakings. When the throne fell vacant at Memphis, Heracleopolis, a prince from middle Egypt, founded a new royal line. Princes from Upper Egypt responded by establishing a rival line of kings at Thebes. This period of internal conflict came to an end when Mentuhotep II of Thebes reunited all Egypt under his rule.

During the *Middle Kingdom* (2134–1778 B.C.)—the eleventh and twelfth dynasties—Egypt experienced a period of peace, effective government, and considerable prosperity. Amenemhet I, founder of the twelfth dynasty, established a new administrative center just south of Memphis. Egypt extended its control as far as the second Nile cataract and established trading posts in the region of the third. New and larger copper mines were worked at Sarabit el-Khadem in Sinai. A series of forts were established along Egypt's Sinai frontier to defend the land from enemies to the north. It was during this period that famine led Abraham to visit Egypt in search of food (Gen. 12:10).

The *Second Intermediate Period* (1778–1567 B.C.)—the thirteenth through seventeenth dynasties—began with a rapid succession of kings and a corresponding weakening of the power of the throne. Ranking dignitaries (viziers) exercised the power represented by the pharaoh. Semitic people from Asia began to gain in strength and numbers in the delta area and eventually overthrew the reigning pharaoh, establishing the fifteenth dynasty. These people, about whom we know very little, are called Hyksos, meaning "foreign rulers." They ruled Egypt from their delta capital first at Memphis and later at Zoan (Avaris/Tanis) until about 1570 B.C. The Hyksos' strength stemmed in part from their skillful use of a new weapon, the war chariot. It has been suggested by some that Joseph rose to power under Hyksos rule (Gen. 41:14–45), but this is unlikely, since Joseph died about 1805 B.C. However, the Israelites who journeyed to Egypt with Jacob in 1876 B.C. were apparently favorably treated by the Hyksos, with whom they shared a common Semitic origin.

Egypt entered into the period of the *New Kingdom* (1580–1085 B.C.) when Ahmose I, founder of the eighteenth dynasty, drove the Hyksos from the land. This became the age of Egypt's supreme power, expansion, and wealth. It was during this period that the great temples were built at Luxor, Karnak, Abu-Simbel, and Abydos. The Israelites experienced their bondage and oppression in Egypt at this time, although—because of debate regarding the exact date of Israel's exodus from Egypt—caution must be exercised in linking biblical events with the reigns of specific pharaohs. We can, however, suggest some reasonable possibilities.

Assuming a 1446 B.C. exodus, it is likely that the pharoah who "did not know Joseph" (Exod. 1:8) was Ahmose I, who drove out the Hyksos. Ahmose (1580–1548 B.C.) and probably his successor, Amenhotep, (1548–1528 B.C.) began to carry out oppressive measures against the Israelites, probably to prevent them from gaining greater strength and joining the recently expelled Hyksos in rebellion against the Egyptian regime (Exod. 1:9–10). The famous female pharaoh, Hatshepsut, may have been the "daughter of pharaoh" who rescued and cared for Moses (Exod. 2:5). Hatshepsut married her brother, Thutmose II, and succeeded him on the throne. She ruled until her stepson, the great conquerer Thutmose III, took power. According to Manetho's chronology, Amenhotep II (1448–1423), son of Thutmose III, was most likely the pharaoh of the exodus. A significant link with the biblical record is noted in the fact that Amenhotep's eldest son did not succeed him to the throne (Exod. 12:29). Instead, his successor was Thutmose IV (1423–1410), who left the famous "Dream Stele," which records that he had been told by the Great Sphinx that—although he was not his father's oldest son—he would be Egypt's next pharaoh.

Those who date the exodus in the mid-thirteenth century B.C. (see chapter 4) usually identify Ramses II (1290–1223 B.C.) as the pharaoh of the exodus, arguing that the cities built by the enslaved Israelites (Exod. 2:11) were named for this ruler. However, it appears more likely that the name in the biblical text is merely a scribal modernization of an ancient place-name. The Israelites may have built at Zoan, which Ramses later named after himself.

The *Late Dynastic Period* (1085–332 B.C.)—the twenty-first through the thirtieth dynasties—ended with the conquest of Alexander the Great. During this period, three pharaohs had significant contact with Israel. The first was Sheshonk, the biblical Shishak (945–924 B.C.), who invaded Judah and took treasures from Jerusalem in the time of Rehoboam (1 Kings 14:25). The second was Necho II (610–595 B.C.), who marched north to help Assyria against rising Babylonia. Josiah of Judah attacked him at Megiddo and was killed (2 Kings 23:29–30). The third was Hophra (Apries) (589–570 B.C.), apparently the pharaoh who came to Zedekiah's assistance when he was under attack by Nebuchadnezzar (Jer. 37:5, 7, 11).

After the death of Alexander the Great, Ptolemy, one of his generals, assumed rule in Egypt (304 B.C.). A long line of Hellenistic rulers emerged, and their conflicts with the Seleucid rulers in Syria are described in Daniel 11. Cleopatra was the last of the Ptolemaic rulers. After she and her lover, Mark Antony, were defeated at the battle of Actium (31 B.C.) by Octavian (Augustus), Julius Caesar's appointed heir and Antony's political rival, Egypt was annexed as a Roman province. The Roman domination lasted for almost seven centuries thereafter.

The Sites of Egypt

Memphis

Memphis (biblical Noph) was founded by Menes, who united Upper and Lower Egypt about 3200 B.C. This city, which has now almost completely disappeared, was the adminstrative and religious center of Lower Egypt. It served as the capital of Egypt during the first two dynasties and the Old Kingdom. The Hyksos ruled from Memphis for a time, but later moved their capital to Avaris. Located on the west bank of the Nile, about fifteen miles south of Cairo, Memphis was distinguished by a fine harbor and many temples, palaces and royal tombs. Only Thebes was comparable to Memphis in religious, political, and economic importance.

Memphis was the center of worship of Ptah and his living emblem, the Apis bull. Ptah was regarded as the oldest of the gods and the creator of mankind. Tombs of these sacred bulls are found at nearby Sakkara. The golden calf worshiped by the Israelites in the wilderness (Exod. 32:1–20) may have arisen from an association with the bull cult of Memphis.

Strategically located at the head of the delta, Memphis was quite vulnerable to invaders. The city was periodically attacked by Assyrian and Babylonian rulers and was eventually captured by Cambyses, son of Cyrus. The recorded history of Memphis continues into Roman times, when Emperor Theodosius (A.D. 379–395) ordered the destruction of its temples and statues. The city was utterly destroyed, as the prophets had predicted (Jer. 46:19; Ezek. 30:13). Stones from the buildings of Memphis were later used to build the city of Cairo. Two great statues of Ramses II have been uncovered at Memphis, along with an alabaster and a red granite sphinx. Little else remains of the once-great city.

Giza Pyramids

The Giza Pyramids, located about eight miles southwest of modern-day Cairo, were built during the fourth dynasty (2680–2560 B.C.), about five centuries before Abraham. The three great mortuary pyramids at Giza were built by Khufu, Khafre, and Menkure, known to the Greek historian Herodotus as Cheops, Chephren, and Mycerinus. The largest, that of Khufu (Cheops) covers thirteen acres, is 450 feet high (originally 481 feet), and is composed of 2,300,000 blocks of limestone. It is estimated that it took 100,000 slaves twenty years to build this great pyramid.

To the southwest, Khafre (Chephren) built a slightly smaller pyramid, (447 feet high). This structure retains some of the smooth surface stone near its summit. To the east, under his direction, the Great Sphinx was carved out of natural rock. The sphinx has the body of a lion and the head of a man. The depiction of a royal beard and royal headdress suggests that the head is of a king, probably that of Khafre himself. The Great Sphinx is 240 feet long and 66 feet high and lies in repose as the "guardian" of the pyramids. The third pyramid, built by Menkure (Mycerinus) is dwarfed by the others, being only 204 feet high. Six much smaller pyramids—"pyramids of the queens,"—are also situated at the Giza complex.

Close to each pyramid are the mastabas—flat-roofed, free-standing tombs of the royal officials and priests. Also associated with each pyramid is a funerary temple where the priests conducted regular services on behalf of the dead kings.

Alabaster sphinx at Memphis. *JCL.*

Thebes

Thebes, biblical No or No-Amon (Jer. 46:25; Ezek. 30:14–16; Nah. 3:8), is located approximately four hundred miles up the Nile from Cairo. It rose to prominence as the administrative center of Upper Egypt during the eleventh dynasty and became the capital of the New Kingdom (1580–1085 B.C.) at the beginning of the eighteenth dynasty. Not only was Thebes an important political center, it was the central place of worship of Amon (Amun), who was later linked with the sun god Re (Amon-Re).

Ancient Thebes was situated on the east bank of the Nile. Just across the river is the Valley of the Kings, notable for its many mortuary temples and royal tombs. It was here that the treasure-laden tomb of the now-famous, "King Tut" (Tutankhamen) was discovered. On the west bank of the river are the two great temple complexes of Karnak and Luxor. Covering about one hundred acres, Karnak is said to be the largest temple complex in the world. It was built, enlarged, and modified by Egyptian rulers over a period of nearly two thousand years. The largest temple at Karnak is the Great Temple of Amon. An avenue of sphinxes constructed by Ramses II in 1292 B.C. links Karnak with the temple complex at Luxor, two miles to the south.

After about 1000 B.C., Thebes began to decline in influence. The political center of Egypt had moved north to the delta region. Yet Thebes remained a proud religious center until it was sacked by the Assyrian ruler Ashurbanipal in 663 B.C. (Nah. 3:8–10). Although efforts were later made to restore the city, it never regained its former glory.

Other Egyptian Cities

Many other Egyptian cities of lesser importance are mentioned in Scripture. Genesis 41:45 reports that Joseph married the daughter of a priest of On *(Heliopolis)*. The Israelites built the storage cities of *Pithom* and *Raamses* (Exod. 1:11). After the destruction of Jerusalem, many Jews fled to *Tahpanhes* (Jer. 43:7). *Alexandria* was the birthplace of the converted Jewish preacher, Apollos (Acts 18:24). The land of Egypt provides a rich historical and cultural background for biblical studies especially as they relate to the Israelites' sojourn in that ancient empire and the exodus that was to follow. Egyptian people and places have also been at least indirectly significant in other Old and New Testament events.

4

The Wilderness Wanderings
1446 to 1406 B.C.

After their exodus from Egypt, the people of Israel spent the first forty years of their national history wandering in the barren wastelands of the Sinai Peninsula. There they received the law, which served as their national constitution (Exod. 19–24), and there, too, God instituted the priesthood under the direction of Aaron and his sons (Lev. 8–10). It was in the wilderness that the tabernacle was erected for the first time as that place where God would "dwell" among his people (Exod. 25–40). It was in Sinai that the people rebelled against the Lord and were judged with forty years of wilderness wanderings (Num. 14). Many years later, Sinai became a place of refuge for that troubled prophet, Elijah (1 Kings 19:1–14).

What was this place where the mountains trembled and God answered with thunder? A thorough understanding of the geography and history of Sinai is necessary for an appreciation of Israel's growth as a nation and an understanding of many of the references to this region in Israel's history (Ps. 95:8–10; Ps. 114:4, 8; Judg. 5:4–5; Ps. 68:7–8).

The Land of Sinai

In the Bible, the name *Sinai* is used variously to refer to a specific mountain (Ps. 68:8), a mountain range (Deut. 33:2; Judg. 5:5), and a

69

View of Judean wilderness from the monastery on Mount Sinai.

desert, or wilderness. It most commonly refers to the peninsula that serves as the land bridge connecting Egypt with Palestine.

The Sinai Peninsula is a vast triangle of desert lying south of the Negev between the two northern arms of the Red Sea. To the east lies the Gulf of Aqaba (Num. 14:25; Deut. 1:40). This gulf, also known as the Gulf of Eilat, was named after the port city in this region. The western arm is the Gulf of Suez, which today leads to the Suez Canal (Exod. 10:19; Num. 33:10–11). Both of these bodies of water are referred to in the Bible as "Red Sea" and are differentiated only by context.

The peninsula is approximately 235 miles from its southern tip to the shores of the Mediterranean Sea. A distance of 160 miles spans the wider northern portion from the Suez Canal to the southern tip of the Dead Sea. This gives Sinai a land area of about 18,800 square miles.

The Regions

Northern and southern Sinai are vastly different in their geography and geology. The northern half of the peninsula is a broad wasteland of limestone and low chalk hills. The ground covering is mostly gravel and sand. Along the northern coast are many sand dunes, which are blown by the Mediterranean winds and present no small problem in keeping the roads clear. Northern Sinai averages 2,000 to 2,500 feet in elevation, lower in elevation than the region to the south. The higher

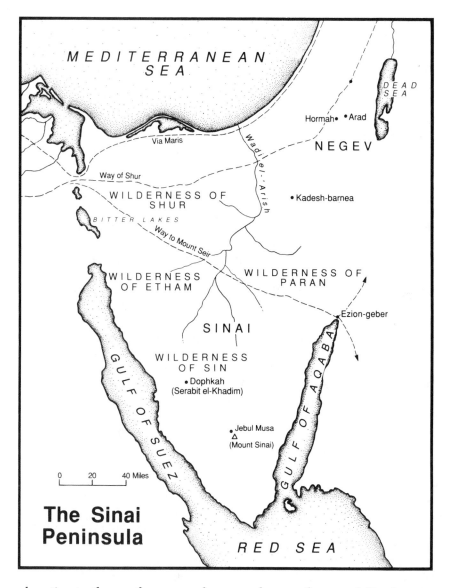

MEDITERRANEAN
SEA

DEAD
SEA

Hormah• •Arad

Via Maris

NEGEV

Wadi el-'Arish

Way of Shur

WILDERNESS OF
SHUR

• Kadesh-barnea

BITTER LAKES

Way to Mount Seir

WILDERNESS
OF ETHAM

WILDERNESS OF
PARAN

Ezion-geber

SINAI

GULF OF SUEZ

WILDERNESS
OF SIN

• Dophkah
(Serabit el-Khadim)

• Jebul Musa
△
(Mount Sinai)

GULF OF AQABA

0   20   40 Miles

**The Sinai
Peninsula**

RED SEA

elevation to the south, east, and west makes north-central Sinai something of a basin, drained by the Wadi el-'Arish.

Three travel routes penetrated this region in ancient times. The Via
Maris ("way of the sea") advanced along the northern coast of Sinai
into Israelite territory and on to Damascus. It is also referred to in the
biblical record as "the way of the land of the Philistines." "The way to

Shur" paralleled the Via Maris from Goshen through northern Sinai, but then continued east to Beersheba in the central Negev (Gen. 16:7). Still farther south was "the way to Mount Seir," which extended through north-central Sinai and linked Goshen with Ezion-geber and Arabia.

The southern half of the Sinai Peninsula is mountainous, and its red and gray granite mountains were important in ancient times as sources for turquoise and copper. The mountains of Sinai reach their loftiest point on 8,660-foot Jebel Katarina near traditional Mount Sinai (7,363 feet).

The Exodus narratives identify five wilderness regions along the route used by the Israelites in Sinai: Shur, Etham, Sin, Paran, and Zin. The Wilderness of Shur was that region in the northern Sinai across the "Reed Sea," immediately east of Goshen. The Hebrew name *Shur* means "wall" (Gen. 49:22) and may refer to the wall of mountains that appear to enclose the central plateau of Sinai. The Wilderness of Etham, "on the edge of the wilderness" (Exod. 13:20), appears to have bordered the Wilderness of Shur on the south. The Wilderness of Sin was in south-central Sinai. (The oasis of Dophkah, identified with Serabit el-Khadim, was in this region.) The Wilderness of Paran (Deut. 1:19) lay in the east-central region of the peninsula, bordered by the Arabah (see below) and the Gulf of Aqaba. The Wilderness of Zin was situated southwest of the Dead Sea but north of the Wilderness of Paran. Kadesh-barnea, from which the spies sent by Moses entered Canaan, is situated on the southern border of this wilderness (Num. 13:21). It was primarily in this region that the Israelites spent thirty-eight years as God's discipline for their faithless refusal to enter the Promised Land (Num. 14:26–35).

One other region of Sinai that cannot be ignored is the Arabah ("dry land"), a term used regularly in Scripture to describe the desolate Rift Valley extending both north and south of the Dead Sea (Deut. 1:7; 3:17; Josh. 11:2). In the Sinai, this region begins at the Dead Sea at 1,300 feet below sea level and then stretches south. Just west of Petra (now part of Jordan), it rises to 300 feet above sea level. The Arabah extends about a hundred miles from the Dead Sea—which was sometimes referred to as "the Sea of the Arabah" (Deut. 4:49; Josh. 3:16; 12:3; 2 Kings 14:25)—to Eilat, at the northern end of the Gulf of Aqaba.

Climate of the Sinai

Along the Mediterranean coast, the Sinai receives four to eight inches of rainfall annually. The average annual rainfall in the north is only about two and a half inches and is even less in the south. The oases in the Sinai region provided water for the needs of the biblical Israelites and sustains Bedouin life there today. The oases in the valleys of the south, and particularly those of the Wadi Feiran, owe their existence to the strata of marl (a deposit of lime, clay, and sand) deposited in sections of these valleys. The water from sudden rainstorms, which rushes down the impervious granite walls of the mountainsides, is captured and retained by the porous marl. Water can be found by digging in the apparently dry wadis to a depth of two to three feet.

As elsewhere, the temperature in Sinai varies according to season and elevation. It is cooler in the mountains and during the winter. The average monthly temperature in January is about 64°F., with an average of 77°F. in July. The sun is always hot, but the desert cools rapidly at night, thus accounting for the prevailing moderate temperature even during the summer months.

Economy of the Sinai

The Sinai is not agriculturally productive except in the sandy areas along the Mediterranean coast and at the oases, where date palms are cultivated. The Sinai provides, as in earlier times, a suitable locale for Bedouin nomads, who camp with their camels and flocks of sheep and goats at the desert oases. It was in the southern wilderness of the Sinai that Moses was pasturing Jethro's flock when God appeared to him in the burning bush (Exod. 3:1–2).

Since antiquity, the Sinai has been regarded as a region rich in mineral wealth. The Egyptians prized Sinai's turquoise, for their jewelry and also mined copper, important for the production of tools and weapons. Ancient copper mines and refineries have been discovered at Serabit el-Khadim (probably biblical Dophkah), at Ezion-geber on the Gulf of Aqaba, and at Timnah, about fifteen miles north of the gulf.

History of the Sinai

Date of the Exodus

The biblical history of the Sinai Peninsula focuses on the Israelites' entrance into the region, following the miraculous deliverance of God's people from Egyptian bondage. Although the actual date of Israel's departure from Egypt and entrance into the land of Sinai is debated, determining the precise date is important for providing us with a historical setting of the Book of Exodus. Some would suggest a date in the mid-fifteenth century B.C. Others opt for a 1290 B.C. exodus and a 1250 B.C. conquest of Canaan. The "early" date of 1446 B.C. is suggested by the biblical data and harmonizes well with recent archaeological discoveries.

According to 1 Kings 6:1, Solomon began to build the temple in the fourth year of his reign, 480 years after the exodus. Solomon reigned forty years (970–931 B.C.), and the fourth year of his reign would be 966 B.C. (Albright suggests 958 B.C.). Using 966 B.C. as a base, the date of the exodus can be simply calculated by going back 480 years. Hence: 1446 B.C. The forty-year wilderness wanderings would then place Joshua's conquest in the year 1406 B.C.

Other biblical and archaeological data serve to confirm these dates. First, in Judges 11:26, Jepthah reminds the king of Ammon that the Israelites had been in Ammon for three hundred years. Since Jephthah's judgeship can be dated no later than 1100 B.C., Israel's arrival in Transjordan could be no later than 1400 B.C. Second, the Amarna Letters (c. 1400–1366 B.C.), mention the Ahibiru (apparently etymologically equated with the "Hebrews") as invading southern and central Palestine. Abdi-Hiba, governor of Jerusalem, wrote numerous letters to Pharaoh Akhnaton (1370–1353 B.C.) to request aid against the encroaching "Habru" if the region was to be saved for Egypt. Third, John Garstang's excavations (A.D. 1930–36) at the site of Jericho resulted in the discovery of a violent destruction that could be dated to around 1400 B.C.

The Route of the Exodus

The most direct route to Canaan from Egypt was the Via Maris, designated "the way of the land of the Philistines" (Exod. 13:17). Since the fleeing people were neither physically prepared for battle nor spiritually ready to occupy the land (Exod. 13:17; 3:12), the Lord led them south through the wilderness toward *yam suph*, "the sea of reeds." They journeyed from Raamses to Succoth (probably Tell el-Maskuta), west of Lake Timsah, and then camped at Etham (Exod. 13:20).

From Etham, the Israelites turned north "back" to Pi-hahiroth (meaning "region of salt marshes") between Migdol ("watchtower") and the sea (Exod. 14:2). Their second camp was at Baal-zephon. Both Migdol and Baal-zephon are unidentified but were probably fortresses at the northeast corner of the Nile delta. It was here that the fleeing Israelites were overtaken by the Egyptians (Exod. 14:9).

The Lord delivered his people from certain destruction by the greatest miracle of the exodus—the crossing of the Red Sea. Although the Hebrew term *yam suph*, used to describe this body of water, is used elsewhere to designate the Red Sea, the Gulf of Aqaba, or the Gulf of Suez (Exod. 10:19; Num. 14:25; 33:10–11; Deut. 1:40; 1 Kings 9:26), the reference in Exodus 13:18 is *not* to the Red Sea proper. First, its western arm, the Gulf of Suez, is too far south to have provided a logical place to exit from Egypt. Second, the biblical account indicates

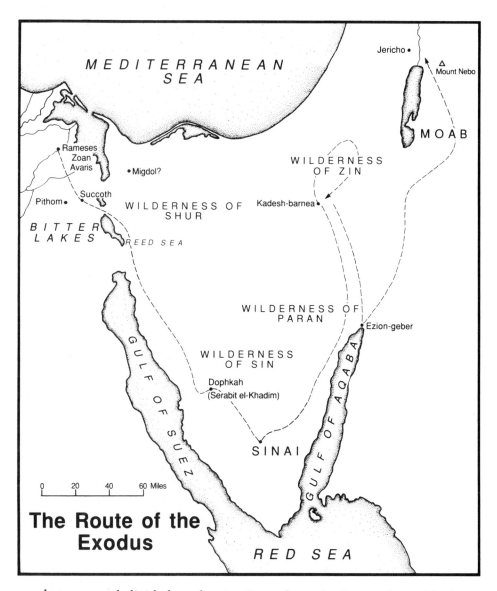

The Route of the Exodus

that *yam suph* divided productive Egypt from the desert. If Israel had gone directly south to the Gulf of Suez, they would have encountered much desert before crossing any water. Third, when they crossed *yam suph*, they found themselves in the "wilderness of Shur" (Exod. 15:22), which we have already located in northern Sinai, roughly south of Canaan.

Some argue that the Israelites crossed a sandy strip along the north side of Lake Menzaleh, but it seems more accurate to view *yam suph* ("sea of reeds") as a marshy area north of the Gulf of Suez, comprising the Bitter Lakes and Lake Timsah. The exact location would be impossible to identify in view of the major geographical changes engendered by the construction of the Suez Canal.

After crossing "the Red Sea," the Israelites entered the Wilderness of Shur (Exod. 15:22). They complained at Marah about the bitter water and then camped at Elim (unidentified). From there the Israelites set out again and entered the Wilderness of Sin (Exod. 16:1). While passing through this region, they camped at Dophkah (Num. 33:12), which means "smeltery," a site identified with the Egyptian mining center of Serabit el-Khadim.

Then the Israelites journeyed inland, probably through the Wadi Feiran, camping at Rephidim (Exod. 17:1) and finally at the foot of Jebel Musa, commonly identified as Mount Sinai (Exod. 19:1–2) –three lunar months after their departure from Egypt. The Israelites spent ten days short of a year (Num. 10:11) at Mount Sinai, where God reaffirmed his covenant with the nation and instructed them as to the law, the tabernacle, and the priesthood. Journeying north from Mount Sinai, the Israelites passed through the Wilderness of Paran to Kadesh-barnea, an oasis on the edge of the Wilderness of Zin. There they received from their spies a discouraging report of "giants" dwelling in the land (Num. 13:32). Rejecting the leadership of Moses, the faithless spies and most of the waiting congregation sought to return to Egypt. God sentenced the unbelieving generation to forty years in the wilderness. And, of the spies, only Joshua and Caleb were spared God's wrath (Num. 14:36–38).

Israel's disobedience resulted in fruitless desert years for an entire generation, as decreed by God. (Deuteronomy 2:14 rounds this period to thirty-eight years.) Most of this time appears to have been spent at Kadesh-barnea (Num. 33:36–38). After the old generation died off, the Israelites left the Wilderness of Zin and journeyed north to the Plains of Moab in preparation for their conquest of the Promised Land.

Sites of the Sinai

Many of the Sinai place-names mentioned in Scripture were only campsites, which provided no remains for archaeological investigation. Most of the sites listed in the Numbers 33 account of the Israelites' itinerary must be left unidentified. Some, however, can be given consideration.

Dophkah

As previously mentioned, the name *Dophkah* (Num. 33:12) means "smeltery" and has been identified with the Egyptian mining center of Serabit el-Khadim. This site was first excavated by W. F. M. Petrie in 1905, and archaeologists have successfully uncovered an Egyptian temple dedicated to Hathor, goddess of the land and minerals. A stele in this temple records a history of the mining expeditions there. A second important find at this site was a small statue inscribed with letters that are recognized as being the earliest Semitic alphabetic script. It has been dated about 1500 B.C.

Mount Sinai

Israel spent almost a year camped in the plain before Mount Sinai, also known as Mount Horeb (Exod. 19:1, 18; Deut. 4:10). Early Christian tradition from the time of the fourth century A.D. identifies biblical Mount Sinai with 7,363-foot Jebel Musa in southern Sinai. At the foot of this mountain lies a monastery, which Justinian I dedicated to Saint Catherine about 527 A.D. The monastery was built on a site where Helena, Constantine's mother, erected a small church two centuries earlier (326 A.D.). There are several factors favoring this identification of Mount Sinai: (1) the early tradition; (2) the mountain's distance from the starting point of Israel's exodus from Egypt; (3) its distance from the entrance to Canaan, an eleven-day journey to Kadesh-barnea ((Deut. 1:2); (4) its proximity to Serabit el-Khadim. (Moses' father-in-law was a Kenite ["smith"], and the mines there could account for his presence); and (5) just to the north of the mountain is a large 400-acre plain, where the Israelites could have camped.

Eusebius and some modern scholars identify Mount Sinai with Jebel Serbal, twenty miles northwest of Jebel Musa. Still others locate the holy mountain further north at Jebel Halal, about thirty miles west of Kadesh-barnea. Some would even reject the Sinai Peninsula as its location, opting instead for a site in northwestern Arabia. In light of the debate, the site with the strongest tradition seems preferable. Despite the uncertainty regarding its precise location, a visit to traditional "Mount Sinai" is well worth the trip. A climb to the top of Jebel Musa allows one to reflect on the events associated with the giving of the law to the people of Israel. Saint Catherine's monastery at its base is famous for Tischendorf's 1859 discovery of the fourth-century Codex Sinaiticus.

Kadesh-barnea

Kadesh-barnea was an oasis in the Wilderness of Zin in northern Sinai. There Moses, at the Lord's command, told the rock to bring forth

water, but he lost the privilege of leading Israel into the Promised Land
by striking the rock twice (Num. 20:2–13). Two sites in close proximity,
lying about fifty miles southwest of Beersheba, qualify by their general
position and water supply as Kadesh-barnea: Ain Qudeis and Ain
Qudeirat. The first retains the basic name *Kadesh* and the second
boasts the best springs. Water flows year round at Ain Qudeirat, and
good pastureland lies nearby. Situated only five miles apart, both sites
may have provided water for the large encampment of Israelites. We
are told that Miriam, Moses' sister, died at Kadesh (Num. 20:1).

Excavations on a small tell near the spring at Ain Qudeirat resulted
in the discovery of an Israelite fortress from the period of the kingdom
of Judah. It appears to have been intended to guard Judah's southern
border, possibly in the days of Jehoshaphat or Uzziah.

Ezion-geber

Ezion-geber is the last place mentioned in the route of the Israelites
before they passed into Transjordan (Deut. 2:8; cf. Num. 33:35). It is
described as "near Eloth," on the shores of the Gulf of Aqaba, the
northwest arm of "the Red Sea" (1 Kings 9:26). The site has been
identified with Tell El-Kaheleifeh, midway between Jordan's Aqaba
and Israel's Eilat and about five hundred yards from the shore. Ezion-
geber was later to become Israel's gateway to Arabia, Africa, and India.
Solomon maintained a fleet of ships at this harbor town (1 Kings
9:26–28). Jehoshaphat's ships were wrecked here (1 Kings 22:48), shat-
tering his hopes of engaging in maritime trade.

5

The Transjordan Settlement
1406 B.C.

Joshua 18:7 reports that Gad, Reuben, and half the tribe of Manasseh received their inheritance "beyond the Jordan eastward." Although the Transjordan tribes sought to maintain their identity with the tribes west of the Jordan (cf. Josh. 22), the Rift Valley provided too great a barrier to such unity. Gilead was the only Transjordan site colonized by the Israelites that had any significant role in intertribal history. Apart from Israel's journey through this region en route to Canaan and occasional military expeditions into the area (Judg. 8; 1 Sam. 11; 2 Sam. 11:1), Transjordan remained "foreign" land throughout the biblical period. In New Testament times, this area was regarded as "gentile" territory. Nevertheless, a study of the Bible lands is incomplete without a survey of Transjordan.

The Land of Transjordan

Transjordan includes the territory east of the Jordan River, extending about 150 miles from the southern shore of the Dead Sea to the base of Mount Hermon. This land falls within the modern state of Jordan. The region is made up of an elevated plateau that becomes higher as it extends southward, rising from two to five thousand feet in elevation. The average width of the Transjordan territory stretches about twenty-five miles from the eastern edge of the Jordan Valley to the Arabian Desert. The border between Transjordan and the desert was not fixed by definite geographical barriers but fluctuated according to climatic and political conditions. In times of drought or political instability, the borders would retreat westward with the advance of the desert nomads (cf. Judg. 6:3–5).

Regions of Transjordan

Four great canyons drain the western slopes of the Transjordan highlands, dividing the land into the major geographical regions significant in biblical times: Bashan, Gilead, Ammon, Moab, and Edom.

North of the Wadi Yarmuk and east of the Sea of Galilee lay the territory of Bashan. This region was noted for its rich volcanic soil and copious rainfall, which provided abundant grasslands for grazing cattle (Ps. 22:12; Amos 4:1; Ezek. 39:18). Wheat was the primary crop of the region, and Bashan was regarded in New Testament times as one of the great granaries of the Roman Empire. Bashan's southern border, the Yarmuk, is the largest eastern tributary of the Jordan. It flows southwest, entering the Jordan Valley about five miles south of the Sea of Galilee.

South of Bashan is a broad limestone dome known as Gilead. The term *Gilead* seems to be used rather loosely in the Old Testament, sometimes referring to the region north of the Jabbok River gorge and sometimes to the regions on both sides of the Jabbok (cf. Num. 32:1; Deut. 3:15–16; Josh. 12:2). Since Ammon (see below) is regarded as lying south of the Jabbok (Josh. 12:2; Deut. 3:16), we will place Gilead to the north. The territory of Gilead was about forty miles from north to south and was famed in the biblical period for its forests (Jer. 22:6), pasturelands (Num. 32:1–4), and medicinal balm (Jer. 8:22; 46:11).

The deep gorge of the Jabbok served as the northern border for the land of Ammon, home of the Ammonites (cf. Gen. 19:36–38), who were frequently at war with Israel. Ammonite territory had its center at the very edge of the Arabian Desert at Rabbah (Modern Amman), about twenty-three miles east of the Jordan. In the New Testament period, Rabbah was known as Philadelphia, an important trading center in the Decapolis.

The Wadi Arnon, which empties itself into the Dead Sea about twenty miles south of the entrance of the Jordan River, served as the northern border of Moab, land of the Moabites (Num. 21:13; cf. Gen. 19:36–38). This territory extends about thirty-five miles south to the Wadi Zered. Although the region is considerably more barren than the Transjordan territory to the north, the land was apparently suitable for grazing, as evidenced by the fact that the king of Moab was a sheep

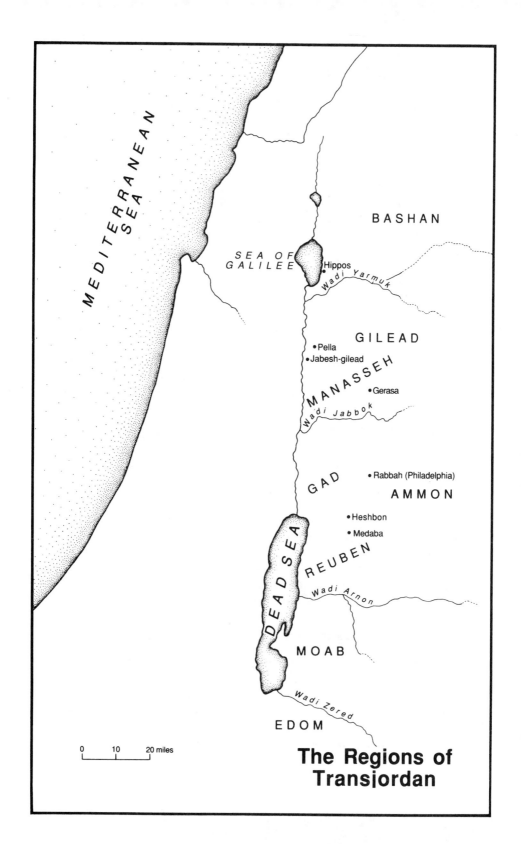

MEDITERRANEAN SEA

BASHAN

SEA OF GALILEE

• Hippos

Wadi Yarmuk

GILEAD

• Pella
• Jabesh-gilead

MANASSEH

• Gerasa

Wadi Jabbok

GAD

• Rabbah (Philadelphia)

AMMON

• Heshbon

• Medaba

DEAD SEA

REUBEN

Wadi Arnon

MOAB

Wadi Zered

EDOM

0   10   20 miles

The Regions of Transjordan

breeder (2 Kings 3:4). The area is about 3,000 feet above sea level and 4,300 feet above the shores of the Dead Sea.

The land of Edom lay south of the Wadi Zered (Num. 21:12). This was the territory of the descendents of Esau and is also known as Mount Seir (Gen. 36:8–9). Edom was bordered by the Arabah on the west, the Arabian Desert on the east, and the Gulf of Aqaba on the south. The region's barren territory was conducive to neither agriculture nor cattle raising, but its hills were a source of copper, and its location on the King's Highway (Num. 20:17) was a commercial advantage. The Transjordan mountains reached their highest elevations in Edom, rising to heights of 5,000 to 5,700 feet.

Climate of Transjordan

Since Transjordan is situated between the arid Rift Valley and the Arabian Desert, it is a land influenced by the moisture-laden Mediterranean winds. Annual rainfall is heaviest in the upper reaches of Bashan (30 to 40 inches) and on the heights of Gilead (20 to 30 inches) but diminishes in the territories further south (5 to 15 inches).

The Transjordan areas receive the full blow of the sirocco winds, which blast out of the desert as out of an oven during the transitional seasons (April through June, September through October). These winds bring a steep rise in temperature (16 to 22°F.) and a drop in relative humidity as much as 40 percent. The ferocity of the sirocco winds increases the farther one goes toward the east.

Economy of Transjordan

Where rainfall provided sufficient moisture for grasslands, cattle raising was an important part of the Transjordan economy, and wheat was grown in the rich and well-watered soil of Bashan. But undoubtedly the most important contribution to Transjordan culture and economy was the famous King's Highway (Num. 20:17), which passed through the region and provided commercial opportunities in the markets of Damascus, Elath, and Arabia. These trade opportunities had enriched the Edomites and filled their treasuries (cf. Obad. 6).

The History of Transjordan

When the Israelites were about to embark on the conquest of their Promised Land, the Moabites occupied the area between the Zered and the Arnon rivers. To the north were the territories of the two Amorite kings, Sihon and Og. The kingdom of Sihon, who ruled from Heshbon, extended from the Arnon to the Yarmuk. The kingdom of Og was to the north, in Bashan. On the borders of the Arabian Desert were the nomadic Midianites (Num. 25, 31; Josh. 13:21) and the more set-tled Ammonites (Josh. 13:10). How were the Israelites to deal with these obstacles to their entrance into the Promised Land?

While still at Kadesh-barnea, Moses sent messengers to the king of Edom, requesting permission to pass through Edomite territory along the King's Highway (Num. 20:14–17). However, the Edomites, though distant relatives of the Israelites, refused them passage (Num. 20:18–21), forcing the travelers to head south to Ezion-geber (Deut. 2:8) and detour around Edom. Following God's instructions not to provoke war with Moab (Deut. 2:9) or with Ammon (Deut. 2:19), the Israelites skirted these territories and encountered their first major confrontation with Sihon, whose land stood between the Israelites and the Jordan. In the battle that ensued, Sihon was defeated and the Israelites occupied his territory from the Arnon to the Yarmuk (Deut. 2:32–37). The Israelite forces achieved a similar victory over Og, king of Bashan (Deut. 3:1–11), and captured all his territory. The Israelites engaged in one more major battle before entering Canaan—a holy war against Midian to execute the Lord's vengeance for tempting his chosen people into idolatry and sin (Num. 31).

The land in Transjordan was suitable for pasture, and at their re-quest Moses granted the conquered territory to the tribes of Gad, Reuben, and the half-tribe of Manasseh (Num. 32:2–33). Reuben was allocated the territory from the Arnon to the northern tip of the Dead Sea; Gad received the territory north to the Jabbok; and Manasseh settled the land north of the Jabbok, including all of Bashan (Josh. 13:8–33).

As a witness to their unity with the tribes west of the Jordan, the Transjordan tribes erected a large altar by the Jordan River (Josh. 22). This gesture was misunderstood as an act of religious apostasy and almost resulted in intertribal warfare! Yet, it indicates the attempt of the Transjordan tribes to maintain a relationship with their kinsmen to the west, despite the barrier of the Jordan Rift.

During the years that followed the conquest, Transjordan territory was squeezed from the north by the Arameans, from the south by the Moabites, and from the east by the Ammonites. King David was later able to reestablish Israelite control over the Transjordan territory (2 Sam. 8), but after the division of the kingdom, much of this territory was lost. Most of the area returned to Israelite control during the reign of Jehoash (2 Kings 13:25), but the Jordan Rift made it virtually im-possible for Transjordan to become integrally united with Samaria and Judah on a permanent basis.

Transjordan rose to prominence during the intertestamental period (430–5/4 B.C.), under the influence of the Greek rulers to the north and south (the Seleucids and the Ptolemies). Having surmised that founding new cities was the best way to spread Greek culture, the Greeks established such cities as Gerasa and renamed others, such as Philadelphia (Rabbah), granting them a large measure of autonomy. (The territory occupied by Greek cities became known as the Decapolis after the successful campaign of Pompey to establish Syria as a Roman province.)

Transjordan once again came under Jewish control during the time of the Maccabees. The kingdom of Alexander Janneus (130–76 B.C.) extended north from the Wadi Zered to include all Bashan until the area's conquest by Pompey in 63 B.C.

In the time of Jesus, the territory from the Wadi Arnon north to Pella was called Perea. The Decapolis extended northward to just beyond Hippus and spilled west across the Jordan to include Scythopolis. North of Hippus, along the northeast shore of the Sea of Galilee, lay Gaulanitis.

The Cities of Transjordan

Rabbah

Rabbah (Rabbath-Ammon), modern Amman, was the capitol of the Ammonites. It was located northeast of the Dead Sea (east of "Gilead"), twenty-two miles east of the Jordan. Here Uriah was sent to his death, making possible David's marriage to Uriah's wife, Bathsheba (2 Sam.

The Roman amphitheatre at Amman. *Levant.*

11). Rabbah was an important trade center since it was situated at the junction of desert roads leading north, south, east, and west. Recognizing its commercial and strategic importance, the city was rebuilt by Ptolemy Philadephus (285–246 B.C.) and renamed "Philadelphia."

Gerasa

Situated on the King's Highway about twenty miles north of modern-day Amman lies the site of Gerasa (modern Jerash), a city that rose to its greatness during the Hellenistic and Roman periods. The walled city enclosed an area of about two hundred acres. Not only was Gerasa of commercial importance, it was a worship center for Zeus. A succession of temples dedicated to this god was erected on the hills south of the city's forum. Later, a temple to Artemis was built in the heart of the city. Although located thirty-five miles south of the Sea of Galilee, there is evidence that Gerasa had a controlling interest in territory extending to the southeastern shore of the Sea of Galilee. Its fame among the Greeks apparently led Luke to mention the city in connection with Jesus' healing of the demoniac (Luke 8:26–39).

Medaba

Although not particularly significant in biblical history (Num. 21:30; Josh. 13:16), Medaba, located in the Moab region about twelve miles from the northeastern corner of the Dead Sea, became an important town in the Byzantine period. The site has become famous for the 1896 discovery of a sixth century A.D. mosaic floor depicting the Bible lands. That early map is an extremely helpful source of information about the topography and sites of the Holy Land as it was understood in that time.

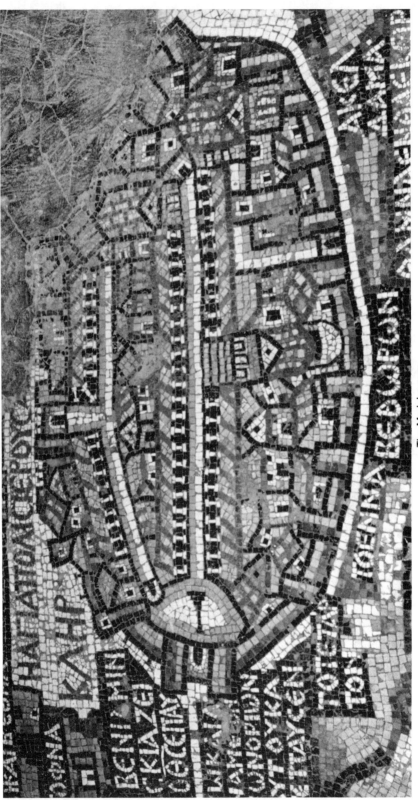

The Medaba map.

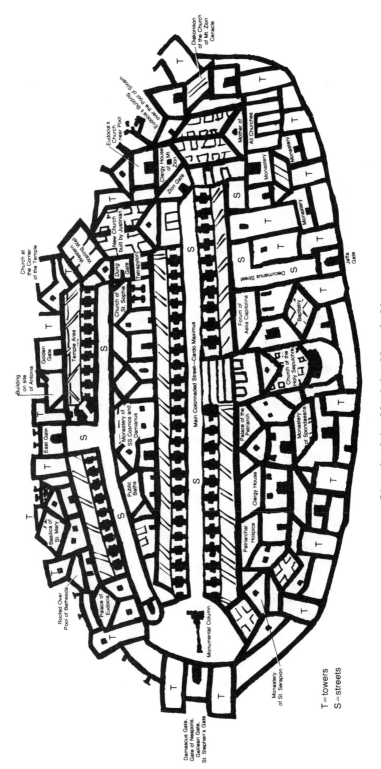

Sketch of the Medaba Mosaic Map

T = towers
S = streets

Diakonikon of the Church of Mt. Zion Cenacle

Eudocia's Building over the Pool of Siloam

Eudocia's Church near Pool

Clergy House of Mt. Zion

Zion Gate

Mother of All Churches

Monastery

Monastery

Monastery

Church at the Corner of the Temple

Western Wall

New Church built by Justinian

Dung Gate

Tetrapylon

Church of St. Sophia

Building on site of Antonia

Golden Gate

Temple Area

East Gate

S

S

S

S

S

S

S

S

S

S

Monastery of SS Cosmas and Damianus

Main Colonnaded Street—Cardo Maximus

Decumanus Street

Jaffa Gate

Forum of Aelia Capitolina

Baptistry

Church of the Holy Sepulchre

Palace of the Patriarch

Monastery of Spondaeans

Public Baths

Basilica of St. Mary

Roofed Over Pool of Bethesda

Palace of Eudocia

Patriarchal Hospice

Clergy House

Monumental Column

Monastery of St. Serapion

Damascus Gate, Gate of Neapolis, Galilean Gate, St. Stephen's Gate

6

The Conquest of Canaan
1406 to 1375 B.C.

The land west of the Jordan River provides the setting for most of the biblical events. This region provides the geographical background for the conquest, the period of the judges, the monarchy, the restoration after the exile, the life of Christ, and the early church. Although significant because of the biblical events with which it is associated, this region is important quite apart from the biblical record, since it has long served as a land bridge between the great powers of Asia, Europe, and Africa. In early times, virtually all of the traffic between these continents had to cross the territory of Palestine. Those who controlled this land bridge had great influence over the destinies of other nations. (In this chapter, we will use the terms *Canaan, Israel,* and *Palestine* interchangeably.)

Another Look at Canaan

Although we introduced the Promised Land—Canaan—when considering the patriarchal period, (chapter 2), a brief review will be helpful as we begin our study of Israelite territories west of the Jordan. Palestine extends north from the Wadi el-'Arish to the southern slopes of the Lebanon Mountains, a distance of about two hundred miles. The land is bordered by the Rift Valley on the east and the Mediterranean

Sea on the west. Because the coastline reaches out toward Egypt in the south, the land is wider in the southern region. It is about thirty-five miles wide in northern Galilee and about eighty-five miles wide at the latitude of the southern end of the Dead Sea. The expression "from Dan to Beersheba" (Judg. 20:1) is used in Scripture to refer to the occupied land as measured from its northern to southern extremities. The Israelite territories west of the Jordan divide into three distinctive geographical regions: the *coastal plain*, the *hill country*, and the *Rift Valley*. (We have considered a fourth region, the *Transjordan*, in chapter 5.)

Several generalizations regarding the climate of Israel will prove helpful in our survey of the land. The region's climate is determined by two major factors: distance from the sea, and elevation. Areas closer to the Mediterranean are more humid in contrast to the arid regions near the desert. And, generally speaking, places of higher elevation have cooler temperatures. To the west of the central mountain range, the climate of Palestine is predominantly influenced by the sea. To the east, the desert is the principal determinant of the area's climate.

Rainfall in Palestine generally increases toward the north (mountains) and toward the west (sea). The rainfall diminishes to the south and east, predominantly lowlands and desert. There are two primary seasons—a wet winter and a dry summer. Rain falls principally during the months of November through March, and the dry season extends from May through September. The "early rain and the later rain" (Deut. 11:14) occur during the seasonal transitions at the beginning and the end of the wet months. The "early" rains, usually falling in October, soften the soil after the long summer drought, enabling the farmer to plow and plant winter wheat. The "later" rains, mainly in April, cause the ripening heads of grain to swell, providing the farmer with a heavy crop of wheat. Both transitional rains are essential to agricultural prosperity (Jer. 5:24; Joel 2:23).

The climate is strongly influenced by the Mediterranean sea-to-land breeze, which brings cooling relief from the hot sun. This sea breeze is felt along the coastal plain about mid-morning, as the hot air rises and the cooler sea air rushes in to fill the space. The wind is felt in the mountains around noon and reaches the Rift Valley about two hours later. During the transitions between the wet and dry seasons, Palestine may feel the effects of the hot, dry sirocco winds that blast out of the Arabian Desert. The spring siroccos do extensive damage to winter grass and crops if they come too soon (Ps. 103:16; Isa. 40:6–8; James 1:11).

Since Israel lies between 30 and 33 degrees latitude, the summer sun is almost directly overhead. This results in relatively high temperatures, but they are somewhat moderated in the higher elevations and by the cooling effect of the sea breeze. Summer temperatures average between 65 and 85°F. in the mountains and between 80 and 105°F. on the coastal plain and in the Rift Valley.

The Hill Country

The hill country encompasses the central mountain range that runs north and south through Palestine, extending from the Negev to the foot of the Lebanon Mountains. This mountain range is formed by an upwarp of limestone about twenty miles wide and averages about 2,500 feet above sea level. A number of valleys pierce the hill country from the east and west. The largest of these is the Valley of Jezreel (Esdraelon). For the purposes of this study we will focus our attention on the hill country allocated to the tribes of Judah, Benjamin, and Ephraim—considering Galilee at a later time (chapter 14).

A view of the Judean hills from the Jordan Valley.

The hill country of Judah began just north of the Beersheba basin and ran to a point just south of Jerusalem—a distance of thirty-five miles. The mountains are about fifteen miles wide at this point. The highest elevation is near Hebron, where the mountains reach 3,373 feet above sea level. An ancient highway connecting Beersheba, Hebron, and Jerusalem follows the central range of this mountain area.

Just north of Judah's hill country lay the tribal territory of Benjamin. This was a smaller region, measuring about ten miles from north to south. The boundary between the two regions was more polit-

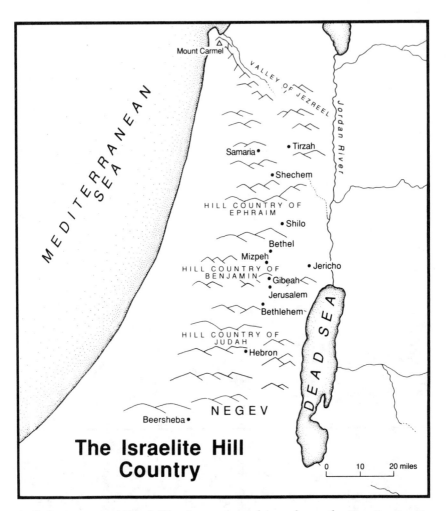

The Israelite Hill Country

ical than geographical. The important thing about the Benjamin territory was the strategic access it provided into the hill country of
Judah. Benjamin was accessible from the west by a road that ascended
from the Aijalon Valley to the Beth-horon ridge. This served as the
main approach to Jerusalem from the coastal plain. Since the control
of this access was crucial for the defense of Jerusalem, this land was
eventually absorbed into Judah's territory.

The border between Benjamin and Ephraim ran between the cities
of Mizpah and Bethel. The land from Bethel north to the Jezreel Valley
was occupied by Ephraim and one-half of the tribe of Manasseh. This
entire area was later known as Samaria and is today called Mount
Ephraim. The land measures thirty miles north to south and twenty

miles east to west. The highest part of Mount Ephraim is just northeast of Bethel at Ba'al Hazor (3,000 feet). The elevation descends toward the north to Shechem (2,000 feet) and on to Dothan (1,000 feet) near the Jezreel Valley's southern edge. The hill country of Ephraim is considerably more open than the mountains to the south, and many wide valleys penetrate its central region. While this feature provided more land for cultivation, it also made Ephraim more accessible to enemy invaders. Since this was a harder area to defend, it fell to the Assyrians in 722 b.c., whereas Judah survived for another 135 years.

Climate of the Hill Country

The hill country is generally a pleasant region in terms of climate. The winters are cool, but there is ample warm sunshine. The hot summers are moderated by a breeze from the sea. The Mediterranean breeze reaches the hill country about midday, bringing cooling relief and keeping the annual mean temperature between 59 and 66°F. The hill country receives twenty-five to thirty inches of rain annually, with most of the rain falling during about forty-five days in January and February. An occasional snowfall occurs in the hills around Jerusalem and Hebron.

Geology of the Hill Country

One of Palestine's most important resources is its rock. The hill country is dominated by a large exposure of Cenomanian limestone, which for centuries has provided building stones for its inhabitants. This variety of limestone breaks along even lines and can be easily shaped for building.

The unique composition of this limestone also makes it a natural water reservoir. It permits the rapid seepage of rainwater, which is absorbed until it reaches a nonporous stratum of rock. It then flows horizontally until it reaches the surface, breaking forth in the springs so prevalent in this region (cf. Jer. 2:13). Cenomanian limestone weathers into a fertile, reddish-brown soil *(terra rossa)*. Much of this fine soil has been lost through erosion due to deforestation (Deut. 20:19–20; Josh. 17:15). Terracing the hillsides continues to be an effective method of retaining the soil and converting hilly regions into agricultural land.

Economy of the Hill Country

The residents of the hill country were primarily an agricultural and pastoral people. They raised sheep and goats and grew the Mediterranean staples—wheat, grapes, and olives (cf. Deut. 7:13; Neh. 5:11; Ps. 104:15). They also produced nuts, pomegranates, dates, and figs. The hill country around Hebron still abounds with productive vineyards, and the wide valleys of Samaria are especially suited for the cultivation of wheat.

The main travel routes through the hill country followed the water line at the crest of the mountains and then joined the major highways by way of east-west valley roads. This system of roads united this rather isolated region with the other areas and was useful for communication, trade, and travel. Yet, since the roads also gave access to advancing armies, the valleys had to be fortified (cf. 2 Chron. 11:5–12).

The History of the Conquest

At the time of the Israelite conquest, most of the Canaanites lived in valleys and along the coastal plain. There were a few important cities in the hills, such as Hebron, Jebus, Bethel, and Shechem. These cities were strongly fortified and defended by well-equipped Canaanite warriors. The Canaanite culture in the fourteenth century B.C. was remarkably advanced. There were skilled craftsmen, experienced merchants, and knowledgeable farmers. In fact, the Canaanites were more advanced culturally than the Israelites, who had spent their previous forty years in the wilderness.

The Canaanite religion was essentially a fertility cult, founded on the belief that the blessings of progeny and abundant harvest were a direct result of the sexual relations of the gods. To encourage such activities, the worshipers engaged in sacred prostitution. The rituals would be performed at a high place—in either a temple or grove of trees. El was the supreme god of the Canaanite pantheon and Baal, his son and successor, the central figure in Canaanite worship. Fertility goddesses included Anath, Asherah, and Ashtaroth. The religious culture of Canaan was ripe for judgment (Gen. 15:16; Lev. 18:24–25). God commanded the complete destruction of the Canaanites by Joshua to punish the wicked inhabitants (Deut. 9:4) and protect the Israelites from involvement in such pagan worship (Deut. 20:17–18).

The Entrance into Canaan

After the death of Moses, the mantle of leadership passed to Joshua, who was to lead God's people into Canaan. The Israelites approached the land from the east, apparently with plans to divide the hill country and conquer the north and south separately. Before crossing the Jordan, Joshua sent spies out to reconnoiter the city of Jericho (Josh. 2). Since news of Israelite victories over Sihon and Og had reached the ears of the Canaanites, the spies were able to report that the citizens of

Jericho were overcome with terror (Josh. 2:9). After the miraculous crossing of the Jordan River at flood stage—an event on the par of the crossing of the Red Sea—the Israelites set up camp at Gilgal (identified with Khirbet el-Mefjer) and celebrated Passover (Josh. 5:10). The day after they had eaten some of the produce of Canaan, the manna ceased. Now they must claim the land God had promised them.

The Central Campaign

Joshua's central campaign (Josh. 6–9) began at Jericho, the oldest known fortified city in the world. The capture of Jericho was strategically important, for it gave access to valleys ascending into the hill country. According to the biblical account, the destruction of Jericho was accomplished by the Lord, totally apart from the efforts of the people. The feat was designed to show the people that this was God's war and that he would lead them to victory (cf. Josh. 5:13–15).

The Israelites experienced a serious setback at Ai on account of sin in the camp (Josh. 7). (Ai has been identified with et-Tell, about two miles east of Bethel [Beitin]. The problem with this identification is that Ai was apparently unoccupied at the time of the conquest. Perhaps the site has been misidentified and should be located elsewhere.) In close association with Joshua's victory over Ai (Josh. 8) was his conquest of Bethel (Josh. 8:17; 12:16). The Israelites then marched north to Shechem, where they observed ceremonies designed to reaffirm their commitment to the law (Josh. 8:30–35).

The Southern Campaign

Joshua's southern campaign (Josh. 10) was precipitated by his unwise alliance with the Gibeonites (Josh. 9). Since Joshua was deceived into believing the Gibeonites to be wanderers from a distant land, he did not realize he was ignoring God's command not to covenant with the people of Canaan (Deut. 7:1–2). He then discovered that they actually lived at el-Jib, just six miles north of Jerusalem! When news of the Gibeonites' capitulation reached Adonizedek, king of Jerusalem, he organized the five kings of the Amorites into attacking Gibeon, forcing Joshua to defend those with whom he had become mistakenly allied. He led his troops on a twenty-four-mile night march from Gilgal to Gibeon and took the attackers by surprise. The enemy fled west down the ascent of Beth-horon, and the Israelites captured and put to death the five kings who had attacked the city. This victory sealed the fate of southern Palestine. Joshua's warriors continued south, conquering cities in the Shephelah, southern hill country, and the Negev (Josh. 10:28–43).

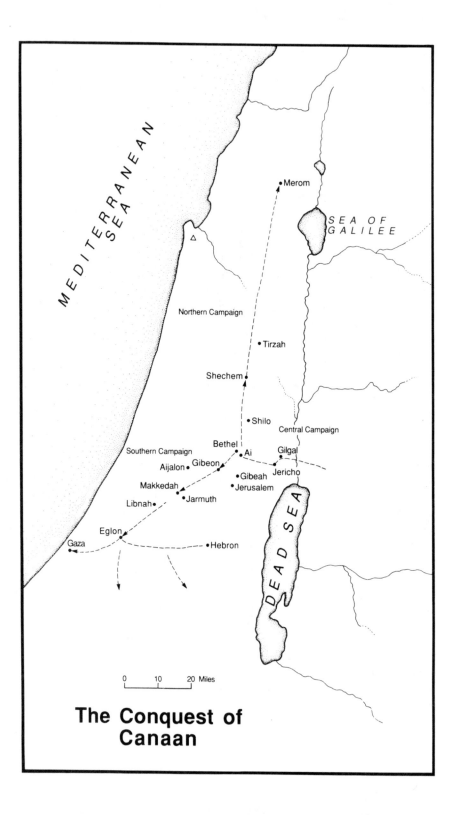

MEDITERRANEAN SEA

SEA OF GALILEE

• Merom

Northern Campaign

• Tirzah

Shechem •

• Shilo

Central Campaign

Bethel •
Southern Campaign • Ai   Gilgal •
Aijalon • Gibeon •   Jericho
Makkedah •   • Gibeah
Libnah •   • Jerusalem
    • Jarmuth
Eglon •
Gaza •   • Hebron

DEAD SEA

0   10   20 Miles

The Conquest of Canaan

The Northern Campaign

The news of Joshua's overwhelming victory in southern Canaan soon reached the ears of Jabin, king of Hazor, a strategic fortress city north of the Sea of Galilee. Fearing attack, he organized a coalition of cities to protect the northern territory. The gathering point for Jabin's confederacy was the waters of Merom, a copious spring about seven miles northwest of Hazor (Josh. 11:1–5). Joshua did not wait for the enemy to come to him, but led the Israelite warriors to the battlefield for a surprise attack. The Lord gave his people a great victory over Jabin's forces and the mighty fortress of Hazor, the only city in northern Canaan that Joshua burned (Josh. 11:13). Joshua completed the conquest of the north, capturing many cities and taking plunder. Thus Joshua took the whole land, as God had promised—and the Israelites had rest from war.

Dividing the Inheritance

Joshua's conquest, which took about six years to complete (cf. Josh. 14:7–10), broke the military strength of the Canaanites, but the land had to be subjugated and settled by the individual tribes according to territorial allotments. Many tribes failed to fulfill this responsibility (Josh. 15:63; 16:10; 17:12–26; 19:47; Judg. 1:1—2:5).

The land was divided by casting lots and according to tribal size (Num. 26:54–56). The general vicinity of a tribe's inheritance was apparently determined by lot, and the actual boundaries by need. The larger tribes received more territory. Joshua 14–19 describes the territories assigned to the nine and one-half tribes west of the Jordan. Reference to the map is the most helpful way to get a sense of the tribal territories.

The Years that Followed

The Bible records that the people of Israel served the Lord all the days of Joshua and the elders who succeeded him (Josh. 24:31; Judg. 2:7), but then there arose a generation "who did not know the Lord" (Judg. 2:10). The new generation forsook the Lord and took up the worship of Baal, the Canaanite fertility deity.

Seduction into false worship was a problem that pursued the Israelites down through the ages. This sin was disciplined by God through the Assyrian destruction of Samaria in 722 B.C., after which time the northern tribes were taken into captivity and never returned to the land. Later, God used the Babylonians as his instrument of judgment on Judah and Jerusalem. In 586 B.C. Jerusalem was captured and the temple burned. The Judeans were then exiled to Babylon, but God graciously restored them under the decree of Cyrus in 538 B.C.

God had given the land of Canaan to the people Israel. But the privilege of living in the land and enjoying its blessings was conditional on their obedience. This was the lesson God was to teach his people throughout their history in the land of promise.

Cities of the Hill Country

Many cities of the hill country are worthy of in-depth consideration. The few selected here are representative of those that have a significant place in the history of the Israelites. (Jerusalem, an obvious omission, will be considered in chapter 12.)

Shechem

Identified with the ancient mound known as Tell Balatah, Shechem was situated between two mountains, Ebal and Gerizim, in central Ephraim. The site was strategically located at the junction of the main north-south road through the hill country and the valley leading to the coastal plain and the Via Maris. It was here at Shechem that Jacob had bought a piece of land and dwelt among the Canaanites (Gen. 33:18–20). There is no record of Joshua's having engaged Shechem in battle, but there the Israelites affirmed their allegiance to God and his law (Josh. 8:30–35). It is thought that because of ancient ties, Shechem may have been peacefully absorbed by the invading tribes. Joseph's mummified body was later buried there (Josh. 24:32).

During the Maccabean period (Hasmonean dynasty), Shechem was destroyed by John Hyrcanus (129 B.C.) in a campaign to establish his sovereignty as high priest and hereditary ruler. It was never rebuilt. Nablus, just one mile to the east, was established in 72 B.C., and Shechem was virtually forgotten until uncovered by archaeological investigation. It was near Shechem that Jesus met the Samaritan woman at "Jacob's well" (John 4:5–43). Her village of Sychar (identified with modern Askar) was located about half a mile to the north of Shechem.

Shiloh (Shilo)

Shiloh was located just east of the main north-south road, about twelve miles south of Shechem (twenty miles north of Jerusalem). Here the Israelites assembled after the conquest of Canaan to erect the tabernacle and complete the division of the land (Josh. 18:1–10). It was here, too, that Eli the priest ministered and Samuel the prophet grew up and first knew the Lord (1 Sam. 1–3). Shiloh remained the center of

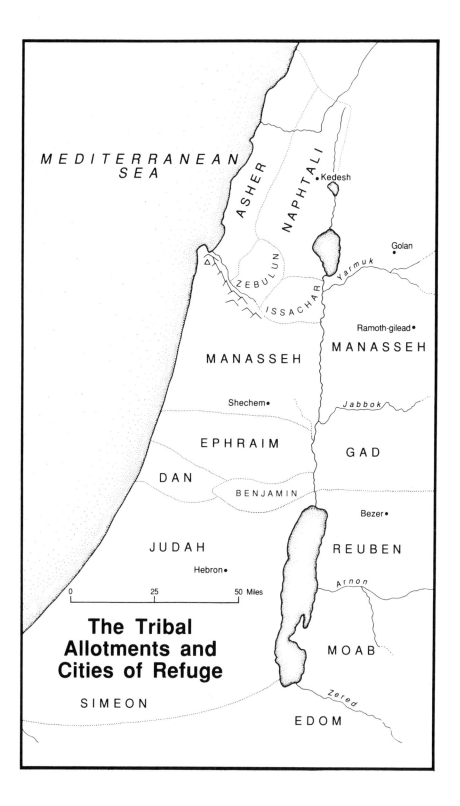

MEDITERRANEAN
SEA

ASHER

NAPHTALI

• Kedesh

• Golan

ZEBULUN

ISSACHAR

Yarmuk

Ramoth-gilead •

MANASSEH

MANASSEH

Shechem •

Jabbok

EPHRAIM

GAD

DAN

BENJAMIN

Bezer •

JUDAH

REUBEN

Hebron •

Arnon

0   25   50 Miles

**The Tribal
Allotments and
Cities of Refuge**

MOAB

SIMEON

Zered

EDOM

A columned street of Samaria, now called Sebaste. *Guy P. Duffield.*

Round Hellenistic tower at the western entrance to Samaria. *John McRay.*

Israelite tribal worship until its destruction in 1050 B.C., probably by the Philistines (cf. 1 Sam. 4; Jer. 26:6). Excavations at the site indicate that the town was reestablished in the Hellenistic period and prospered during Roman and Byzantine times.

Gibeah

Gibeah (Tell el-Ful) was situated on a hill just three miles north of Jerusalem. Lying in the center of Benjaminite territory, it became a town of considerable importance. In its early history, Gibeah gained a rather bad reputation for tolerating evil (Judg. 19–20), which resulted in its destruction by the other tribes. Later, it was rebuilt and became a royal city. Gibeah was King Saul's hometown and became his capital (1 Sam. 10:26; 15:34). (This site was first excavated by W. F. Albright in 1922–23 and 1933.)

Tirzah

About seven miles north of Shechem is Tell el-Farah, identified with ancient Tirzah. The ancient city was strategically located at the head of Wadi Fari'a, a deep valley leading east to the Jordan River. Tirzah is first identified as a royal city during the reign of Baasha (1 Kings 15:21, 33; 16:6). Noted for its beauty (Song of Sol. 6:4), Tirzah served as the capital for the kingdom of Israel until the days of Omri, who established a new capital at Samaria in the seventh year of his reign (1 Kings 16:23–24). Tirzah was destroyed by the Assyrians about 725 B.C. and eventually abandoned in 600 B.C. (Excavations at Tizrah were directed by Roland de Vaux, 1946–60.)

Samaria

The city of Samaria, seven miles west of Shechem, was founded by Omri about 800 B.C. to serve as a new capital for the northern kingdom, Israel (1 Kings 16:24). Omri selected a site on an easily defensible hill (three to four hundred feet above the valley), which commanded a major trade and travel route between the coastal plain and the hill country of Ephraim. Ahab, Omri's son, is known for commissioning the rich ivory inlays that embellished the walls and furnishings of the royal palace there (1 Kings 22:39).

Although the city was unsuccessfully attacked a number of times throughout its history, it was finally besieged by Shalmaneser and captured by Sargon II of Assyria in 722 B.C. Samaria later flourished in the Hellenistic and Roman periods. Herod the Great built a theater, stadium, and temple there around 25 B.C. and renamed it "Sebaste" in honor of Emperor Augustus.

7

The Period of the Judges
1375 to 1050 B.C.

After the death of Joshua, the Israelites were without centralized leadership and entered into a period of political chaos, religious confusion, and moral compromise. In the words of the author of Judges, "In those days there was no king in Israel; every man did what was right in his own eyes" (Judg. 17:6; 21:25).

The people of Israel were finally dwelling in the land that had been promised them. Why, then, did they not enjoy the blessing of God during this period? The Book of Judges tells the story—an account of a failed mission. The people were unable to completely drive out the original inhabitants (Judg. 1:1–2:5) and soon became involved in the trappings of their pagan worship. Israel "forsook the LORD, and served the Baals and the Ashtaroth" (Judg. 2:13).

As a consequence of Israel's disobedience, the Lord gave his people into the hands of oppressors and plunderers, a discipline meant to turn them from sin and back to God (Judg. 2:14–15). Most of Israel's oppressors were local enemies from the border areas, for the major powers of the ancient Near East were not yet of sufficient strength to engage in active domination of Palestine. The foreign oppressors whom God used to discipline his people included the Mesopotamians, the Canaanites, the Midianites, the Ammonites, and (most serious of all) the Philistines.

Once the Israelites recognized their faithless backsliding and repented, the Lord raised up judges to give leadership to his chosen people and deliver them from their oppressors (Judg. 2:16, 18). Twelve of these judges are identified. They served in various regions of the land of Israel as the demand for their leadership arose. One geographical region where at least two of the judges were active was the Valley of Jezreel, an important region of northern Israel that we will examine before considering its relationship to the history of Palestine at this time.

The Valley of Jezreel

The broad, fertile Valley of Jezreel is the only major gap in the great upwarp of Cenomanian limestone that extends from the Negev to the Lebanon Mountains. The name *Jezreel* ("God sows") was taken from the name of a royal city that flourished there during the rule of Ahab (1 Kings 18:45; 21:1). The valley is also known by the Greek form of the name, "Esdraelon" (Judith 1:8; 3:9; 4:6). Josephus calls it "the Great Plain." It is popularly referred to as the "Valley of Armageddon" on the basis of Revelation 16:16. According to Revelation, the nations will gather for an apocalyptic battle at a place called (in Hebrew) "Har-Magedon" (hence, "Armageddon"). This appears to be a reference to the hill of Megiddo, an ancient site that commands the Valley of Jezreel.

The Valley of Jezreel angles through the Cenomanian upwarp in the same direction as the Carmel range, which serves as its southwestern boundary. The valley begins about ten miles from the Mediterranean coast, extending southeasterly from the plain of Haifa to the Jordan Valley. The portion of the valley between the ancient site of Jezreel and the Jordan is usually referred to as the Harod Valley, after the prominent spring (Judg. 7:1) that waters the region. Since no major topographical feature serves to demarcate these two valleys, they will be considered as one. The Jezreel Valley thus extends about twenty-five miles from the post-biblical Jewish city of Beth She'arim to Bethshean at the junction with the Jordan Valley. At its widest point, south of the hills of Nazareth, the valley is approximately fifteen miles wide.

Rivers of the Jezreel

The greater part of the Valley of Jezreel is nearly level and lies about 150 feet above sea level. The valley is drained to the west by the Kishon River and to the east by the Harod. In the past, the Kishon was inadequate to drain the valley, particularly during the rainy season, when the river would become a raging torrent (Judg. 5:21). Runoff

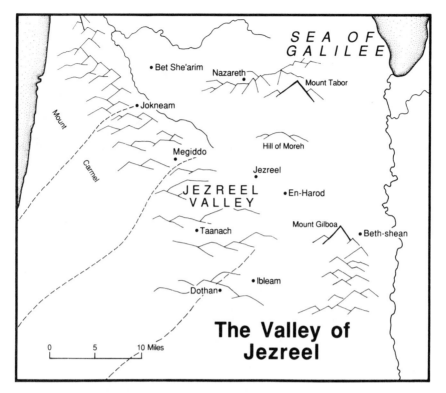

The Valley of Jezreel

from the surrounding mountains would turn the rich, alluvial soil into a marshy quagmire, making the valley almost impassable. Travelers caught in a heavy rain might find themselves knee deep in clinging mud.

To the east, the Jezreel descends toward the Jordan, passing below sea level near En-Harod and reaching 500 feet below sea level at Beth-shean. The Harod flows another four miles, dropping another 250 feet before emptying into the Jordan.

Mountains of the Jezreel

There are three important mountains that rise from this valley and break its continuity. Mount Tabor (1,843 feet) is a cone-shaped hill north of the valley, about five miles west of Nazareth. The prominence of this mountain is highlighted in a number of Old Testament poetic texts (Ps. 89:12; Jer. 46:18; Hos. 5:1). From the heights of Mount Tabor, Deborah and Barak descended upon the Canaanites and achieved a great victory (Judg. 4–5). Although not mentioned in the New Testament, the mountain has traditionally been associated with the transfiguration of Christ.

Mountains of Gilboa from the Valley of Jezreel (Esdraelon, Armageddon).

Mount Moreh (1,815 feet), about five miles to the south of Tabor, is of volcanic origin. The "hill of Moreh" is mentioned as the campsite of the Midianites when they were attacked by Gideon and his army (Judg. 7:1). At the foot of the hill to the north is the village of Nain, where Christ raised the widow's son (Luke 7:11–17). Just a mile and a half northeast of the hill is Endor, where Saul met with a medium and requested communication with the long-dead Samuel (1 Sam. 28).

Mount Gilboa (1,696 feet), in the southeast sector of the Valley of Jezreel, is actually a small mountain range eight miles long and three to five miles wide. Gilboa is a geological continuation of the hill country of Ephraim and the mountain is composed of Eocene limestone. Nowhere in Israel is there such a concentration of springs as are found along the northeast base of Mount Gilboa. The springs provide abundant sources for irrigating this area.

Situated on a western spur of Gilboa was the once royal city of Jezreel (1 Kings 21:1). At the foot of the mountain in the north is "the spring of Harod" (En-Harod), where Gideon camped before his night attack on the Midianites (Judg. 7:1). It was on the slopes of Mount Gilboa that Saul and his three sons met their deaths while campaigning against the Philistines (1 Sam. 31).

One other mountain must be considered in relationship to the Jezreel Valley. Paralleling the valley to the southwest is the Mount Carmel range, extending thirty-five miles from its slopes near Haifa to the Dothan Valley, which separates Carmel from the hill country of Ephraim. Mount Carmel reaches 1,790 feet at its highest point, but the range is sliced into three sections by the mountain passes linking the Jezreel Valley with the coastal plain. Each of these passes was guarded in ancient times by a fortress city. The passes are spaced about eight miles apart. The central and most important of the three is Megiddo pass, where Josiah met Pharaoh Neco (2 Kings 23:29). To the northeast is Jokneam pass, and to the southeast is the Dothan pass. Each of these narrow valleys and the cities that guarded them were strategically important for the control of the Jezreel.

Climate of the Jezreel

The Valley of Jezreel is well watered, averaging twenty to twenty-five inches of rainfall annually. Mount Carmel, higher in elevation and nearer to the sea, receives between thirty and thirty-five annual inches at its summit. The valley is relatively open to the sea from the northwest and receives the cooling benefit of the Mediterranean sea-to-land breeze. July and August temperatures are around 80°F., with temperatures in January and February averaging around 55°F.

Economy of the Jezreel

The Jezreel has long been recognized as a rich and fertile valley (cf. Isa. 28:1). It has been estimated that the alluvial soil in the valley reaches depths of 330 feet. The Jezreel served as the granary for Palestine throughout the biblical period. It was only after the Arab conquest in A.D. 634 that the Jezreel, due to neglect, became a malaria-infested swamp. Recent conservation efforts have returned it to its former productivity.

The most important factor contributing to the culture and economy of the Jezreel was the numerous travel routes that passed through the region. The mighty Via Maris passed right through the Carmel range at Megiddo pass and then angled between Mount Tabor and the hill of Moreh toward Damascus. From Megiddo, another important road went east to Beth-shean. A coastal highway extended northwest to Acre, Tyre, and Sidon. Those living in the Valley of Jezreel benefited enormously from the resulting trade and travel opportunities.

The History of the Judges

There seems to be somewhat of a problem with the chronology of the judges, a discrepancy that can be simply stated, and possibly just as simply solved. Although the terms of service performed by the judges total 410 years, 1 Kings 6:1 states that 480 years elapsed between the exodus and Solomon's fourth year, when he began to build the temple. That apparently leaves just a seventy-year gap for the wilderness wanderings, the conquest, the reigns of Saul and David, and the first four years of Solomon's rule—all of which actually total 145 years. The 410-year total for the events of the Book of Judges is about seventy-five years too long!

The problem dissolves, however, if we assume that the careers of some of the judges overlapped. Since each judge ruled a particular region, several could have given leadership to the nation at the same time (cf. Judg. 10:1–5). For example, it appears that Jephthah, busy with the Ammorites in Transjordan, and Samson, concerned with Philistine activity to the west, were contemporaneous in their activity. The period of the judges, then, spans about 325 years—from the death of Joshua (c. 1375 B.C.) to the anointing of Saul (1050 B.C.).

The Cycles of Apostasy

The Book of Judges records seven cycles of apostasy. The cycles always began with a relapse into sin and idolatry, which was then disciplined by the Lord. Sin brought ruin and servitude under a foreign power. After the Israelites cried out to the Lord in repentance, God would raise up a spirit-empowered "deliverer," or judge. These judges provided military, and sometimes spiritual, leadership for the distressed people. After being restored through a judge's leadership, the people would enjoy a period of peace, only to fall into apostasy once again and repeat the cycle.

1. *Mesopotamian Oppression* (3:8–11). The first punishing oppressor, Cushan-rishathaim, came from the far north. "Mesopotamia" literally translates "Aram of the two rivers," a reference to the Tigris-Euphrates valley. After eight years of servitude to these foreign oppressors, the people repented and God raised up *Othniel*, Caleb's younger half-brother, to deliver Israel. Then the people enjoyed peace for forty years.

2. *Moabite Oppression* (3:12–30). Israel's Moabite neighbors in Transjordan captured Jericho and subjugated the people for eighteen years before the Lord raised up *Ehud*, a left-handed Benjamite, to deliver them. Ehud, the cloak-and-dagger judge (Judg. 3:16) slew Eglon, king of Moab, and the Israelites quickly destroyed the Moabite army. Eighty years of peace followed—the longest such time in the period of the judges.

3. *Canaanite Oppression* (4–5). Israel's next apostasy was followed by twenty years of oppression under Jabin, king of Canaan, who reigned at Hazor. Joshua had conquered Hazor, but the Canaanites apparently rebuilt the city. When Israel cried out for help, the Lord raised up *Deborah*, a godly woman who was already serving in a judicial capacity in Israel. She called on *Barak* to take command of the Israelite forces and draw Jabin's army into battle. Barak and Deborah assembled their forces on Mount Tabor in the Valley of Jezreel. Sisera, Jabin's general, gathered the Canaanite chariot force "at Taanach by the waters of Megiddo" (5:19), crossed the upper reaches of the Kishon, and then proceeded toward Mount Tabor. As the Israelites descended

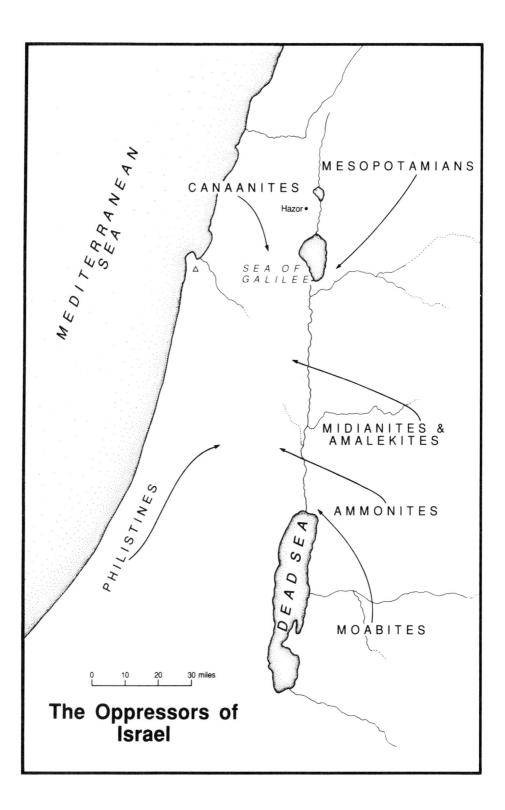

MEDITERRANEAN SEA

MESOPOTAMIANS

CANAANITES

Hazor •

SEA OF GALILEE

MIDIANITES & AMALEKITES

AMMONITES

PHILISTINES

DEAD SEA

MOABITES

0   10   20   30 miles

The Oppressors of Israel

upon the Canaanites from the mount, a sudden rainstorm caused the Kishon to swell and overflow. The Canaanite war chariots became stuck in the mire, and General Sisera fled on foot before meeting death at the hands of Jael. Forty years of peace followed Israel's deliverance by Deborah and Barak.

4. *The Midianite Oppression* (6:1–8:28). The fourth oppression brought upon Israel was led by the Midianites, aided by some desert tribesmen, the Amalekites. After seven years of unhindered pillage, the people once again repented. For their deliverance, God raised up *Gideon*, who lived in the village of Ophrah, located in the Valley of Jezreel where the attacks had been centered. He gained recognition and a new name, Jerubbaal ("let Baal contend"), by delivering his town's people from the influence of Baal worship. When the Midianites and their allies assembled in the Valley of Jezreel for battle, Gideon gathered his army of 32,000 at the foot of Mount Gilboa and camped at the spring of Harod (7:1). The Midianites were just across the valley on the north side of the hill of Moreh. As the Lord had commanded, Gideon surprised the enemy with a night attack by his much-reduced army of three hundred men. The remnants of the Midianite troops were pursued back to Transjordan, and the Israelite people enjoyed another forty years of rest.

5. *Abimelech's Oppression* (8:33–10:5). After the death of Gideon, his son by a concubine, Abimelech, claimed the kingship that his father had rejected. He secured his throne by killing Gideon's other sons and reigned for three years at Arumah between Shechem and Shiloh. He suffered an ignoble death while besieging Thebez. Israel's restoration after the rebellion of Abimelech probably took place under the leadership of *Tola* and *Jair*, who appear to have ruled contemporaneously.

6. *Ammonite Oppression* (10:6–12:7). Judges 10:6 reports that the Israelites served not only the false gods of Canaan, but also those of Aram, Sidon, Moab, Ammon, and Philistia. Adopting the religious customs of their neighbors brought God's discipline once again to the people of Israel. God delivered his people into the hands of the Philistines and Ammonites, the latter being the more significant in this period. In response to Israel's cry of repentance, God gave his people deliverance through *Jephthah*, one of the most interesting and problematic judges. His daughter's fate after Jephthah's victory is a subject of considerable debate (Judg. 11:34–40).

7. *Philistine Oppression* (13:1–16:31). The last major cycle of apostasy recorded in Judges resulted in forty years of oppression by the Philistines, most of whom had migrated from the Aegean Islands around 1168 B.C. They eventually settled on Israel's southern coastal

plain and gained control of the coastal plain north to Mount Carmel, including the Jezreel Valley all the way to the Jordan. To deliver Israel from the Philistines, the Lord raised up *Samson*. This mighty man had great potential for leadership and service, but his spiritual unfaithfulness and unbridled passions prevented him from fully delivering the Israelites from the Philistine menace.

History of the Jezreel

When the Israelites first conquered Palestine, they occupied the hill country, but the Canaanites and their powerful chariot forces maintained control of the plains and lowlands, including the Jezreel. Most of the valley was allotted to the half-tribe of Manasseh (Josh. 16:8-11), although the tribal territories of Zebulun and Naphtali shared the northern reaches of the valley. Neither of these tribes took full possession of the Jezreel because of the militarily superior Canaanites living in the land (Judg. 1:19, 27, 30, 33). The Valley of Jezreel continued as a battlefield and "no-man's land" until the conquests of David, whose expansive kingdom (1 Kings 4:24) Solomon was privileged to inherit. It is probable that at this time the Levitical cities in the Jezreel (Jokneam, Taanach, Kishion, and Daberath) became functional as cities of refuge (cf. Josh. 21). When Solomon later organized his kingdom into twelve administrative units, the Jezreel was divided among the fifth, ninth, and tenth districts.

At the division of the monarchy (931 B.C.), the Valley of Jezreel fell to the northern kingdom. A fragment of a stele indicates that the Egyptians captured Megiddo in the time of Pharaoh Shishak (924 B.C.). The plain was again under Israelite control in the days of Omri and Ahab, who maintained a winter capital at Jezreel. It was in 733 B.C. that the Assyrian forces of Tiglath-pileser III captured Galilee and the Jezreel from the northern kingdom (2 Kings 15:29). The Valley of Jezreel, with Galilee, became an Assyrian province and continued as such until the days of Josiah, who took advantage of Assyria's weakness at this time and extended his rule into Samaria, the Jezreel, and possibly Gilead.

After Nebuchadnezzar's victory at the battle of Carchemish in 605 B.C., all the land of Israel fell under the domination of Babylon. Nebuchadnezzar would have passed through the Valley of Jezreel in 597 and 586 B.C. on his way to pillage and besiege Jerusalem.

There is some debate as to whether the Valley of Jezreel belonged to the political district of Galilee during the Roman domination. Some have suggested that the whole plain belonged to Galilee. On the basis of Josephus' description, it has been suggested that the district, which separated the more mountainous regions of Galilee and Samaria, was neutral territory. It may be that while the official boundary ran through the middle of the valley, the region was popularly regarded as neither Galilean or Samaritan. This popular view is reflected in Josephus. The valley was administered, at least in part, by Herod Antipas during the time of Jesus. The eastern extension of the Jezreel (the Harod Valley) was part of the Decapolis. Jesus grew up in the hills of Nazareth, which overlooked the Valley of Jezreel, and there is at least one reference to his traveling through the valley to Nain (Luke 7:11).

The Cities of Jezreel

Of the many important ancient cities in the Valley of Jezreel—Megiddo, Beth-shean, Jezreel, Taanach, Ibleam, and Dothan–the first two stand head and shoulders above the rest in historical significance.

Megiddo

The ancient Canaanite and Israelite city of Megiddo, located on the southern side of the Jezreel Valley about twenty-two miles southeast of today's Haifa, was strategically situated to guard the major pass through Mount Carmel and control travel along the Via Maris. The site also served as a junction with the road going northwest to Acco and southeast to Beth-shean.

The first historical mention of Megiddo occurs in the annals of Tuthmose III, who defeated a Canaanite army nearby in 1468 B.C. Megiddo was a strong Canaanite city-state at the time of Joshua's

Solomonic Gate at Megiddo. *JCL.*

conquest and was among the Canaanite cities not originally taken by the Israelites (Judg. 1:27). The city later became an Israelite possession in the time of David and was fortified by Solomon (1 Kings 9:15). The multiple defense gate at Megiddo is identical to the gates at Hazor and Gezer. Excavations at Megiddo have uncovered a large palace, probably the governor's residence. Also uncovered were numerous structures containing feeding troughs, thought by some to mark Solomon's stables (cf. 1 Kings 10:26), although others have interpreted the chambers to be storage facilities (1 Kings 9:19).

Megiddo had a well-planned water system, with a 224-foot tunnel leading from the interior of the city to a spring outside the city walls. This ensured safe access to water in time of siege. The Israelite city of Megiddo fell to the Assyrians in 733 B.C. Josiah was killed near Megiddo in 609 B.C. In post-biblical times, both Napoleon (1799) and Allenby (1918) defeated Turkish forces at Megiddo. It appears that a great apocalyptic battle is destined to occur at the site (Rev. 16:16).

Beth-shean

The ancient city of Beth-shean was situated at the crossroads of two valleys—the eastern (Harod) extension of the Jezreel and the Jordan. This strategic site was controlled north-south traffic through the Jordan Valley and east-west traffic between the Jezreel and Transjordan. The site is mentioned in Egyptian sources from the time of Tuthmose III (15th century B.C.). Beth-shean—along with Taanach, Dor, Ibleam, and Megiddo—was one of the Canaanite cities not captured by the Israelites at the time of the conquest (Judg. 1:27). During Saul's reign, the city was in the hands of the Philistines, and the bodies of Saul and

Mound at Beth-shean, now being excavated. *John McRay.*

his sons were displayed on the walls of Beth-shean after they were killed in battle (1 Sam. 31:10, 12). David appears to have captured the city as his kingdom expanded northward, and it later belonged to the fifth administrative district of Solomon (1 Kings 4:12).

Beth-shean benefited from the rich soil, abundance of water, and warm weather that produced agricultural abundance. One of the sages of Israel said, "If the garden of Eden is in the land of Israel, then its gate is at Beth-shean."

Despite its choice location, strategically and agriculturally, the city of Beth-shean was deserted about 700 B.C. and not reoccupied until the Hellenistic period, when it became known as Scythopolis ("city of the Scythians"). The city rose to its greatest period of prosperity when it was taken by Pompey in 63 B.C. and became the capital of the Decapolis, although it was the only city of that district located west of the Jordan River.

Excavations at Beth-shean have uncovered eighteen levels of occupation. One interesting discovery was a series of temples (1400–1200 B.C.) built by the Egyptians in honor of various deities, including the god Mekal, named as "Lord of Beth-shean" on a dedicatory inscription. The site is also noted for having the best-preserved Roman theater in Palestine.

8

The United Monarchy
1050 to 931 B.C.

The prophet Samuel functioned as a transitional figure between the period of the judges and the beginning of the monarchy. In response to Israel's request for a king God led Samuel to anoint Saul, a handsome young Benjamite, to rule his people (1 Sam. 8:4–10:24). Thus, as Ezekiel records, the nation "came to regal estate" (Ezek. 16:13).

International politics was a significant factor in the rise of the monarchy. This was a time of transition, during which Palestine was less disturbed by outside world powers than during its previous history. This allowed the Israelite monarchy to develop nationally without external restraint. After being conquered by Tiglath-pileser I (1115–1077 B.C.), the Hittites of Asia Minor had passed into insignificance. The death of Tiglath-pileser I left Assyria in a state of decline from which it did not recover for nearly two hundred years—about the time of Ahab (874–853 B.C.). Egypt did not interfere with the monarchy while Saul, David, and Solomon ruled, for weakness, stagnation, and internal conflict characterized its own national government. After Ramses III (1195–1164 B.C.), no Egyptian ruler crossed the borders of Palestine until the time of Rehoboam (931–913 B.C.). We can conclude that Israel's first three kings were unaffected by other national powers, making possible the great expansion of its boundaries during this period.

The Philistines, having migrated from the Aegean Islands and Asia Minor under the pressure of the Dorian Greeks (c. 1168 b.c.), constituted Israel's main foreign threat during this period. However, this potential danger was an impetus to the nation to unite under the leadership of Saul and David.

Chronology of the United Monarchy

Three reasons were given by the elders who came to Samuel at Ramah to request that he anoint a king: the desire to conform to the pattern of the Gentile nations; the need for a faithful judge, probably in light of the corruption of Samuel's sons; and the need for a military commander to fight Israel's battles (1 Sam. 8:5, 20). While God had made a provision in the law for the appointment of a king (Deut. 17:14–20), Samuel recognized the people's error in failing to recognize God as their true king (1 Sam. 8:7; 12:12). Although warned by Samuel of the price of kingship—taxation, military draft, loss of personal liberty—the people insisted on having a king, and God granted the people their wish. Saul, from the tribe of Benjamin, was anointed by Samuel. But, while the nation got the king they desired, they also got the discipline they deserved. Since Saul was from the tribe of Benjamin, rather than the royal line of Judah (cf. Gen. 49:10), his kingship would not endure, and the monarchy did not really blossom until the time of King David, born of the tribe of Judah.

The Reign of Saul (c. 1050–1010 b.c.)

Saul's major task after his anointment as king was to unify the Israelite tribes into a nation. This was basically an internal task that was necessitated by the ongoing Philistine threat, against which Israel's loosely organized tribes could not cope. The Philistines had a powerful military organization and ruled a predominantly Canaanite population on the coastal plain and in the Negev and Valley of Jezreel.

Saul's entire reign was spent at war (1 Sam. 14:52). His initial military victory came with the defeat of the Ammonites who had besieged Jabesh-gilead (1 Sam. 11:1–11). This successful campaign served to unite Israel, organize the military, and bring about Saul's acceptance by the people as their king.

From his capital at Gibeah, Saul's military campaigns took him north to defeat Zobah, east to defeat the Ammonites and the Moabites, south to defeat the Edomites and Amalekites, and west to defeat the Philistines. In his battles with the Philistine forces, Saul sought to prevent further Philistine subjugation by completely removing their yoke of oppression. Although not an imperialist (as some would suggest), Saul was an aggressive-minded defender of the young nation of Israel at a crucial time in its history.

Saul's great spiritual failure as king is linked to his lack of obedience to the directives God gave him through the prophet Samuel. Instead of waiting for Samuel's arrival as he had been directed (1 Sam. 10:8), Saul took matters into his own hands and sacrificed at Gilgal (1 Sam. 13:8–9). Then, instead of acknowledging his sin when Samuel arrived, the king offered some weak excuses to justify his conduct. Saul's greatest disobedience occurred in the Amalekite war, which resulted in his being rejected by God as Israel's king (1 Sam. 15). Samuel then anointed David, a man after God's own heart, to rule God's people Israel.

The Reign of David (1010–970 B.C.)

David's rise to power began while Saul was still on the throne. Before long, Saul began to hear of the acclaim David was receiving and sent for the young man. Although David's presence had a soothing effect on Saul's "evil spirit," the king's periodic jealousy of David led to suspicion, fear, and hostility. David eventually had to flee Saul's court to preserve his own life. During the disintegrating last days of Saul's rule, David was a fugitive in the wilderness. Although David had several opportunities to take Saul's life, David was not an usurper and refused to lift up his hand against the Lord's anointed king. In due time, God allowed Saul's life to end during a battle with the Philistines (1 Sam. 31), and David was then free to accept the kingship offered to him by the leaders of Judah in the south. After ruling over Judah for seven and a half years at Hebron, the elders of Israel (the northern tribes) came and anointed David king over all the land. He established his capital at Jerusalem, where he reigned for another thirty-three years. Since Jerusalem was in Benjaminite territory, the move from Hebron served to solidify the northern and southern tribes under David's leadership.

David stands primarily responsible for the unification and development of the kingdom of Israel. Although his initial dominion was a relatively insignificant section of politically divided hill country, David bequeathed his son Solomon a virtual empire. Excavations have corroborated the implications of Scripture (2 Sam. 24:5–8; 1 Kings 4:7–9) that Canaanite holdings along the coastal plain and in the Jezreel and Jordan valleys were brought under Israelite control during David's reign. David established his rule from north of the Sea of Galilee to Beersheba and on both sides of the Jordan River and then turned to foreign affairs. Having subjugated the Philistines, he was free to convert his kingdom into an empire.

David's expansionist policies were probably due to his concern for protecting Israelite settlements in Transjordan. He extended the kingdom to the north, south, east, and west (2 Sam. 8:1–14). In addition to military conquest, David was the first of the Israelite kings to use marriage alliances as an important part of his foreign policy (2 Sam. 3:3). In the ancient Near East, marital arrangements between royal houses were often used to conclude treaties and cement political relationships. As elsewhere and more recently, such alliances were based on the premise that if the families of heads of state intermarried, more friendly relationships could be pursued and hostilities avoided. David's conquests and alliances gave him control of territory from the River of Egypt (Wadi el-'Arish) to the Euphrates. For a time, Israel was as strong as any power in the ancient world.

The great turning point in David's brilliant royal career was his sin with Bathsheba and the murder of her husband, Uriah (2 Sam. 11). Although David confessed his sin and was forgiven by the Lord (2 Sam. 12:13; Ps. 51), a great deal of family and political turmoil followed, including Absalom's attempt to usurp his father's throne. An accession crisis took place at the end of David's reign, when Adonijah, David's fourth and oldest surviving son, proclaimed himself king (1 Kings 1:5). Bathsheba, with the assistance of Nathan the prophet, was able to orchestrate events with David so that their son Solomon succeeded to the throne.

The Reign of Solomon (970–931 B.C.)

Although Solomon's reign was not entirely peaceful, he is not known to have engaged in major military conflict. Most of his activities tended toward strengthening and developing David's achievements through political, economic, and administrative means. While David had transformed the land of Israel from a small state into a powerful kingdom, Solomon developed the country into an international center that boasted one of the most advanced cultures of his day.

Militarily, Solomon sought to defend rather than expand his territory. He fortified key cities and military bases, including Hazor (to defend Israel from the Arameans), Megiddo (to control the Via Maris and the Jezreel), and Gezer (to control the coastal plain and guard the western approach to the hill country). In addition, Solomon strengthened the military through the introduction of chariots and horses (1 Kings 10:26). The king maintained security and discouraged aggression by building a military establishment that few would care to challenge.

The cornerstone of Solomon's foreign policy was his widespread use of international marriages to conclude treaties and cement relations with neighboring kings and rulers. Through his own multiple diplomatic marriages, Solomon secured treaties with Egypt, Moab, Ammon, Edom, Sidon, and the Hittite nation (1 Kings 11:1). Since this practice was a violation of God's law for the king (Deut. 17:17), it proved quite destructive for Solomon spiritually. The foreign wives brought their pagan gods to Israel, and Solomon's heart was turned from the Lord (1 Kings 11:3–8).

Solomon is perhaps best-remembered for his unrivaled wisdom (1 Kings 10:23–24), significant literary contributions (1 Kings 4:32), and for his building of the Jerusalem temple (1 Kings 6). Yet his spiritual failure, which resulted from acquiring foreign wives, overshadows the great accomplishments of his reign. Because of this unfaithfulness, God announced to Solomon that the kingdom would be divided between Solomon's son, Rehoboam, and his servant, Jeroboam (1 Kings 11:9–13). The days of the united Israel were glorious but short-lived.

The Wilderness of Judah and the Dead Sea

The Wilderness of Judah and the western shores of the Dead Sea provide the geographical setting for many of the events in the lives of Saul and David. Growing up in Bethlehem, David would have tended his father's sheep in the wilderness area to the east. Later, as a fugitive from Saul's court, David took refuge in the caves and strongholds of the Wilderness of Judah. He also fought military engagements in this area. The Wilderness of Judah and the Dead Sea have very unique geographical features that make them quite interesting to study.

Geography of Judah's Wilderness

The Wilderness of Judah was a distinct geographical region of the tribal territory of Judah (Josh. 15:61–62). This area lies just east of the Judean watershed and extends about twelve miles eastward to the shores of the Dead Sea. The region lies parallel to the Dead Sea, stretching about fifty miles from north to south. The wilderness southeast of Hebron in the vicinity of Ziph is sometimes referred to by the name *Jeshimon*, meaning "waste" or "desert" (1 Sam. 23:19, 24; 26:1).

The desolate and broken Wilderness of Judah makes a very steep descent from the Judean mountains to the shores of the Dead Sea. The

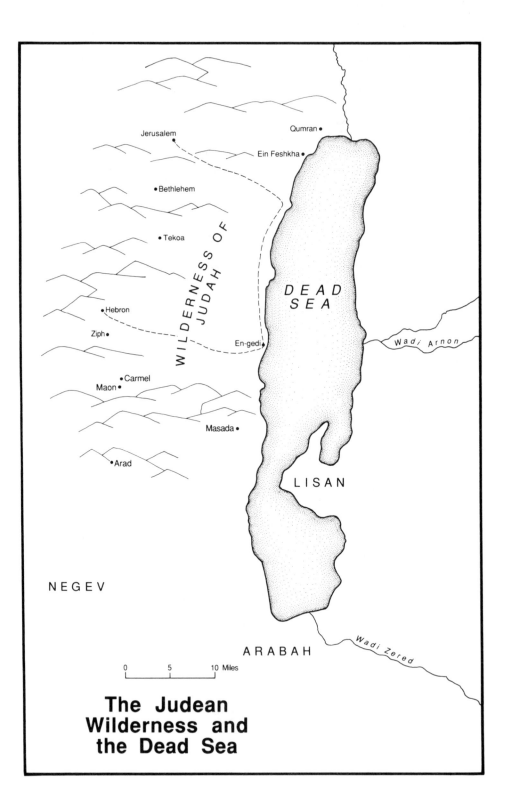

Jerusalem

Qumran

Ein Feshkha

Bethlehem

Tekoa

WILDERNESS OF JUDAH

DEAD SEA

Hebron

Ziph

En-gedi

Wadi Arnon

Carmel

Maon

Masada

LISAN

Arad

NEGEV

0   5   10 Miles

ARABAH

Wadi Zered

The Judean
Wilderness and
the Dead Sea

elevation drops 4,300 feet in roughly twelve miles—from 3,000 above sea level to 1,300 below. Most of the slope is covered by an outcrop of soft and porous Senonian limestone, which is chalky and has a low resistance to erosion. This characteristic has contributed to the formation of the deep wadis and ravines that slice through the region. The limestone rock underlying this region serves as a natural reservoir, absorbing and storing water until it eventually breaks forth as springs along the shores of the Dead Sea.

Climate of the Wilderness of Judah

Palestine is generally noted for its abundance of sunshine, and this is especially evident in the Judean wilderness. The moisture-bearing clouds, which ascend the hill country from the Mediterranean, dissipate as they pass over the wilderness and the Jordan Valley. The hot sun causes the summer temperatures to soar into the 90's. The mean temperature in January is 62°F. The mean annual temperature at the southern end of the Dead Sea is about 78°F. and a few degrees cooler at the northern end. On a cloudless June day in 1942, the temperature reached a record 122°F. at the Dead Sea.

Rainfall in the Wilderness of Judah averages between three and twelve inches annually. Since cultivation of crops requires a least twelve inches of rain per annum, this area is not suitable for agriculture except near the springs. The wilderness and Dead Sea regions are reached by the Mediterranean sea-to-land breeze, but the air is heated as it passes through the wilderness and ravines. A moist and perspiring body is momentarily cooled by the breeze, but its cooling effect diminishes as one's skin dries.

Economy of the Wilderness of Judah

The Judean wilderness was primarily useful as a place to graze sheep and goats, since the ground is too steep, rocky, and infertile for planting. Except in the vicinity of an oasis, there is insufficient water for agriculture. Along the shores of the Dead Sea, the water that has flowed underground from the hill country breaks out in a number of springs. Ein Feshkha and En-gedi are two of the more prominent and productive of these oases. In antiquity, the salt of the Dead Sea was important to the economy of the region, as salt was extracted and sold as a preservative. One city along the western shores of the Dead Sea was known as "the City of Salt" (Josh. 15:62).

The lack of water, the steep terrain, and the general barrenness of this wilderness rendered the hill country almost inaccessible from the east (cf. 2 Chron. 20:1–28). However, there were two known routes through the Wilderness of Judah to the hill country. Both began at En-gedi. One went north along the shores of the Dead Sea to the Kidron Valley and then west to Bethlehem, and the other went directly west through the wilderness to Hebron.

The Dead Sea

The Dead Sea, which occupies the deepest part of the Rift Valley, is about fifty miles long and ten miles wide. It is referred to as "the Salt Sea" (Gen. 14:3; Num. 34:3) as well as "the Sea of the Arabah" (Deut. 3:17; Josh. 3:16) and "the Eastern Sea" (Ezek. 47:18; Zech. 14:8). The Dead Sea lies 1,274 feet below sea level and is about 1,300 feet deep at its northern end. The southern part (south of the Lisan, a tongue-shaped peninsula attached to the eastern shore) is quite shallow. The sea narrows between the Lisan and the western shore to about two and one-half miles and was known to have been a passable ford in antiquity. The water level of the Dead Sea has decreased in recent times, and the ford appears once again passable.

The Jordan River and numerous wadis flow into the Dead Sea, but it has no outlet. The inflow is balanced by evaporation from the sea's 380-square-mile surface. Over the years, the evaporation has caused the minerals, brought to the sea by the rivers, to become increasingly concentrated. This mineral content now amounts to about 28 to 33 percent, depending upon the depth of the water, making the Dead Sea a vast resource of mineral wealth. Two of the minerals presently being extracted from the Dead Sea are bromine (used in pesticides and fumigants) and potash (used as a fertilizer). The Dead Sea is also known to have contained vast amounts of magnesium and lithium.

Scientists are now experimenting with the development of solar ponds, using saltwater from the Dead Sea. These ponds are capable of generating electricity from the sun as the water heats and releases vapor that turns a turbine connected to a generator. Engineering planners anticipate that within a few years, solar ponds will provide all the electricity necessary for the entire Dead Sea basin.

Sites of the Wilderness of Judah

David's wanderings in the wilderness as a fugitive from Saul took him to a number of sites, including Ziph, Maon, En-gedi, Carmel, and Masada (cf. 1 Sam. 22:3–26:12). Several of these sites are worthy of special consideration.

En-gedi

En-gedi is an oasis on the western shore of the Dead Sea, directly across from where the Wadi Arnon enters the sea. The site is named for the copious spring that waters the area. En-gedi was allotted to the territory of Judah (Josh. 15:62). During David's flight from Saul, he hid out in the "strongholds of Engedi" (1 Sam. 23:29), also referred to as the "wilderness of Engedi" (1 Sam. 24:1). It was here that Saul went into a cave in which David was hiding. David could have killed Saul, but he refused to lift up his hand against the Lord's anointed. (1 Sam. 24:3–7). The cave at En-gedi may also provide the background of David's experience as recorded in Psalm 142.

En-gedi was known in ancient times for its beauty, spices, and vineyards (cf. Song of Sol. 1:14). Josephus states that the finest palm trees and balsam grew there. En-gedi was also at the head of a travel route through the wilderness to the hill country. During the reign of Jehoshaphat, the Ammonites and the Moabites began their ascent to the hill country from En-gedi to attack the southern kingdom of Judah.

Masada

Masada is a natural rock fortress on the western shore of the Dead Sea just across from the Lisan. The fortress was formed by erosion in the surrounding wadis, which eventually isolated Masada from the other mountains in this area. The cliffs surrounding Masada rise up almost vertically 1,320 feet to a plateau of approximately twenty acres. The name *Masada* is a transliteration of the Hebrew word for "mountain fortress" or "stronghold." David frequented a mountain fortress in the wilderness while fleeing from Saul (1 Sam. 22:4; 24:22). Although the term is also used of Jerusalem (2 Sam. 5:9, 17), the earlier references most likely refer to Masada.

Although the site might have been used by David and others as a fortress in the biblical period, it was first fortified by the high priest Jonathan (103–76 B.C.), a Hasmonean ruler of Judea. The fortress was later acquired by Herod and used as a place of refuge for his family while he was struggling for power. When he secured his rule over Judea in 37 B.C., Herod completely rebuilt the fortress to give him a place of refuge in case of Jewish revolt or foreign attack. Surrounding the plateau with a double wall, Herod built a fine palace, cisterns for water, and storerooms. Following Herod's death, a small Roman garrison appears to have been maintained at Masada, until the Romans were expelled by the Zealots at the beginning of the Jewish Revolt. Masada soon became a symbol of Jewish resistance, and the Romans went to great lengths to overthrow its defenders. They finally built a ramp to the top of the plateau so that siege equipment could be used against the walls. The Jews held Masada until May 2, 73 A.D., when the Tenth Roman Legion succeeded in breaking through the gate, only to

ON MONDAY, 21ST OF TAMMUZ
5729 (7 JULY 1969) THE REMAINS
OF THE LAST DEFENDERS OF
MASADA, WHO HAD FALLEN
THREE YEARS AFTER THE
DESTRUCTION OF THE TEMPLE
(73 C.E.), WERE BURIED
IN THIS PLACE.
  THEY WERE BURIED
ACCORDING TO THE
DECISION OF THE
GOVERNMENT OF ISRAEL
AND IN FULL MILITARY
HONOURS.

Above: Fortress of Masada showing
Roman ramp on the right. *Guy P. Duffield.*
Middle: Ruins of the northern palace,
middle terrace, at Masada. *Charles
Pfeiffer.* Bottom: Marker commemorating
final resting place of defenders of Masada.
JCL.

discover that the 960 defenders had taken their own lives rather than be enslaved. Josephus reports the events of Masada's final hours, having received the account from one of the seven survivors. Today's Israeli soldiers take the oath of allegiance to their country on Masada, vowing that the mountain fortress will never fall again.

Qumran

About eight miles south of Jericho, along the northwest shore of the Dead Sea, is Qumran. The site, which has been identified by some as Judah's "City of Salt" (Josh. 15:62), is located just north of the oasis Ein Feshkha and the Wadi Qumran. The name *Qumran* found its place in the vocabulary of modern Jews and Christians with the discovery of the Dead Sea Scrolls there in 1947. These scrolls have been acknowledged as the most important discovery for biblical scholars in this century. They provide scholars with Old Testament manuscripts a thousand years older than any manuscripts previously available. The scrolls date from around 200 to 100 B.C. and confirm the accuracy of the Masoretic text that is used in the translation of most of our modern versions.

There has been much discussion about the nature of the community of Qumran, where the scrolls were found. Josephus describes a sect of Jews known as "Essenes," and the residents of Qumran seemed to fit

Qumran Cave 4, marked by a circle, contained what seems to have been the bulk of the library of the Qumran community.

the description well—except for the fact that although the Essenes were celibate, there were some women found buried at the site.

Whether they were actually Essenes or merely Essene-like, these people separated from established Judaism and devoted themselves to copying and preserving the biblical scrolls. In the excavation by Roland de Vaux, a hall *(scriptorium)* was discovered where the scrolls were apparently copied, since tables with inkwells were found. The dwellings at Qumran were abandoned in 68 A.D. during the First Jewish Revolt, when the Romans destroyed the site. Anticipating this attack, the scrolls were carefully placed in clay jars and hidden in caves, the residents probably expecting to recover the scrolls after the Romans departed. Although the inhabitants never returned to the site, the clay jars and arid conditions preserved the scrolls for discovery and use by modern scholars. Most of the scrolls were written on parchment (leather) and a few on papyrus. Except for the Book of Esther, every book of the Old Testament is represented in part or in its entirety among the scrolls found at Qumran.

9

The Divided Monarchy
931 to 722 B.C.

The vast empire that David and Solomon had united under their reigns soon disintegrated following Solomon's death. The northern tribes went into revolt, leaving David's dynasty with only Judah and Benjamin. The resultant division of the monarchy almost led the tribes into open civil war, but armed conflict was averted by the Lord's intervention (1 Kings 12:21–24).

It is important to distinguish between the reason for the division and the circumstances under which it took place. The underlying cause was Solomon's apostasy, idolatry, and disobedience. Having built high places for the gods of his heathen wives, Solomon was told by the Lord: "Since this has been your mind and you have not kept my covenant and my statutes which I have commanded you, I will surely tear the kingdom from you and will give it to your servant" (1 Kings 11:11). The circumstances that God used to bring about this judgment are recorded in 1 Kings 12. Rehoboam, Solomon's son, forsook the advice of his wise counselors to become a servant of the people. Instead, he promised to make their burdens heavier. In response, Jeroboam, who had formerly served the administration of Solomon, led the ten northern tribes in revolt. The northern kingdom is known as "Israel," and the southern kingdom retains the name "Judah."

In this chapter, we shall survey the history of the divided monarchy

(931–722 B.C.) and then consider a region of which both kingdoms held a part—the coastal plain.

Highlights of the Divided Monarchy

The political history of the divided monarchy falls into four main periods, characterized by conflict, alliance, parallel independence, and Assyrian domination.

The Period of Conflict: 931–875 B.C. (1 Kings 12:1–16:28)

Although the Lord's intervention prevented the outbreak of hostilities immediately following the rebellion by Jeroboam (1 Kings 12:24), the spirit of mutual toleration did not last long. The biblical record indicates that "there was war between Rehoboam and Jeroboam continually" (1 Kings 14:30). The first sixty years of the divided monarchy were characterized by military conflict between the northern kingdom (Israel) and the southern kingdom (Judah). The warfare finally ceased when the border between the two kingdoms was firmly established between Mizpah and Bethel.

After leading the northern tribes into rebellion, it occurred to Jeroboam that Judah's possession of Jerusalem and the temple gave the southern kingdom a distinct advantage in providing a rallying point for the people. He feared that the citizens of the northern tribes would travel to Jerusalem for religious festivals and soon recognize and support Rehoboam's rule. Jeroboam's solution was to establish worship centers in Dan and Bethel—the northern and southern extremities of his kingdom (1 Kings 12:26–29). He proceeded to institute golden-calf worship in the religious centers and to establish a priesthood not of the tribe of Levi. Jeroboam also appointed a feast to be observed one month after the traditional Feast of Tabernacles. The pagan religion, substitute priesthood, and supplementary feast served to unite the people of the northern tribes under Jeroboam's rule. The sin of idolatrous worship was perpetuated by his successors, who "walked in the way" of Jeroboam (1 Kings 15:26; 16:34).

Rehoboam, Solomon's son, did not do much better with his people than did his neighbor to the north. Judah, too, neglected the law and was led into idolatry. The idolatrous activities tolerated by Rehoboam constituted a revival of Canaanite religion in the southern kingdom (1 Kings 14:23–24). It was not until the rule of Asa, Judah's first great religious reformer, that the trend toward religious apostasy was reversed (1 Kings 15:9–15).

After brief periods of rule by leaders as ineffective as Jeroboam had been, the northern kingdom's army made their general, Omri, king of

Israel. Omri is best known for his founding a new capital for the northern kingdom at Samaria (1 Kings 16:24). He was succeeded by his son, Ahab, perhaps the most faithless of the northern kings.

The Period of Alliance: 874–835 B.C.
(1 Kings 16:29–2 Kings 11:16)

A period of alliance between Israel and Judah began when Jehoshaphat, king of Judah, made peace with Ahab, king of Israel (1 Kings 22:44). The two kingdoms then carried on several joint military campaigns (1 Kings 22:1–36; 2 Kings 3:1–27). This alliance had disastrous spiritual consequences, for the treaty was sealed by the marriage of Athaliah, Ahab's daughter, to Jehoram, Jehoshaphat's son (2 Kings 8:18, 26–27). When Athaliah came to live with Jehoram, she brought the idols of her mother, Jezebel, and Baal worship took hold of the kingdom of Judah.

Jezebel, wife of the powerful King Ahab, had brought the worship of Baal-melqart ("Baal, king of the town") from Phoenicia. This god was identical with the Canaanite Baal and claimed power over fertility, rain, vegetation, fire, death, and progeny. Jezebel's efforts to make the Baal cult the official religion of Israel brought her into conflict with Elijah, and both Elijah and his successor, Elisha, functioned as general antagonists against the paganism introduced by Jezebel. These prophets defended the orthodox faith and attacked the commonly held beliefs about Baal. Their miracles demonstrated that Yahweh was the one true God and that Baal was no god at all—that the gifts of grain, oil, rain, fire, and life itself were from Yahweh, not Baal.

Toward the end of this period, characterized mostly by religious failure, both Israel and Judah suffered some major political setbacks. Samaria, capital of the northern kingdom, was besieged by the Arameans. The terrible famine that resulted led to the horror of cannibalism (2 Kings 6:24–29). During this same period, Edom and Libnah revolted from Judah's control (2 Kings 8:20–23). The overly zealous enthusiasm of Israel's King Jehu for purging the political and religious order of both kingdoms brought the period of alliance to a bloody conclusion (2 Kings 9:11–10:28).

The Period of Parallel Independence: 835–740 B.C.
(2 Kings 11:17–15:26)

A period of independence for each of the kingdoms was brought about by two main events: the slaying of Ahaziah, king of Judah, by Jehu (2 Kings 9:27–28); and the killing of Athaliah, Ahab's daughter, by the captains of Judah when Joash was installed as king (2 Kings 11:13–16). During this period, the kingdoms experienced an occasional clash (2 Kings 14:8–14), but for the most part each tolerated the other's existence and grew very powerful. The later part of this period has been regarded as the golden era for both Israel and Judah.

This prosperous period began with spiritual reform in Judah under the direction of Jehoiada, the priest who served as counselor to the boy king, Joash. The system of Baal cult worship was destroyed, and the priests of Baal killed (2 Kings 11:17–18). When the Jerusalem temple was repaired, true worship was reinstituted in Judah. Sadly, after Jehoiada's death, Joash permitted the people to abandon the temple and return to pagan worship.

The highlight of this period was the great territorial expansion undertaken by both kingdoms. Jeroboam II secured for Israel the regions as far north as Damascus and Hamath (2 Kings 14:25–28). Uzziah (Azariah) was able to extend Judah's border as far south as Elath on the Gulf of Aqaba (2 Kings 14:22). He also expanded his kingdom west into Philistine territory and east into the Transjordan (2 Chron. 26:6–8). The combined territories of Israel and Judah were as expansive as Solomon's kingdom at the peak of his prosperity. Yet the glory of the two independent Israelite kingdoms quickly faded in the advance of the powerful Assyrians. Soon, Menahem, then king of Israel, was forced to pay tribute to the king of Assyria (2 Kings 15:19–20). By so doing, he retained his throne but became his throne but became an Assyrian vassal.

The Period of Assyrian Domination: 740–722 B.C. (2 Kings 15:27–17:41)

It was under the leadership of Tiglath-pileser III (754–727 B.C.) that the kingdom of Assyria grew to become an empire that eventually swallowed up the petty kingdoms of Aram and Israel. Tiglath-pileser was not satisfied with the mere surrender of kings and receipt of tribute. He initiated the annexation of conquered territories to the Assyrian state by reducing them to provinces governed by Assyrian deputies. Potential opposition to Assyrian rule was overcome by exiling the noble classes of the conquered regions and resettling other populations in their place. Although both Israel and Judah fell under Assyrian dominion, for Israel it meant the end of the kingdom.

As the Assyrian threat increased, Pekah of Israel and Rezin of Damascus formed an alliance to resist the aggressors. Ahaz, king of Judah, refused to join the anti-Assyrian coalition and was attacked by Pekah and Rezin (Isa. 7:1–7). Ignoring the warnings of Isaiah, Ahaz appealed to Assyria for help. Tiglath-pileser responded with three devastating campaigns against both Israel and Damascus (734–732 B.C.). Assyria captured portions of northern Israel (2 Kings 15:29) and exiled a number of captives to Assyria. After the conquered regions were divided into Assyrian provinces—Dor, Megiddo, and Gilead, the days of the kingdom of Israel were numbered. It was roughly during this period that Amos, Hosea, and Micah rebuked Israel's apostasy and called the nation to repentance.

The end was precipitated when Hoshea, king of Israel, joined Egypt in a revolt against Assyria and refused to pay the annual tribute. In response, Shalmaneser V (727–722 B.C.) marched on the northern kingdom and besieged Samaria for three years (2 Kings 17:1–5). Sargon II (722–705 B.C.) succeeded Shalmaneser and finalized the capture of Samaria. He then exiled 27,290 of the citizens of Israel to the distant regions of the Assyrian Empire and repopulated Samaria with idolatrous foreigners (2 Kings 17:24–33), standard practice for Assyria.

The captivity of Samaria brought the period of the divided monarchy to an end. The people of the northern kingdom had broken the covenant. They had taken the path of death and adversity rather than the way of life and prosperity (Deut. 30:15–20). Having broken the stipulations of the covenant (2 Kings 17:7–23), they inherited the consequent judgment (Deut. 28:15–68), including exile from the Promised Land. Would Judah learn from this lesson or continue the sinful ways of her fallen sister to the north?

The Coastlands

There was one geographical region that both Israel and Judah shared—the coastal plain. The tribes of Asher, Manasseh, Ephraim, Dan, and Judah had all been allotted territory along the Mediterranean coast, a plain that extended north from the Wadi el-'Arish (River of Egypt) to Rosh-Ha Niqra ("the ladder of Tyre"), a distance of about 150 miles. The coastal plain varies in width from about three miles in the north to approximately twenty-five miles in the south, where the coastland swings eastward toward Egypt.

Regions of the Coastal Plain

The Plain of Asher. Extending about twenty-five miles from 1,700-foot Mount Carmel to Israel's northern boundary at Rosh Ha-Niqra is the Plain of Asher. The region averages about eight miles in width but narrows in the north and virtually disappears where "the ladder of Tyre" juts out into the Mediterranean Sea. The region was originally inherited by the tribe of Asher, but since the Israelites never really controlled it (Judg. 1:31–32), the territory played an insignificant role in their history. Sand and marshlands were characteristic of this re-

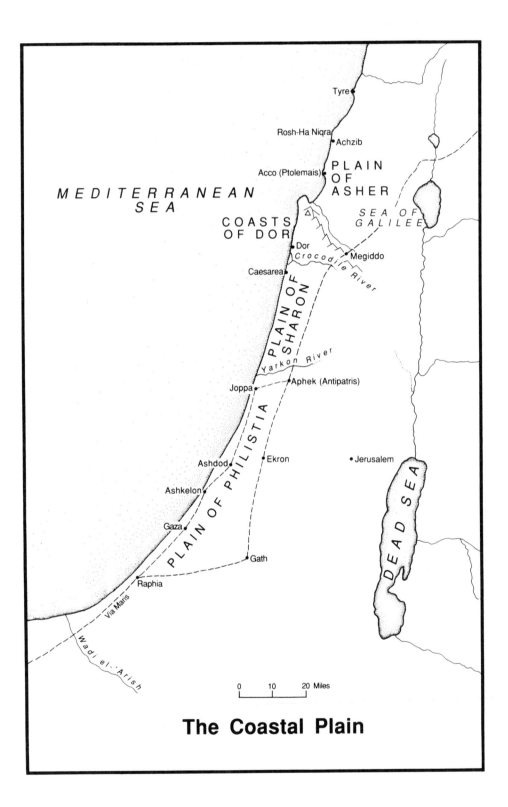

The Coastal Plain

gion in the biblical period. The major cities were Acco (New Testament "Ptolemais") and Achzib. The Bay of Haifa, which forms an important deep water port today, occupied the southern eight miles of the Plain of Asher.

The Coasts of Dor. Extending about twenty miles south from Mount Carmel to the marshes of the Crocodile River (Nahal Tannimin) is an area known as the Coasts of Dor. Here, the coastal plain is only about two miles wide, for Mount Carmel extends west and lies very close to the coastline. Dor was part of the inheritance of Manasseh, but the tribe did not gain possession of the land for several generations (Judg. 1:27). The region is characterized by low hills and sand dunes, which blocked the streams flowing from Mount Carmel and made the land swampy in the lower sections. Only one town in the region is mentioned in the Bible, the important harbor city of Dor (Judg. 1:27).

The Plain of Sharon. The fertile Plain of Sharon extends south about fifty miles along the Mediterranean Coast from the Crocodile River to Joppa (Jaffa). The plain is about ten miles wide and made up largely of sand dunes and alluvium. The Yarkon River cuts across the plain from Aphek (Antipatris) to Tel Qasile (just north of Joppa), where it empties into the Mediterranean Sea. Arising from a spring at Aphek, the Yarkon is the largest river on the coastal plain that discharges into the Mediterranean Sea.

The Plain of Sharon, inherited by the tribe of Manasseh, is the only section of the coastal plain that the Israelites effectively controlled during this period. Six references to the Plain of Sharon suggest its luxuriance (1 Chron. 5:16; 27:29; Song of Sol. 2:1; Isa. 33:9; 35:2; 65:10). The region was richly forested in biblical times and supports fabulous orange groves today. Important biblical cities of this region include Caesarea, Aphek, Lydda, and Joppa.

The Plain of Philistia: Extending south toward Gaza from Joppa to the Wadi el-'Arish, a distance of seventy miles, is the Plain of Philistia. This region of the coastal plain varies from ten to twenty miles in width. Some sections are over a thousand feet above sea level, due to the rise of mountains to the east. The sand dunes that border the area reach inland as much as two miles. Although not as well watered as the plain to the north, the rainfall was sufficient to make Philistia a very productive granary (Judg. 15:5). The difficulty with living in biblical Philistia was that—since the Via Maris went right through the region—armies from both north and south had easy access and faced no natural barriers to thwart their plan of attack. The powerful Philistines found the region to their liking, but the tribe of Dan (which had been allocated the northern reaches of Philistia) eventually abandoned their inheritance and migrated to Galilee (Judg. 18). The tribe of

Judah had been assigned the rest of Philistia but found the hill country preferable. Major population centers of this region were the Philistine cities of Ashdod, Gaza, Ashkelon, Gath, and Ekron (1 Sam. 6:17).

Climate of the Coastal Plain

The coastal land encompasses the subtropical arid zone of Egypt and the subtropical wet zone of Lebanon. This helps explain the rather light rainfall on the southern coastal plain in contrast with the heavier rainfall to the north. The annual rainfall in the vicinity of the Wadi el-'Arish is about six inches. Gaza, further north, receives about fifteen inches of rain annually. The Plain of Sharon and Coasts of Dor receive around twenty inches annually, several inches more than Philistia to the south. Acre (Acco), on the Plain of Asher, receives an annual average of twenty-six inches of rain. In addition to the rainfall, moisture reaches the plain in the form of dew, which forms 200 nights per year. This is especially important for the production of crops in the summer, when there is no rainfall.

The mean annual temperature in the coastal regions is around 70°F. Since coastal temperatures are constantly moderated by the sea, seasonal temperature fluctuations are less here than elsewhere in Israel. (Fluctuations increase with the distance from the sea and elevation.) While the coastal temperatures are comfortable most of the time, the relative humidity is higher here than elsewhere. The coastal plain is noted for its mild sea breeze, which picks up during the morning hours and continues throughout the day. During the summer, a light land-to-sea breeze may be experienced when the land cools below the Mediterranean's temperature, usually late at night or in the early morning.

Economy of the Coastal Plain

The cities of the coastal plain became early centers for textile production due in part to the availability of the Murex shells used in making Tyrian purple. Texts found at Ugarit, dating from the 14th century B.C., mention textiles imported from Acco, Ashdod, and Ashkelon. The two latter cities are also mentioned as export centers for the fish-preserving industry that existed in many coastal cities in the south. Other ports on the coastal plain involved in shipping and travel included Joppa and Dor. Beyond the sand dunes that fringe the coast, the Plain of Philistia was noted for its grain fields. Further north, in the Plain of Sharon, were heavily forested areas.

The coastal plain reaped both the benefits and hazards of being situated along the route of the Via Maris. The highway approach to Philistia from the south was divided at Raphia into coastal and inland routes. The two roads rejoined at Aphek, and the Via Maris continued north near the foothills of Samaria through Mount Carmel to Megiddo. There the highway divided again, with the inland route going northeast to Damascus and the coastal route passing through the Plain of Asher, then on to Tyre, Sidon, and Ugarit. Although this network of roads brought caravans and trading opportunities, the route was also used in military campaigns that left desolation and destruction in their wake.

Cities of the Coastal Plain

Many important cities occupied the coastal plain during the biblical period. An examination of several of these sites will give us a better appreciation of this region.

Acco (Ptolemais/Acre). Acco was located on the Plain of Asher at the north end of the Bay of Haifa. The ancient city was situated at Tell El-Fukhkhar, a little more than a mile to the east of the present site, Acre, which dates back to the fourth century B.C. Acco possessed the best and most important harbor in northern Palestine and served Galilee and the Jezreel. Although assigned to the tribe of Asher, the city did not become an integral part of the Israelite territory until the time of David. During Solomon's reign, it was transferred to Tyrian control (1 Kings 9:10–13) and remained part of Phoenician territory until its conquest by Alexander the Great. The city was known as Ptolemais in Hellenistic times and was granted the status of a Roman colony in A.D. 67. Paul stopped over for one day at Ptolemais at the end of his third missionary journey (A.D. 57), on his way from Tyre to Caesarea (Acts 21:7). There he fellowshiped with a local group of believers. After the fall of Jerusalem to Islamic forces, Acre functioned for some time as the capital of the Crusaders' "Christian Kingdom" (1187–1287). It was the last city held by the Crusaders in Palestine.

Caesarea. Located midway along the Mediterranean coastline between Joppa and Acco, Caesarea began in the middle of the third century B.C. as a small fortified anchorage built by the Phoenicians. It was then called Strato's Tower. The city rose to greatness under Herod the Great, who (in 22 B.C.) began construction of a port city to be named Caesarea in honor of Caesar Augustus. Herod's building projects at Caesarea created the first artificial harbor in the ancient world. His engineers erected wooden forms and then poured concrete to build two breakwaters extending 1,500 feet into the Mediterranean Sea. The city also boasted a Roman theatre, hippodrome, Roman baths, a temple dedicated to Augustus, and an amphitheater larger than Rome's. Since the city is lacking in natural springs, aqueducts were built to bring water from springs on the southern slopes of Mount Carmel and from the Crocodile River. Caesarea was the seat of Roman rule for

the province of Judea. When Pilate was prefect of Judea, he occupied
the governor's residence in Caesarea. The city also served as the headquarters for the Roman legions stationed in the province.

Philip the Evangelist brought the Christian faith to Caesarea (Acts
8:40) and later entertained Paul and his companions there (Acts 21:8).
Caesarea was also the home of Cornelius, the God-fearing centurion of
the Roman army (Acts 10:1). Paul landed at Caesarea when returning

A view of the Mediterrean Sea from the ruins of the old city of Caesarea. *JCL.*

House of Simon the tanner at Joppa. Peter prayed on the roof of this house. *Guy P. Duffield.*

from his second and third missionary journeys (Acts 18:22, 21:8) and was imprisoned there for two years before sailing to Rome (see chapter 15).

Aphek (Antipatris): Aphek is located twenty-five miles south of Caesarea, at the headwaters of the Yarkon River. The site is especially strategic, for here the Via Maris passes along a narrow gap between the city and the hills to the east. Occupation of Aphek meant control of this important trading route. The king of Aphek was one of the Canaanite rulers defeated by Joshua (Josh. 12:18). It was near Aphek that the Israelites were defeated by the Philistines and suffered the loss of the ark of the covenant (1 Sam. 4). During the Roman period, the city was rebuilt by Herod the Great, who named it Antipatris in honor of his father, Antipater. The city served then as a military post between Jerusalem and Caesarea. After Paul's life was threatened in Jerusalem, he was taken by night by military guard to Antipatris (Acts 23:31) and on to Caesarea the next day.

Joppa. One of the most ancient ports on the Palestinian coast, Joppa (Jaffa) is located thirty-five miles northwest of Jerusalem. (The ancient site of Joppa has been engulfed by the expanding borders of Israel's modern Tel-Aviv.) Although the city was assigned to the tribe of Dan (Josh. 19:46), it did not come under Israelite control until David gained effective control of the coastal plain. Timber from Lebanon was brought by rafts to the port of Joppa and then carried to Jerusalem for Solomon's temple (2 Chron. 2:16; cf. Ezra 3:7). It was from Joppa that the disobedient prophet Jonah embarked for Tarshish in order to avoid going to Nineveh (Jon. 1:3). In New Testament times, Joppa was the home of Tabitha, whom Peter raised (Acts 9:36–43). It was in Joppa at the home of Simon (the tanner) that Peter received the vision that prepared him to minister to the Gentiles (Acts 10).

Ashkelon. Another important Philistine city during the Old Testament period was Ashkelon, located on the seacoast about thirty miles south of Joppa. The city was temporarily occupied by Judah during the period of the judges (Judg. 1:18) but reverted to Philistine rule by the time of Samson (Judg. 14:19). Located on the Via Maris, Ashkelon was conquered by the Assyrians under Tiglath-pileser III (734 B.C.) and Sennacherib (701 B.C.) and later destroyed by the Babylonian ruler Nebuchadnezzar around 604 B.C. (Jer. 47:5–7). Ashkelon was the birthplace of Herod the Great, who later embellished the city with ornate buildings, temples, and colonnaded courts.

10

The Solitary Kingdom of Judah

722 to 586 B.C.

The kingdom of Judah survived the northern kingdom (Israel) by about a hundred and forty years (722–586 B.C.), but this period was far from trouble free.

Judah's Periods of Foreign Oppression

During those years of solitary existence, Judah was subject to the yoke of three foreign powers: Assyria, Egypt, and Babylon.

Assyrian Domination (722–609 B.C.)

The fall of the northern kingdom did not quench Assyria's thirst for greater dominion. And although Judah was saved from such a fate by King Ahaz's submissive alliance with Tiglath-pileser III of Assyria (2 Kings 16:7), there was considerable unrest among most of the subject kingdoms in the eastern Mediterranean world. The winds of rebellion were in the air. In 712 B.C., the Ethiopian pharaoh, Shabaku, revolted against Assyrian domination. According to the inscriptions of Sargon II (722–705 B.C.), Judah, Edom, and Moab were involved in this revolt but quickly surrendered. Most of Assyria's wrath was vented upon Ashdod, which became an Assyrian province. As the territorial borders of the Assyrian Empire reached the River of Egypt (Wadi el-'Arish), there remained little hope for an independent Judah.

Judah's King Hezekiah (728–686 B.C.) reversed the policy of submission to Assyria introduced by Ahaz and prepared for rebellion by extending Judah's border to the west (2 Kings 18:8) and strengthening fortifications in Jerusalem (2 Chron. 32:1–8). He also ordered the preparation of a tunnel to carry water from the Gihon Spring to Jerusalem (2 Chron. 32:30). Yet, it was not until after the death of Sargon, who had by then captured Samaria, that Hezekiah joined in full-fledged revolt against Assyria.

Sennacherib succeeded Sargon II in 705 B.C. and, after putting down rebellion in the eastern regions of Assyria, led his warriors against Philistia and Judah (701 B.C.). According to Assyrian annals, he was able to subjugate Philistia and capture forty-six cities of Judah. While Sennacherib was besieging Lachish, Hezekiah submitted to Assyria and met his demand for tribute (2 Kings 18:13–16). Still not satisfied, Sennacherib sent Rabshakeh, his royal emissary, to demand the full surrender of the city. Sennacherib boasted of Hezekiah, "Himself I made a prisoner in Jerusalem, his royal residence, like a bird in a cage."

At the eleventh hour of the siege, God miraculously intervened for Judah, and "the angel of the LORD" killed 185,000 Assyrian warriors during the night (2 Kings 19:35). Sennacherib retreated and was later slain at Nineveh by his sons while worshiping in the temple of his god, Nisroch.

The expansion of Assyria reached its height during the first half of the seventh century B.C. Esarhaddon (681–669 B.C.), Sennacherib's son and designated successor, conquered Lower Egypt (Noph) in 669 B.C., and his son Ashurbanipal conquered Upper Egypt (Thebes) in 663 B.C. These conquests gave the Assyrians control of the Fertile Crescent and all the territory from Upper Egypt to the Persian Gulf. During those days, Judah continued its existence as a vassal kingdom under Assyrian authority.

This period of Assyrian domination is noted for two periods of apostasy and two periods of religious reform in Judah. The idolatry under Ahaz was followed by reform during Hezekiah's reign. Later, the apostasy under Manasseh and Amon was followed by sweeping reforms under Josiah. The prophets ministering in Judah during this period included Isaiah, Micah, Nahum, Zephaniah, and Jeremiah all of whom called for repentance and warned of coming judgment on Judah and Jerusalem.

Egyptian Domination (609–605 B.C.)

Despite the sweeping territorial expanse under its control, the Assyrians began to experience a decline of power toward the end of Ashurbanipal's reign. First, Egypt managed to overthrow the Assyrians' yoke and expel their garrisons by about 650 B.C., under the leadership of Psammetichus I. Then, in 626 B.C., the city of Babylon was led in revolt by Nabopolassar, who then began a destructive campaign against Assyria. The combined Babylonian and Medes armies captured Nineveh in 612 B.C. (The divine judgment and destruction of Nineveh, the defiant capital of the Assyrian Empire, had been predicted by the prophet Nahum.) After Assyria's last stronghold, Harran, fell to Babylonia shortly thereafter, the once-mighty Assyrian Empire ceased to exist.

King Josiah, Judah's greatest religious reformer, took advantage of Assyria's decline to extend his influence north into territories that had been Assyrian provinces. Not only did he initiate reform in Judah and Jerusalem, he took steps to eradicate idolatry from "the cities of Manasseh, Ephraim, Simeon, and as far as Naphtali" (2 Chron. 34:6). Yet, as Judah began to flourish again after the years of submission to Assyria, the rulers of two other nations—Babylonia and Egypt—began to weigh the advantages of ruling Palestine. Egypt was the first to have this opportunity.

While Assyria's power was gradually weakening, Pharaoh Necho in Egypt felt threatened by the rapid rise of the aggressive new power, Babylonia. In order to equalize the balance of power and keep the Babylonians in their place, the pharaoh went to the aid of Ashuruballit of Assyria, who made an ill-fated effort to recapture Harran in 609 B.C. King Josiah, assuming that any friend of Assyria was an enemy of Judah, led his army to Megiddo and lost his life to Necho's forces in an attempt to stop the enemy's advance (2 Kings 23:29). Thus he was spared the sadness of witnessing the deterioration and ultimate destruction of Judah.

Upon Josiah's death, his second son, Jehoahaz, was elevated to the kingship of Judah, but his evil reign lasted only three months (2 Kings 23:30). When Pharaoh Necho returned from his campaign against Babylon, Jehoahaz was deposed and Josiah's oldest son (Eliakim) was installed as king, a mere puppet of Egypt. Necho collected tribute and changed Eliakim's name to Jehoiakim, in keeping with a suzerain's prerogative over a vassal (2 Kings 23:33–34). This was often done to demonstrate a king's authority over a lesser ruler.

Egypt maintained control over Palestine and Syria from 609 until

605 B.C., when the Babylonians defeated Necho's army at Carchemish (cf. 2 Kings 24:7, Jer. 46:2) and again at Hamath. Babylonia had become the new world power, and Nebuchadnezzar (605–562 B.C.) moved quickly to take possession of his newly won territory.

Babylonian Domination (605–586 B.C.)

The Babylonian Empire wrested control of most of the territory previously held by Assyria. In Judah, Nebuchadnezzar handled the situation by marching on Jerusalem and capturing the city (Dan. 1:1–2). Jehoiakim (609–597 B.C.) was allowed to remain on the throne, vessels from the temple and specially selected members of the nobility were taken captive to Babylon (Dan. 1:3–6). This was the first of a series of deportations experienced by the Judeans under Babylonian rule and included Daniel and three companions later known as Shadrach, Meshach, and Abednego. The second deportation took place in 597 B.C. during the rule of Jehoiachin, who reigned only three months before Jerusalem was besieged by Nebuchadnezzar. The king and his family were captured and exiled, the treasuries of the temple and palace were pillaged, and ten thousand Judeans, including the prophet Ezekiel, were exiled to Babylon (2 Kings 24:11–16).

In place of Jehoiachin, Nebuchadnezzar set Zedekiah (597–586 B.C.) on the throne, changing his name from Mattaniah to highlight the fact that the king of Judah was a Babylonian vassal (2 Kings 24:17). After a period of submission, a strong anti-Babylonian group in Jerusalem encouraged revolt. A coalition with Edom, Moab, Ammon, and Phoenicia was formed (Jer. 27:1–3), and Judah, against the warnings of Jeremiah, rebelled against Babylon.

Nebuchadnezzar marched west to quell the uprising and captured most of the fortified cities in the Judean hill country and Shephelah (Jer. 34:7). In December of 588 B.C., Nebuchadnezzar once again laid siege to Jerusalem. Zedekiah attempted to flee but was captured near Jericho and taken to Nebuchadnezzar's headquarters in Riblah. There he was punished, in accordance with Jeremiah's prophecy concerning the faithless kings of Judah (Jer. 22). The walls of Jerusalem were breached several months later and the city, including the temple, was looted and burned (2 Kings 25:4–10). All the surviving residents of Jerusalem, except for "some of the poorest of the land," were deported to Babylon (2 Kings 25:11–12).

Following the destruction of Jerusalem and the third deportation, Nebuchadnezzar appointed Gedaliah, a Judean, to govern Judah as a Babylonian province (2 Kings 25:22–23). From his residence and administrative center at Mizpah, Gedaliah followed the counsel of Jeremiah and encouraged the populace remaining in Judah to submit to Babylonian authority. However, he was slain by the opposition forces of Ishmael, after which the Judean rebels kidnapped Jeremiah and fled to Egypt (Jer. 41:1–43:7). Shadows fell over Jerusalem as the people of Judah entered their period of Babylonian exile.

The Region of the Shephelah

Crucial to the defense and control of the hill country of Judah was the transitional zone to the east known as the Shephelah. The name means "lowland" in Hebrew and was used in a geographical sense to describe a specific region in the territory of Judah (Josh. 15:33–47).

The Shephelah is located between the coastal plain of Philistia and the Judean hill country. It constitutes a strip of foothills about ten to twelve miles wide and forty-five miles long. These gently sloped hills are between 350 and 1,500 feet in elevation. The major valleys of the hill country to the east descend through this region before reaching the coastal plain. The Shephelah begins in the north at the Aijalon Valley and continues south to the border of the Negev just northeast of Beersheba. It is significant to note that there is no comparable "lowland" bordering the hill country of Ephraim. The Shephelah is a feature unique to Judah.

The Shephelah is characterized by a broad outcrop of Eocene limestone, which is divided from the Cenomanian limestone of the Judean hill country by a long, narrow valley of Senonian chalk. This chalk valley, running north and south, has served effectively as a moat defending the fortress of the hill country from the west. Eocene limestone does not break down into the rich, fertile soil that forms from the Cenomanian. Hence, although it receives adequate rainfall (ten to twenty inches annually), the region of the Shephelah is not agriculturally hospitable. It was, however, richly forested in ancient times (1 Kings 10:27).

Valleys and Defenses

Throughout the history of the Promised Land, the Shephelah has been of strategic importance as a buffer zone between Israelite and Philistine territories and was thus regarded as the most valued part of the Judean kingdom. Although the Judeans sought to occupy and fortify the Shephelah, in times of overwhelming attack they could usually retreat safely to the hill country. Even when the Shephelah was under foreign control, the narrow valleys, the "moat" of Senonian chalk, and the fortified cities would often prevent further loss of Judean territory.

The chief topographical characteristic of the Shephelah is a series of valleys leading from the coastal plain into the interior sections of

The Shephelah

Judah. Most of these valleys are broad and fertile as they enter the Shephelah, but they narrow as they begin to ascend the rocky heights of the hill country.

The Aijalon Valley was the most important route into Judah from the coastal plain, for it gave access to the ascent of Beth-horon (Josh. 10:10–15; cf. 1 Sam. 14:31), an easy route into Benjaminite territory from which one could swoop down on Jerusalem. Guarding this important way of access to the Judean capital were the cities of Aijalon, on the north, and Gezer, to the south of the valley. Pharaoh Shishak used the Aijalon Valley to gain access to Jerusalem during the reign of Rehoboam in 924 B.C.

The Sorek Valley, about eight miles south of the Aijalon, is famous for the exploits of Samson (Judg. 16:4). The valley was defended by the fortress cities of Beth-shemesh and Zorah. The Rephaim and Kesalon valleys branch off from the Sorek as it ascends to Jerusalem. David twice defeated the Philistines in the Rephaim as they tried to use the valley to gain access to the Holy City (2 Sam. 5:17–25).

The Elah Valley, five miles south of the Sorek, was the setting for the battle David fought with the Philistine giant, Goliath (1 Sam. 17:2). The valley led directly to the gates of Bethlehem, and the fortress cities of Azekah and Socoh defended this access route.

The Guvrin Valley, known in the biblical period as the Zephathah (2 Chron. 14:10), is located five miles south of the Elah. It provides the shortest route from the coastal plain to Hebron and was defended by the fortress city of Mareshah, home of the prophet Micah. An important battle took place here when Zerah the Ethiopian attempted to use the valley to enter the hill country (2 Chron. 14:9–15).

The Lachish Valley is located four miles south of the Guvrin and was defended by the city of Lachish, a frontier fortress near the southern border of the Shephelah. It may have been through this valley that Samson carried the Gaza gates to Hebron (Judg. 16:3). Both Sennacherib in 701 B.C. and Nebuchadnezzar in 586 B.C. used this valley to gain entrance into the hill country (2 Kings 18:14; Jer. 34:7).

Cities of the Shephelah

The cities of the Shephelah served as strongholds for defense in times of attack from the coastal plain. An appreciation of the defensive value of the Shephelah will be enhanced by a consideration of some of the strategic cities of this region.

Gezer. One of the largest and most important cities of Palestine in Old Testament times, Gezer was situated on the western edge of the Shephelah just south of the Aijalon Valley. Gezer was a fortress city that guarded the junction of the Via Maris and the Aijalon Valley. In addition to its strategic location, Gezer was supplied with a good source of water from springs and deep wells in its southeast section.

The site of Gezer was occupied at least 1,500 years before the Israelites entered the land. Shortly before the Israelite conquest, the Canaanite city reached its peak of prosperity. A ten-foot-wide stone wall with square towers protected the city. Horam, king of Gezer, was defeated by Joshua (Josh. 10:33), and the city was assigned to the Levites in Ephraim (Josh. 21:21), although the Canaanites were never completely expelled (Judg. 1:29). During Solomon's rule, Gezer was officially incorporated into Israelite territory, having been granted as a dowry to the Egyptian pharaoh's daughter when she became Solomon's wife (1 Kings 9:15–17). Solomon proceeded to fortify Gezer along with Beth-horon, which guarded the main ascent to the hill country of Benjamin. When Pharaoh Shishak invaded Judah, he launched his drive by attacking Gezer. After this initial victory, he was able to penetrate the hill country and eventually collect tribute from Jerusalem (2 Chron. 12:1–12).

An interesting feature of Gezer is its well-preserved Solomonic Gate, which is identical to the gates Solomon erected at Hazor and Megiddo. Also found at the site was a Hebrew inscription known as the Gezer Calendar, which describes the annual agricultural activities. Gezer continued to be occupied through the Crusader period and was then abandoned until its rediscovery in 1873 and excavation during the first decade of this century.

Beth-shemesh. Located in a commanding position in the Sorek Valley about fifteen miles west of Jerusalem, Beth-shemesh marked the northern boundary of Judah (Josh. 15:10) and was designated as a Levitical city (Josh. 21:16). The name means "house of Shemesh," indicating that a temple of the sun god Shemesh was originally located there. The city was close to the border of the Philistines, who appear to have exerted a strong influence on its early culture. Samson was born at Zorah, just two miles south of Beth-shemesh. The Philistine city of Timnah, where Samson sought a wife, lay farther down the Sorek Valley, about four miles to the west. When the Philistines returned the ark of the covenant to Israel because they feared its great power, it was sent via the valley to Beth-shemesh (1 Sam. 6:12).

Archaeological evidence indicates that the city was occupied by the Philistines just prior to the establishment of the Israelite monarchy. The city was destroyed about 1050 B.C., probably by Saul, and rebuilt in the style of the Israelites, probably in the time of David. Beth-shemesh was fortified by Rehoboam (2 Chron. 11:5–12), probably in anticipation of Shishak's invasion (924 B.C.). A clash took place at Beth-shemesh between Amaziah, king of Judah, and Jehoash Israel's king (2 Kings 14:11–13). The city was captured from Judah by the Philistines in the days of Ahaz (2 Chron. 28:18). After destruction by the Babylonians in 586 B.C., Beth-shemesh ceased to be a place of significance.

Azekah. On a 350-foot mound overlooking the Elah Valley and about sixteen miles west of Bethlehem, lies the ancient site of Azekah. Joshua pursued the Amorites as far as Azekah after he defeated them at the ascent of Beth-horon with the help of the Lord's "hailstones" (Josh. 10:10–11). The Philistines gathered between Azekah and Socoh to fight the Israelites in the days of Saul (1 Sam. 17:1), and David slew Goliath in the valley below. Azekah was one of the cities fortified by Rehoboam Solomon's son (2 Chron. 11:5–9), and was one of the last two Judean strongholds to fall to the Babylonians just before Nebuchadnezzar attacked Jerusalem in 588 B.C. (Jer. 34:7). The mention of Azekah in inscriptions found at Lachish (the "Lachish letters") suggests that it was an important site at the end of the Judean monarchy. Azekah was among the towns of Judah resettled by the Jews in the time of the restoration (Neh. 11:30). The site was excavated by F. J. Bliss and R. A. S. Macalister at the end of the nineteenth century.

Lachish. Another city prominent in this period was Lachish, located on the south side of the Lachish Valley about fifteen miles west of Hebron. The king of Lachish was one of the five Amorite kings against whom Joshua fought in defense of Gibeon (Josh. 10:3). The king was killed at Makkedah, and the city of Lachish was overthrown and destroyed (Josh. 10:22–32). Evidence of this destruction has been uncovered by archaeologists. The city was rebuilt early in the period of the united monarchy, possibly by David or Solomon. Later, Rehoboam fortified Lachish, probably in anticipation of Shishak's attack (2 Chron. 11:19).

Lachish was besieged by Sennacherib in 701 B.C. as the Assyrians pressed Judah to surrender (2 Kings 18:13–17). The walls from Sennacherib's palace in Nineveh are decorated with scenes from the siege of Lachish. During the decline of the Assyrian Empire, Lachish once again became a Judean stronghold until it was besieged once again— this time by the Babylonians. Along with Azekah, Lachish was one of the last two Judean cities to be captured before the fall of Jerusalem (Jer. 34:7).

Lachish is noted for its "Lachish letters," which are the only existing letters of antiquity in classical Hebrew. They are valued for the light they shed on Hebrew script and vocabulary from the sixth century B.C. The fourth letter reflects the historical situation when most of the cities of the Shephelah had fallen to the Babylonians. It concludes, "We are watching for the fire signals of Lachish, according to all the signs my lord gave, because we do not see Azekah." These words suggest that signals were no longer being sent from Azekah because it had already fallen to its Babylonian attackers.

11

The Babylonian Exile
586 to 537 B.C.

With the fall of Jerusalem and destruction of the temple, the people of Judah entered a period of captivity in a foreign, pagan land. Ironically, this was the land from which the people of Israel had come, generations before. Abraham had journeyed to Canaan from Ur. The sons of Jacob (Israel) had been born in Paddan-aram (northern Mesopotamia). Now, as a result of God's judgment on their sin, the Israelites were back in the land of their origin. It was from this place that they would have their "second birth" as a nation.

The History of the Exile

A short overview of the history of this period will help put the Babylonian captivity in proper perspective.

Duration of the Exile

Through the prophet Jeremiah, God had announced to his people that they would serve the king of Babylon for seventy years, after which he would overthrow Babylon and bring the Judeans back to the Promised Land (Jer. 25:11–12; 29:10). One point in question is whether the seventy years is to be calculated from 605 B.C. (the first deportation, when Daniel and his friends were taken to Babylon [Daniel 1]).

Instead, should the exile be dated from the destruction of Jerusalem in 586 B.C.?

The seventy years can legitimately be calculated from either date. If calculated from 605 B.C., the seventieth year would be 536 B.C., when workers began to rebuild the Jerusalem temple (Ezra 3:1–6). If calculated from 586 B.C., the seventieth year would be 516 B.C., just a few months before the temple was completed on the third day of Adar (February-March) in 515 B.C. It appears that Daniel calculated the seventy years from 605 B.C., for it was in 539 B.C. that he prayed in anticipation of the near-completion of this period (Dan. 9:1–2). For our purposes, we will use the earlier dates and assume that the years of captivity commenced with the deportation of the first exiles and ended when the rebuilding of the temple began.

Experiences of the Jews in Captivity

The people who were taken into captivity settled mainly along the irrigation canals of Babylonia, such as the Chebar (Ezek. 1:1). They settled in such ruined sites as Tel-abib (Ezek. 3:15), Tel Melah, and Tel Harsha (Ezra 2:59; Neh. 7:61), where they were expected to rebuild the towns, cultivate the land, and "multiply" (Jer. 29:4–6). Particularly at the beginning of the exile, there was a great sense of sadness at the prospect of living in a foreign land hundreds of miles from Jerusalem. As a psalmist in exile laments, "By the waters of Babylon, there we sat down and wept, when we remembered Zion" (Ps. 137:1). Tormented by their captors, the exiles hung up their harps, because they could not fathom singing the songs of Zion in a foreign land.

Yet, as time passed, the captives found life in Babylonian captivity to be relatively pleasant if compared to the bondage their ancestors experienced in Egypt. With some exceptions (Esther 3; Dan. 3), they were not generally mistreated and enjoyed a variety of privileges. The prophecy of Ezekiel is the clearest contemporary resource for studying conditions among the Jews during the early years of the exile. Ezekiel had his own home where the elders of Judah were free to visit him (Ezek. 8:1). He apparently enjoyed the privilege of correspondence with the people remaining in Jerusalem (Jer. 29:25). Jeremiah even wrote a letter of counsel to the captives in Babylon (Jer. 29).

Mesopotamia is noted for its fine agricultural land, but cultivation there cannot be successful without irrigation. But, as already noted, the Jews settled along the irrigation canals, where plenty of water was available for their crops. Some exiles, such as the craftsmen and smiths (2 Kings 24:14, 16), were taken captive because of their skills and were undoubtedly encouraged to continue their trades in Babylonia. There is also strong evidence for Jewish involvement in trade and commerce during the captivity. Archaelogists have unearthed clay tablets at Nippur on the Kabari Canal, containing the records of business transactions—buying, selling, and renting. Jewish names among these records indicate that many became merchants. Some grew quite wealthy. In fact, the Jewish historian Josephus reports that at the end of the exile many Jews did not want to leave Babylon on account of their many possessions) (*Antiquities* XI.8). Some Jews, such as Daniel and his compatriots Esther, Mordecai, and Nehemiah, attained important positions in government while living in the land of their captivity. It was perhaps through the influence of such trusted Jewish officials as Daniel that Jehoiachin, the exiled king of Judah, was released from prison and eventually restored to a position of honor in the Babylonian court of Evil-Merodach, Nebuchadnezzar's successor (2 Kings 25:27–30; Jer. 52:31–34).

Beginnings of Judaism

Undoubtedly, the greatest heritage of the Judean exile is the inception of what has become known as Judaism. The spiritual developments, beliefs, and traditions that were initially formulated by the Judeans in exile have become the spiritual heritage of the Jewish people. Deprived of the temple and opportunities for religious ritual, the captives in Babylonia began to focus on personal piety rather than official worship protocol and trappings. The two major results were the synagogue and the Talmud.

Having no temple to centralize their worship, the Judeans began to gather in small groups for prayer, instruction, and devotions. As a result, the synagogue, or "assembly," came into being as a context for corporate study of the Hebrew Scriptures. The synagogue not only kept alive the traditions, institutions, and faith of the Jewish people, but it also had a profound influence on maintaining Jewish identity through the exile and down through the ages until the present day. In general, the northern tribes went into captivity and were assimilated into other national groups. The captive southern kingdom of Judah established synagogues and survived as a corporate people by preserving its heritage. Even after the rebuilding of the Jerusalem temple, the synagogue had become such an integral part of Jewish worship that it continued to flourish as an institution. In the first century A.D., synagogues were situated at Jewish centers throughout the entire Mediterranean world. Archaeologists have uncovered the remains of synagogues in Palestine at Capernaum, Chorazin, Masada, Herodium, Beth She'arim, Hammath, Jericho, and Beth Alpha.

The Talmud (from the Hebrew "to learn") is a collection of rabbinical laws, decisions, and commentary on the law of Moses (the

Torah). The Talmud today is composed of the Mishnah, the oral law that was in existence at the end of the second century A.D., and the Gemara, comments on the Mishnah by the rabbis from A.D. 200 to 500. The Talmud began to be developed in order to accommodate the needs of pious Jews living outside the land of Israel. How was the law to be applied to those Jews living in the Diaspora? How were the holy convocations to be observed when there was no temple? The Talmud, which represents developments in Judaism from the exile to the sixth century A.D., reflects how the law of Moses was adapted, reinterpreted, and applied to meet these changing conditions. The Talmud records the accumulation of traditions, institutions, customs, and beliefs of the Jews during the centuries preceding and following the advent of Christianity. This great work of Jewish literature had its beginnings during the Babylonian exile.

The People in Exile

It is difficult to determine the number of Judeans taken into captivity. The first deportation in 605 B.C. probably involved a very small number, since Nebuchadnezzar was primarily interested at this time in members of the royal family and nobles whom he could train for administrative positions in his court (Dan. 1:1–7). The second deportation (597 B.C.) involved the exile of ten thousand Judeans, including King Jehoiachin, his family, and officials and leading men of Judah (2 Kings 24:10–16). (The lower figure recorded in Jer. 52:28 probably reflects a tally of only adult males.) One might expect the third deportation in 586 B.C. to involve the greatest number of exiles. However, 2 Kings 25 does not record the number deported after the temple was destroyed, and Jeremiah 52:29 mentions only 832, probably adult males. Jeremiah 52:30 also mentions the deportation in 581 B.C. of 745 persons, but this may reflect punishment for the murder of Gedaliah of the Jews still living in the land. The total number of Jews taken into captivity may best be indicated by the numbers of those who returned in 537 B.C.—a total of 42,360 (Ezra 2:24; Neh. 7:66).

We can be more specific about the kinds of people taken into captivity. The Babylonians took those with the best training and highest rank—the craftsmen and artisans, the captains and officials, the high priest and the temple officers. It is recorded that Nebuchadnezzar captured all "except the poorest people of the land" (2 Kings 24:14; cf. 25:12). Not all arrived safely in Babylon. Indeed, some were killed at Riblah along the way (2 Kings 25:18–21).

Some of the more prominent personalities of Judah's exilic history include Daniel, Ezekiel, and Jeremiah. Their lives and activities are worthy of individual consideration.

Daniel

Daniel, whose name means "God is my judge," was born into a family of Judean nobility (Dan. 1:3, 6) during the reign of Josiah (640–609 B.C.). Daniel was probably about fifteen years old when he was taken captive by Nebuchadnezzar and sent to Babylon in 605 B.C. He prophesied in Babylon from 603 B.C. (Dan. 2:1) to 536 B.C. (Dan. 10:1) throughout the Babylonian exile and into the Persian period of rule. Daniel was probably about eighty-five years old at the time of his last recorded vision (536 B.C.).

Virtually all we know about Daniel comes from the canonical book that bears his name. Daniel and his three friends—Hananiah (Shadrach), Mishael (Meshach), and Azariah (Abednego)—were selected to be trained in the language and literature of the Babylonians in preparation for serving in Nebuchadnezzar's court. As they entered this three-year training program, Daniel and his friends were assigned names intended to honor Babylonian deities. Daniel was given the name "Belteshazzar," meaning "may Bel [Baal] protect his life."

In spite of all the tempting food and opportunities placed before him, Daniel determined that he would not defile his character by disobeying God's law (Dan. 1:8). God honored Daniel's commitment and blessed his training so that he was found to be wiser than the magicians and conjurers who served Nebuchadnezzar's court. God even gave Daniel the ability to experience and interpret dreams and visions (Dan. 1:17).

Daniel served in Babylonia about seventy years under at least three different sovereigns. He declared and interpreted the dreams and the tree vision of Nebuchadnezzar (605–562 B.C.). He analyzed the "writing on the wall" for Belshazzar (553–539 B.C.), who served as co-regent with Nabonidus (556–539 B.C.). Daniel survived the transition from Babylonian to Persian rule (539 B.C.) and was appointed a commissioner in the court of "Darius the Mede" (Dan. 6:1–6), who may be identified with Cyrus or perhaps with Gubaru, whom Cyrus appointed governor over Babylon. Daniel so distinguished himself in the Persian court that the king intended to appoint him over the entire kingdom.

Daniel's position in the Babylonian and Persian courts gave him significant influence. As already noted, it may have been through Daniel's influence that Jehoiachin was elevated to a place of honor by Evil-Merodach (Amel-Marduk) in 560 B.C. (2 Kings 25:27–30). Daniel's influence may have also been a factor in the decision by Cyrus the

Great to allow the Jews to return to Judah and rebuild the Jerusalem temple (Ezra 1:1–4). Daniel is an excellent example of the godly influence one person can have on a pagan society.

Ezekiel

The son of a Zadokite priest, Ezekiel was deported to Babylonia with King Jehoiachin and ten thousand other captives in 597 B.C. In contrast with Daniel, who lived in the royal city of Babylon, Ezekiel lived among a colony of exiled Jews at a place called Tel-abib (Ezek. 3:15). He began his prophetic ministry when he was thirty years of age, during the fifth year of King Jehoiachin's exile (593 B.C.). Ezekiel continued his ministry for at least twenty-two years. His late-dated prophecy (Ezek. 29:17) was in the twenty-seventh year of Jehoiachin's captivity (570 B.C.).

Ezekiel's ministry to the colony of exiles can be divided into two main periods. From 598 to 586 B.C., or up to the fall of Jerusalem, Ezekiel's ministry consisted primarily of preaching about the coming judgment on Judah. Ezekiel set forth the sins of the nation that were the grounds for her imminent punishment. After the fall of Jerusalem and the destruction of the temple, Ezekiel's ministry was one of consolation and encouragement, as he predicted the future restoration of the nation. Ezekiel sought to emphasize to the exiles that God's judgment was designed to bring them to a knowledge that Yahweh is the only true God (Ezek. 6:7, 10, 13).

Ezekiel is noted for his use of symbolic pantomimes to bring God's message to his people. He made a model of Jerusalem and acted out a siege of the city (Ezek. 4:1–3). He ate meager rations to portray famine conditions in Jerusalem (Ezek. 4:9–17). He packed his bags and carried them out of his house to warn of the coming exile (Ezek. 12:1–7). Ezekiel's symbolic playacting was necessitated in part by his being mute for the first seven years of his ministry (Ezek. 3:26; 33:22). Until the fall of Jerusalem, Ezekiel was unable to speak except when God opened his mouth to proclaim the divine word. Ezekiel would act out a message, and his audience would inquire as to its meaning (Ezek. 12:9; 24:19). Then the word of the Lord would come through the prophet and reach the people.

Although Ezekiel ministered in a difficult time to a stubborn and obstinate people (Ezek. 3:7), his initial vision (Ezek. 1:1–28) left him with an abiding sense of the glory of God (cf. Ezek. 3:23; 8:4; 10:4; 11:22) that sustained him through the most difficult times of his ministry (cf. Ezek. 24:15–27).

Jeremiah

While Daniel ministered in the royal court of Babylon and Ezekiel ministered in the colony of the exiles, Jeremiah continued his prophetic ministry in Jerusalem, declaring God's imminent judgment on the apostate city.

Jeremiah was born into the priestly family of Hilkiah and brought up in the city of Anathoth, located a few miles northeast of Jerusalem. He was called by God to the prophetic ministry in the thirteenth year of King Josiah's reign (627 b.c.). Jeremiah apparently saw Josiah's reforms as inadequate to prevent judgment on Jerusalem. He announced that Judah would be judged and that the people would go into exile. Because of his rather unpopular preaching, Jeremiah faced increasing opposition and persecution. He was confronted with death threats and plots against his life (Jer. 11:18–20) and was publicly humiliated by being beaten and placed in stocks (Jer. 20:1–2). On several occasions he was arrested and imprisoned (Jer. 26:1–24; 37:11–21). Yet, Jeremiah continued prophesying judgment on Judah and Jerusalem through the reigns of the last kings of Judah—Jehoiakim (609–597 b.c.), Jehoiachin (597 b.c.), and Zedekiah (597–586 b.c.).

When Jerusalem fell to the Babylonians in 586 b.c., Jeremiah was released from the imprisonment he had suffered under Zedekiah and allowed to stay among the people remaining in Judah (Jer. 39:11–14). He went to Mizpah, the headquarters of Gedaliah, who had been appointed governor by Nebuchadnezzar. When Gedaliah was slain, Jeremiah warned the remnant of Judah not to depart but to remain in the land. Against the advice of the prophet, they fled for Egypt, taking Jeremiah with them (Jer. 42:19–43:7). There Jeremiah continued his ministry until his death, predicting judgment on Egypt and other foreign nations, including Babylon (Jer. 43:8–51:64). Because of Jeremiah's call and commitment to ministry, he went on preaching even when the people neither heeded nor appreciated his messages.

The Places of the Exile

Babylon

Babylon, capital of the Babylonian Empire and one of the most famous cities of antiquity, was located on the east bank of the Euphrates River (about fifty miles south of modern Baghdad). Babylon first rose to importance in the first half of the eighteenth century b.c., under Hammurabi, but reached the peak of its glory and became the most important city of Mesopotamia during the reign of Nebuchadnezzar (605–562 b.c.). Nebuchadnezzar built an eleven-mile, double-walled

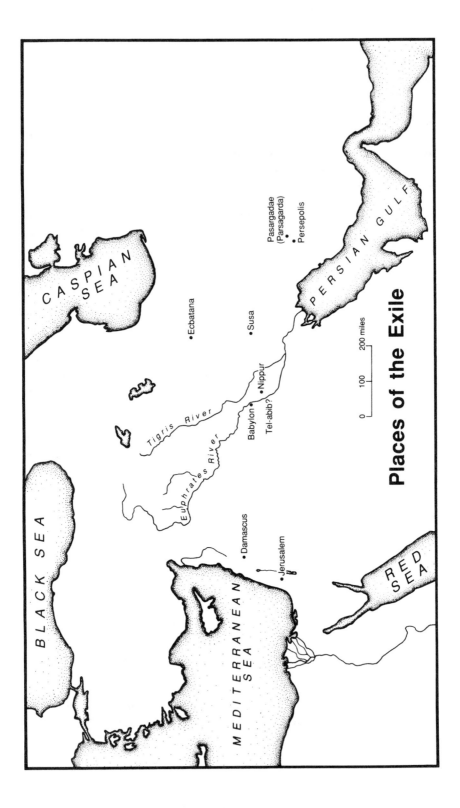

Places of the Exile

CASPIAN SEA

BLACK SEA

MEDITERRANEAN SEA

RED SEA

PERSIAN GULF

Pasargadae (Parsagarda)
Persepolis

Ecbatana

Susa

Tigris River

Euphrates River

Babylon
Nippur
Tel-abib?

Damascus

Jerusalem

0 100 200 miles

Ancient Babylon's Ishtar Gate has been reconstructed in blue tile on its traditional site. *Guy P. Duffield.*

defense system around the city, with inner walls eighty-five feet in thickness. The outer walls were twenty-five feet thick, with strong watchtowers placed every sixty-five feet. An outer moat added to Babylon's defenses.

Within this protective enclosure, Nebuchadnezzar continued the work of his father, Nabopolassar, and reconstructed Babylon into one of the most beautiful cities of the ancient world. He commissioned palaces, temples, and elaborate gateways, and the Hanging Gardens of Babylon were regarded as one of the seven wonders of antiquity. The famous Ishtar Gate, decorated with enameled bricks, gave access to the Processional Way, flanking the palace and the most sacred part of the city, the temple of Babylon's patron god, Marduk (the Esanglia). Excavations have uncovered a thirteen-acre palace compound with several courtyards and other buildings associated with the central structure.

On the site of Babylon, archaeologists have also unearthed the Cyrus Cylinder, an inscribed clay artifact that records details of the city's capture by the Persian king Cyrus. In the rooms of a storeroom near Nebuchadnezzar's palace were found a number of clay tablets that record ration lists, four of them bearing the name "Jehoiachin, king of Judah" (cf. 2 Kings 24:12; 25:27–30).

Babylon fell to Cyrus the Great in 539 B.C., marking the beginning of Persian domination. The city apparently prospered for a time under Cyrus' successors, Darius I and Xerxes I, but it was periodically "punished" for nationalistic uprisings. Babylon suffered a decline after its conquest by Alexander the Great in 330 B.C., and Mesopotamia's capital was moved by Alexander's successors to Seleucia on the Tigris.

Tel-abib

Ezekiel lived in Babylonia among a colony of exiled Judeans at a place called Tel-abib by the River Chebar or "grand canal" (Ezek. 1:1; 3:15; 8:1). This river has been tentatively identified as the "Naru Kabari" or "great river" referred to in two cuneiform texts from Nippur. The name was given to an irrigation canal that brought water from the Euphrates in a southeasterly loop from Babylon via Nippur and back to the main river near Uruk (biblical Erech). The modern name of the canal is Shatt en-Nil.

The name *Tel-abib* probably represents the Akkadian *Tel-abubi*, meaning "mound of the deluge" and suggesting that the site had been previously destroyed by the flooding of the Euphrates River. It appears that the exiles were allowed to rebuild their settlements in Babylon on the sites of ruined cities. The site of biblical Tel-abib has not been identified, but some believe it is located in the vicinity of Nippur, about fifty miles southeast of Babylon.

Susa

Susa, located about 150 miles north of the Persian Gulf at the foot of the Zagros Mountains, was the ancient capital of the Elamite Empire. The city is situated on high ground above the alluvial plain of the Karum River, the biblical "Ulai" (Dan. 8:2). Excavators at Susa have discovered evidence that it was occupied from 4000 B.C. to A.D. 1200, a period of more than five thousand years. During the Persian rule, Susa served as a royal city, along with Ecbatana, Pasargadae, and Persepolis.

Today, Susa is a very large site, with four mounds (tells) covering an area of about three hundred acres. Archaeologists have uncovered the magnificent chief residence of Darius I (522–486 B.C.), decorated with glazed brick. The palace was later reconstructed by Artaxerxes II (404–359 B.C.). The most famous discovery at Susa was the stele of the Code of Hammurabi (c. 1723 B.C.). This law code, which shares many

An aerial view of the mound of the ancient royal city of Susa. *Oriental Institute, Chicago.*

similarities with the Hebrew laws of the Old Testament, was set forth by Hammurabi (1728–1686 B.C.), sixth king of the first dynasty of ancient Babylonia.

Three persons of Old Testament significance are associated with Susa. There, in the days of Ahasuerus (Xerxes I), an exiled Jewess named Esther was elevated to the status of queen to replace Queen Vashti (Esther 1:1–2:17). It was also at Susa that Nehemiah served as cupbearer to Artaxerxes I when he received the disturbing report about the condition of the walls of Jerusalem (Neh. 1:1). Daniel was in Susa "in a vision" (Dan. 8:2) when God revealed the prophetic details of the coming conquests by Persia and Greece.

Ecbatana (Hamadan)

Ecbatana is the Greek name of the city mentioned in the Aramaic of Ezra 6:2 as Achmetha, also known as Hagmatana in ancient times. Hamadan, as it is known today, is located about 180 miles southwest of Tehran, the capital of modern Iran. The site was strategically located

6,000 feet above sea level in the Zagros Mountains, on a caravan route that ran from Mesopotamia to the Persian plateau. Ecbatana became the capital of the Medes in the late seventh century B.C. Because of its pleasant summer weather, it was chosen by Cyrus the Great as his summer capital. Today, it is a popular summer resort, although its winters are long and severe.

It appears that it was from Ecbatana that Cyrus issued the decree allowing the Jews to return to Jerusalem and rebuild the temple. This is suggested by the fact that Darius I later found in the fortress of Ecbatana a scroll containing an official memorandum of this decree (Ezra 6:2). Ecbatana was a city noted for its luxury and splendor. Among the treasures archaeologists have uncovered there is a gold tablet with the inscription of Darius I, as well as assorted objects bearing the names of other Persian rulers. After Ecbatana's destruction by Alexander the Great, the new city of Hamadan was gradually rebuilt. Since the fourth century A.D., Jews have been attracted to the city by its trading opportunities and by the alleged location there of the tombs of Mordecai and Esther (see chapter 12 for the story of these Israelite heroes).

Persepolis

After his accession to the Persian throne in 522 B.C., Darius I moved his capital to Persepolis, a site about three hundred miles southeast of

Man-bulls guarding the eastern doorway, Gate of Xerxes, in Persepolis. *Oriental Institute, Chicago.*

Susa and forty miles from modern-day Shiraz. Darius built a magnificent palace there, on a stone platform forty feet high. Thirteen of the original seventy-two columns of the palace still stand. Near the palace site are the remains of several tombs from the Persian era, believed to be the burial places of Darius and several of his successors, including Xerxes I, Artaxerxes I, and Darius II. The city's rather remote location in a rugged mountain region probably accounts for the Greeks' unfamiliarity with the city until it was taken by Alexander the Great in 331 B.C.

Persepolis' triple defense wall and fortified towers were little protection against Alexander's attack, apparently in revenge against Xerxes I, who had put the torch to Athens 150 years earlier. The city gradually declined in importance until, starting about 200 A.D. (as Istakhr), it acquired significance as the seat of wisdom for the second Persian Empire, although it was later eclipsed by the newer city of Shiraz.

Pasargadae

Located forty miles northeast of Persepolis was Pasargadae, the first capital of the Persian Empire founded by Cyrus the Great. Cyrus established the city on the site of his victory over Astyages the Mede, which gave him control over the empire. There he built lovely gardens and a fine palace. At the southwest edge of the ruined city (identified with "the ruins of Murghab"), lies the tomb of Cyrus. According to the classical writers, the tomb once bore an inscription: "I am Cyrus and I founded the Persian Empire. . . . Grudge me not therefore this monument." Pasargadae was supplanted as capital by Darius I, who preferred Susa and Persepolis as his loyal seats.

Tomb of Cyrus the Great at Pasargadae. *Keith Schoville.*

12

The Restoration of Judah
537 to 430 B.C.

$\mathbf{A}$s God had promised to discipline his people through the Babylonian exile, so he had also promised to restore them to their homeland after seventy years of captivity (Jer. 29:10). The restoration period, chronicled by Ezra and Nehemiah, offered the Judeans a unique opportunity to reestablish on lasting spiritual foundations the temple, their worship institutions, and the city of Jerusalem.

The History of the Restoration

The restoration period covers over a hundred years of Judean history (539–422 B.C.). There are three major returns to be considered and a parenthesis between the first and second—the events recorded in the Book of Esther.

The First Return

The initial return of the exiled Jews was decreed by Cyrus the Great, who conquered Babylon and founded the largest empire the ancient Near East had yet experienced. In 559 B.C., Cyrus inherited the throne of Anshan, a small state near the Persian Gulf, and began unifying the people of Persia. He first attacked the weak and corrupt king of the Medes and took their capital city of Ecbatana (Achmetha) in 550 B.C.

163

without a battle. Unifying the Medes and Persians into one nation, Cyrus went on to defeat the king of Lydia and capture his capital at Sardis in 546 B.C. In its weakened state, the Babylonian Empire was in no condition to resist these combined forces,and Cyrus closed in on the Babylonian capital. According to Herodotus, the fifth century B.C. Greek historian, Cyrus' soldiers managed to divert the waters of the Euphrates, which ran through the city of Babylon. The army then entered the city under the wall through the riverbed and captured Babylon without a battle on October 12, 539 B.C. The Babylonian Empire fell and the Persians took supremacy in the ancient Near East (cf. Dan. 5).

One of the first official acts of Cyrus after the capture of Babylon was to decree the release of the Jewish exiles (2 Chron. 36:22–23; Ezra 1:1–4; cf. Isa. 45:1–13). He did this in his "first year" (Ezra 1:1), which (according to Babylonian reckoning) would be his first regnal year, beginning in 538 B.C., rather than his accession year of 539 B.C. Cyrus reversed the oppressive policies of the Israelites' previous conquerors, the Assyrians and Babylonians, by allowing exiles to return to their homes and reestablish their worship centers. He did this not only for the Jews, but for all the exiles in his realm. Cyrus himself boasts, "I returned to these sacred cities on the other side of the Tigris, the sanctuaries of which have been in ruins for a long time, the images which used to live therein and established for them permanent sanctuaries. I also gathered all their former inhabitants and returned them to their habitations."

It was under the leadership of Sheshbazzar, whom Cyrus had appointed governor of the Persian province of Judah (Ezra 5:14), that the first group of Jewish exiles set out for Judah and Jerusalem, probably in the spring of 537 B.C. Sheshbazzar soon passed from leadership and was succeeded by his nephew, Zerubbabel (1 Chron. 3:19; Hag. 1:1). According to the text of Ezra, over forty thousand Judeans participated in this first return (Ezra 2:64; cf. Neh. 7:66).

The purpose of this return, according to the edict of Cyrus, was to rebuild the Jerusalem temple, the cost of which was to be paid from the Persian treasury (Ezra 1:2; 6:4). Arriving in Jerusalem, the returnees rebuilt the holy altar and laid the foundation of the temple (Ezra 3:1–10). The workmen soon faced stiff opposition from "the adversaries of Judah and Benjamin"—the Samaritans to the north, whom the Jews prohibited from sharing in the rebuilding project (Ezra 4:1–5). This brought the work of the temple to a halt. Sixteen years passed (536–520 B.C.) before the returned exiles once again began to rebuild the Jerusalem temple.

The motivation to continue the restoration of the temple came from two prophets whom the Lord raised up in Judah—Haggai and Zechariah (Ezra 5:1–2). Haggai challenged the people for neglecting their spiritual priorities while spending time and money to panel their own houses (Hag. 1:4). Zechariah declared that genuine repentance was the prerequisite for future blessing (Zech. 1:1–6). The people responded and then began the building in earnest. In spite of further opposition from the Persian governor Tattenai, the original edict of Cyrus was recognized and confirmed by Darius I (522–486 B.C.). The second Jerusalem temple was completed in 515 B.C., and the event was celebrated by a dedication and the offering of sacrifices (Ezra 6:15–17). The temple was not as grand as Solomon's, but Haggai encouraged the people by reminding them of God's promise of future glory and divine blessing on this house of the Lord (Hag. 2:7–9).

The Book of Esther

Between the first and second returns of the Jews (between Ezra 6 and 7) there occurred in Persia a series of events that ultimately resulted in the establishment of the first non-Mosaic Jewish feast. The rule of Persia had by then passed from Darius I to Xerxes I (486–464 B.C.), known in Esther by the name "Ahasuerus." The events of the story of Esther take place in the royal city of Susa during a period of ten years—from the third year of Ahasuerus (483 B.C.) to the feast of Purim in the twelfth year of the king. The purpose of the Book of Esther is both to relate the origin of this feast and encourage the Jews by showing how God delivered and preserved his people in dispersion during the time of the exile.

In 483 B.C., Xerxes I (Ahasuerus) gave a six-month feast in Susa, where (according to Herodotus) he laid plans for his invasion of Greece. It was during the festivities, "when heart of the king was merry with wine," that Queen Vashti was requested to come before the king's guests to display her beauty. (Herodotus notes that Vashti feared for her dignity in the midst of such a drunken group.) She refused the king's command and, as a consequence, was deposed. Vashti's subsequent rejection as queen providentially prepared the way for Esther to receive the crown in her stead.

Apparently a period of three years separates the events of Esther 1 and 2. During this time, Ahasuerus campaigned against Greece and was defeated at Salamis, where the Persian fleet was lost. Upon his return to Susa he set about finding a replacement for Vashti. A "beauty contest" was held, and a lovely Jewess in exile, Esther, was selected as a candidate. Following the instructions of her guardian, Mordecai, she kept secret the fact that she was of Judean descent. When Ahasuerus met Esther, it was love at first sight, and he crowned her queen of Persia (479 B.C.).

Four quiet years passed after Esther's coronation. Then the masterful plot thickened, as Haman "the enemy of the Jews" (Esther 3:10) appeared on the scene. Haman, a favorite prince in the court of Ahasuerus, was angered because Mordecai, due to his Jewish convictions, refused to give him the homage due God alone (Esther 3:3–6). Recognizing that this refusal was based on religious reasons, Haman developed a plan to destroy all the Jews of Persia. By casting lots (*purim*) it was determined that the most favorable time for the destruction of the Jews was the thirteenth day of Adar (March-April), 473 B.C. Offering Ahasuerus financial incentives, Haman secured a royal edict allowing for the destruction of those who "do not keep the king's laws" and the seizure of their property as plunder. All the Jews of Persia, including Queen Esther, were thus put under sentence of death, as Haman planned.

The excitement and suspense of the narrative builds as Esther, with Mordecai's help learns of the plot and seeks to intervene on behalf of her people. Through some carefully calculated moves, the death plot against the Jewish people is revealed to the unwitting king, and Esther points the finger at Haman. Although Haman is punished by the king for his deception—hanged on the gallows he intended for Mordecai— the Jews still stood under the edict of death. The laws of the Medes and Persians were irrevocable, once "sealed with the king's ring" (Esther 8:8). Ahasuerus could not repeal the earlier edict, but he issued a new decree that served to counteract the first—the Jews would be permitted to defend themselves and plunder the spoil of their attackers (Esther 8:11). When the designated day arrived, the Jews were overwhelmingly victorious. Mordecai was elevated to a position of honor and used his authority to institute the feast of Purim still celebrated by Jewish people today (Esther 9:17–31).

The Second Return

About fifteen years after the deliverance of the Jews as recounted in the Book of Esther, a second group of Jews set out for Jerusalem. It was 458 B.C., the seventh year of Artaxerxes I (464–424 B.C.). Sixty years had passed since the first group of Jews had returned to what was now the Persian province of "Yehud." The temple had been rebuilt, but worship had been neglected because of a scarcity of Levites in Jerusalem. The temple was also lacking the proper implements for worship and the people were growing ignorant of God's law. To deal with these matters, God raised up Ezra, a priest and scribe skilled in the law of Moses, to lead a small group (1,500 men) of priests, Levites and temple servants back to Jerusalem. Ezra's activities were officially authorized by Artaxerxes, who appointed him something of a "Secretary of State for Jewish Religious Affairs." The decree of Artaxerxes (Ezra 7:11–26) not only authorized Ezra's work but provided financial support from the royal treasury.

A distance of nine hundred miles separated Ezra and his band from Judah. He carried talents and articles of silver and gold that were worth a small fortune. Since there would be many hazards on such a long journey, especially through the relatively unstable western parts of the Persian Empire, Ezra apparently considered a military escort to be necessary. But, rather than lead Artaxerxes to doubt God's reputed power to protect and deliver his own, none was requested. Instead, Ezra took three days to commit the journey to the Lord before departure (Ezra 8:21–23). Four months later, Ezra and his band arrived safely in Jerusalem and delivered the riches and sacred vessels to the temple officials, after which burnt offerings were made by the returned exiles (Ezra 8:13–34).

In addition to enhancing the temple worship in Jerusalem, Ezra found himself with a moral difficulty to resolve. He had been in Jerusalem about four and a half months when it was brought to his attention that many of "the holy race" had taken "peoples of the land" as wives, although intermarriage between Jews and foreigners was strictly forbidden by Old Testament law (Deut. 7:1–5). (This practice had led Solomon into idolatry and resulted in the division of the monarchy.) The Jewish people had just returned from exile and now were engaged in activities that could once again result in divine punishment and expulsion from the land! Ezra acted with courage and resolve to head off the crisis. After meditation and thorough investigation of each situation, Ezra advised that the foreign wives and their children be "put away" (Ezra 10:1–19; cf. 1 Cor. 7:12–14). Unfortunately, the temptation toward intermarriage continued, and Nehemiah later had to deal with the same problem (Neh. 10:30; 13:23).

The Third Return

Nehemiah, cupbearer of King Artaxerxes I in Susa, led the third return to Jerusalem for the specific purpose of rebuilding the walls of the ruined city. It was probably around 446 B.C. that the adversaries of the returned exiles wrote a letter to Artaxerxes, accusing the Jews of rebuilding Jerusalem's walls and warning of their rebellious ways (Ezra 4: 11–16). The decree issued to Ezra in 458 B.C. had allowed a measure of latitude in how any leftover funds could be spent (Ezra 7:18), but Artaxerxes put a stop to the work on the walls until he could

The Old City of Jerusalem. *Israel Tourist Office.*

thoroughly investigate and issue a specific decree for that purpose (Ezra 4:17–22).

In 445 B.C., Nehemiah received word in Susa of the lamentable situation in the Holy City. Some Jewish travelers reported that "the wall of Jerusalem is broken down, and its gates are destroyed by fire" (Neh. 1:3). Nehemiah wept and mourned, fasted and prayed, in response to this sad news. He then boldly requested of Artaxerxes that he be sent to Jerusalem to rebuild the walled city (Neh. 2:5). The king complied and issued a decree (444 B.C.) that granted Nehemiah a leave of absence and ordained him with the authority to rebuild Jerusalem's walls.

Closeup of a section of Wall of Nehemiah, Along eastern edge of Mount Ophel in Jerusalem, south of Temple Mount. *John McRay.*

Arriving at Jerusalem with officers and horsemen from the king's army, Nehemiah quickly inspected the walls and challenged the leaders of Jerusalem with the task before them (Neh. 2:11–20). Receiving an initial positive response, Nehemiah mobilized Jerusalem for the task. In spite of the opposition from Sanballat, Tobiah, and their wicked associates, the walls of Jerusalem were completed after fifty-two days of work (Neh. 6:15). Josephus stretches this period to two years and four months (*Antiquities* XI.179). Fifty-two days is certainly a short time for such a major project, but even the enemies of the Jews recognized that this work had been accomplished with God's help (Neh. 6:16).

Nehemiah served twelve years as governor of Jerusalem (from 444 B.C. until his return to Artaxerxes in 432 B.C.) (cf. Neh. 5:14; 13:6). During this period, Nehemiah and Ezra instructed the people in the law and the Mosaic covenant was recalled and renewed. The cities of Judah were repopulated and the walls of Jerusalem dedicated. However, during Nehemiah's absence from Jerusalem in 432 B.C., the moral and religious situation greatly deteriorated. The prophet Malachi responded to this situation by rebuking the corruption of the people and priests and calling for repentance (Mal. 4:4). When Nehemiah returned to Jerusalem to begin his second governorship (probably around 431 B.C.), he initiated temple, Sabbath, and marriage reforms (Neh. 13:4–31).

The duration of Nehemiah's second governorship is unknown. By 407 B.C., the office of governor was held by Bogaos, mentioned in an inscription found at Elephantine, a site in Upper Egypt. Artaxerxes I was succeeded in 424 B.C. by less-talented rulers, and the Persian Empire gradually declined until its conquest by Alexander of Macedon (331–323 B.C.).

The City of Jerusalem

Jerusalem! The mere mention of the name stirs thoughts and memories of sacred history. It has been *the* Holy City through the ages, sacred to three great faiths founded in the Middle East—Judaism, Christianity, and Islam. It is difficult to select a specific historical period in which to study Jerusalem since its importance extends throughout the entire biblical era. Yet there was no time during biblical history when Jerusalem was more the center of focus than the restoration period. The exiles returning from Babylon were intent on rebuilding the temple and reestablishing the city as their religious and cultural center. In this section, we will seek to better understand and appreciate the experience of the psalmist who declared. "Our feet have been standing within your gates, O Jerusalem!" (Ps. 122:2).

Location of Jerusalem

The name *Jerusalem* means "foundation of peace." The abbreviated form of the name ("Salem") appears three times in Scripture (Gen. 14:18; Ps. 76:2; Heb. 7:1). The city is situated thirty-three miles east of the Mediterranean Sea and fifteen miles west of the north end of the Dead Sea, at an elevation of around 2,500 feet. Jerusalem is located at the crest of the mountains of the Judean hill country and was originally included in the tribal inheritance of Benjamin (Josh. 18:11–20).

The city lies just east of the north-south watershed of the hill country and was selected for three primary reasons. First, the site has an unfailing water source in the Gihon Spring. Second, the site was very suitable for defense under the conditions of ancient warfare. Deep valleys protected ancient Jerusalem from the east, south, and west. The site was accessible only from the north, where the spur on which the city is situated continues without any change in elevation. Third, Jerusalem lay just east of the north-south travel route that stretched south to Beersheba and north to the Valley of Jezreel. Routes also extended northwest to Joppa and east to Jericho. One thing Jerusalem did *not* have in its immediate vicinity was rich agricultural land. Yet its political and religious importance were sufficient compensation for this lack.

Mountains of Jerusalem

The psalmist declares, "As the mountains are around Jerusalem, so the LORD is around his people . . ." (Ps. 125:2). This is indeed the case. Mountains surround Jerusalem on the north, south, east and west, and the city itself is situated on a 2,200-foot mountain known as Zion. This was the home of "Melchizedek king of Salem," who brought out bread and wine to Abraham (Gen. 14:18; cf. Heb. 7:1). It was also the site of the Jebusite fortress captured by David and made his capital—"the City of David" (2 Sam. 5:7).

Just north of Mount Zion is 2,425-foot Mount Moriah, traditionally identified as the mountain in "the land of Moriah" upon which Abraham offered Isaac (Gen. 22:2). Here David bought the threshing floor from Araunah (Ornan) the Jebusite and erected an altar (2 Sam. 24:18–25). Solomon later built a magnificent temple on this site (2 Chron. 3:1). While Mount Moriah is several hundred feet higher than Mount Zion, the mountain itself is almost indiscernible now, for when Herod built his temple, he erected a twenty-three acre platform that artificially leveled the mountaintop.

A view of the Kidron Valley and the Old City of Jerusalem from the Mount of Olives. *Levant.*

West of Mount Zion is what is known as the Western Hill, the traditional "Zion." When David's original city was abandoned because of its small size, the name *Zion* was transferred to the Western Hill because of its higher elevation (2,550 feet) and dominant position. There the Crusaders located the supposed sites of David's tomb, the "upper room," and Mary's death. The hill may be the "Gareb" of Jeremiah 31:39 and was also the site of the Acra fortress that commanded the temple area during the Maccabean Period. It was during this time that the Western Hill became enclosed within the walls of Jerusalem.

Just east of Jerusalem and across the Kidron Valley is the Mount of Olives (2,700 feet). The "mount" is actually a north-south ridge that parallels the valley. The Mount of Olives was first mentioned in the Old Testament when David is seen ascending it as he flees from Jerusalem during Absalom's revolt (2 Sam. 15:3a). Solomon built high places for Chemosh and Molech, gods of his foreign wives, on the hill "east of Jerusalem" (1 Kings 11:1–7). For this reason, the southern section of the ridge has been known as the mount of "offence," or "corruption" (cf. 2 Kings 23:13). Jesus frequented the mount (John 8:1; Mark 11:1; Matt. 24:3; 26:30), prayed in the Garden of Gethsemane at its foot (Matt. 26:30), and he ascended from its summit into heaven (Acts 1:9–12).

Several miles south of Jerusalem is another hill, on which is now situated a modern U.N. complex. This hill is traditionally known as the Hill of Evil Counsel. From its summit is a splendid view of Jerusalem and the temple area.

Valleys of Jerusalem

The mountains in and around the vicinity of Jerusalem are separated by three valleys, which form the shape of a lopsided pitchfork. The left fork is the L-shaped Hinnom Valley, which curves around the western and southern base of the Western Hill. This valley had an evil reputation in the biblical period, for it was there that Ahaz and Manasseh carried on child sacrifice to Baal and Molech (2 Chron. 28:3; 33:6). The center tine of the pitchfork is the Tyropoeon Valley, mentioned by Josephus and explained as being the valley of the "cheesemakers." It runs in a southeasterly direction between the Western Hill and Mount Zion, joining the Hinnom just south of "Zion," the City of David. This valley has just about been obliterated in the course of time, as it filled with the rubble from the periodic destructions of Jerusalem.

The right fork is the Kidron Valley, which runs north and south between Jerusalem and the Mount of Olives. The pitchfork is considered lopsided because the right fork (the Kidron Valley) continues south, becoming the "handle." South of Jerusalem, both the Hinnom and the Tyropoeon Valleys join the Kidron, which extends southeasterly through the Judean desert to the Dead Sea. David crossed the Kidron as he fled from Jerusalem during Absalom's revolt (2 Sam. 15:23). It was also in the Kidron that Josiah burned the idols of Baal and Asherah (2 Kings 23:4–6). Jesus and his disciples crossed the Kidron Valley after leaving the upper room to pray in the Garden of Gethsemane (John 18:1).

Climate of Jerusalem

Jerusalem has such a pleasant climate that many of today's Israelis work in Tel Aviv and live in Jerusalem. A warm sun penetrates even the winter chill, and a mild Mediterranean breeze reaches the city about noon and brings cooling relief from the hot summer sun. The city of Jerusalem receives about twenty-three inches of rainfall annually. The highest temperatures are reached in July and August, averaging 74° F. The lows come in January and February and average around 48° F. When visiting modern Israel, Jerusalem is probably the most pleasant and convenient place to find accommodations. Most biblical sites, except for those in Galilee, can be reached within an hour and a half of travel time from Jerusalem.

Warren's Shaft goes down to Hezekiah's Tunnel and Gihon Spring. *John McRay.*

Water Sources of Jerusalem

The ancient water sources of the Holy City included springs, cisterns, and pools. The Gihon Spring, which issues from the Kidron Valley just below the City of David, was the main water source of the ancient city. It was here that Solomon was anointed and declared king by Zadok and Nathan (1 Kings 1:33–34). The Gihon still yields clear, cool water. Just south of the junction of the Kidron and the Hinnom valleys is En-rogel, a spring on the outskirts of Jerusalem (Josh. 15:7; 2 Sam. 17:17). This was the coronation site for Adonijah when he attempted to usurp the throne of Judah (1 Kings 1:9).

In preparation for his rebellion against Assyria (701 B.C.), King Hezekiah of Judah blocked access to the Gihon from the Kidron Valley and constructed a 1,600-foot tunnel to channel the water beneath the City of David to a reservoir he built on the south end of Jerusalem—the Pool of Siloam (2 Kings 20:20; 2 Chron. 32:30). The pool is referred to in the Old Testament as "Shiloah" (Isa. 8:6) or "Shelah" (Neh. 3:15). This was the place where Jesus sent the blind man to wash and regain his sight (John 9:1, 7). The construction of the tunnel and the strategically located Pool of Siloam ensured a water supply for Jerusalem during the Assyrian siege and prevented the enemy from using the springs (2 Chron. 32:3–4). An exciting experience for the more adventurous visitor to Jerusalem is to wade through Hezekiah's tunnel from the Gihon Springs to the Pool of Siloam. (Be sure to wear old shoes and carry a flashlight or candle!)

In ancient times, the springs near the city provided sufficient water supply for the inhabitants of Jerusalem. But, as the population grew, these water sources had to be supplemented. This led the Israelites to construct cisterns that were dug into the limestone and plastered to ensure that they were watertight. The mouth was usually about two feet across and the pit about fifteen to twenty feet deep. Rainwater was channeled into the cisterns during the winter, and the stored water could be used during the long, dry summer. Jerusalem is honeycombed with ancient cisterns, many of which are still functional and hold a reserve of water for times of emergency.

There were many pools in Jerusalem during the biblical period. The Old Testament mentions "the upper pool" (2 Kings 18:17), "the lower pool" (Isa. 22:9), "the old pool" (Isa. 22:11), "the King's Pool" (Neh. 2:14), and "the Pool of Shelah" (Neh. 3:15). In the New Testament, there was "the Pool of Bethzatha [Bethesda]" (John 5:2), located near the Sheep Gate (cf. Neh. 3:32; 12:39) north of the temple area. This double pool, noted for its five covered porches, was the place where Jesus healed the lame man who had been sick for thirty-eight years. The so-called "Solomon's Pools" (cf. Eccles. 2:6) were built about nine miles

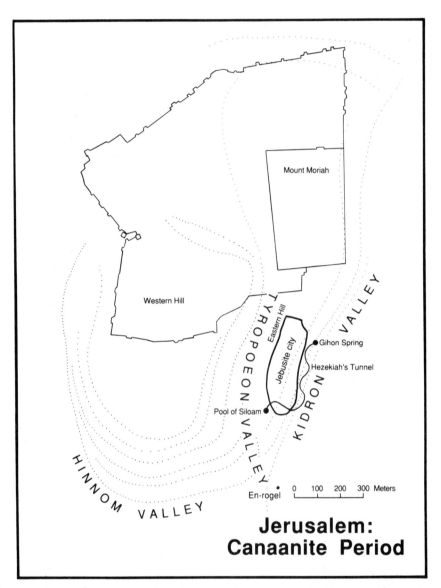

Mount Moriah

Western Hill

T
Y
R
O
P
O
E
O
N

V
A
L
L
E
Y

Eastern Hill

Jebusite city

● Gihon Spring

Hezekiah's Tunnel

Pool of Siloam ●

K
I
D
R
O
N

V
A
L
L
E
Y

V
A
L
L
E
Y

H
I
N
N
O
M   VALLEY

● En-rogel

0   100   200   300 Meters

Jerusalem:
Canaanite Period

south of Jerusalem during the second-temple period to store the water
that issued forth from the strong springs in the vicinity. This water was
channeled from the three pools via stone conduits to Jerusalem.

The History of Jerusalem

The history and expansion of the Holy City can be considered under
six major historical periods: Canaanite, Israelite, Post-Exilic, Intertestamental, Herodian, and Post-Biblical (A.D. 70 to the present).

1. *Canaanite Period* (2100–1010 B.C.) The first historical mention of Jerusalem in Scripture is in Genesis 14:18 ("Salem"), where it is recorded that Abraham honored Melchizedek, its king-priest, by giving him a tenth of the spoil he had captured. On Mount Moriah, just north of the site, Abraham later offered up Isaac (Gen. 22:2). At the time of the conquest, Jerusalem's King Adoni-zedek headed a confederacy of the southern Canaanite kings who opposed Joshua (Josh. 10:1). The reappearance of names ending in "Zedek" indicates that Jerusalem had been ruled by generations of kings who were also priests. Although Adoni-zedek was killed (Josh. 12:10), Jerusalem does not appear to have been captured by the Israelites at this time. The city was later taken by the tribe of Judah (Judg. 1:8), only to be reoccupied by the Canaanite-affiliated Jebusites (Judge. 1:21). During this early period, only the small fortress of Zion was occupied.

2. *Israelite Period*, (1010–586 B.C.). Jerusalem remained a Jebusite fortress until David conquered the city and made it his capital, after reigning seven and a half years in Hebron (2 Sam. 5:6–11). Zion—the City of David—was a choice location for the capital, since the site was not only easily defended but centrally located. David built a house for himself in the city and brought the ark there (2 Sam. 6:12–19). He died and was buried in Jerusalem after reigning there for thirty-three years.

Solomon was responsible for the expansion of the city northward to include the environs of Mount Moriah. There, with the aid of Hiram and the Phoenicians, Solomon built the first Jerusalem temple (966–960 B.C.). The walls of the city were extended northward to surround and protect the temple area. During the divided monarchy, Jerusalem continued to serve as the capital of the southern kingdom without significant changes until its destruction by the Babylonians in 586 B.C.

3. *Post-exilic Period* (539–424 B.C.). After the seventy-year Babylonian captivity, Jerusalem was repopulated with Jewish exiles during "the first return" under the leadership of Sheshbazzar and Zerubbabel. Later, as we have already seen, the temple was rebuilt, the worship institutions were reestablished, the city itself was restored and fortified. But Jerusalem remained within the same basic confines established by the original Israelite occupation. From the restoration period has come the most complete description of the walls, towers, and gates of Jerusalem (cf. Neh. 3).

4. *Intertestamental Period* (424–40 B.C.). (See chapter 13 for general historical details of this period, which spanned the decline of Persian rule, Alexander the Great, Ptolemaic and Seleucid rule, Hellenization, the Maccabean revolt, the Hasmonean era, and the beginnings of Roman domir ation.) Twelve years after the relatively peaceful entry of Alexander the Great into Jerusalem (332 B.C.), Ptolemy I of Egypt par-

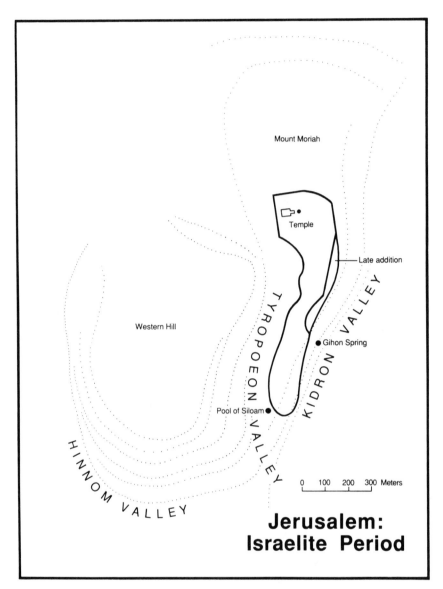

Mount Moriah

Temple

Late addition

TYROPOEON VALLEY

KIDRON VALLEY

Western Hill

Gihon Spring

Pool of Siloam

HINNOM VALLEY

0   100   200   300 Meters

Jerusalem: Israelite Period

tially demolished its fortifications. When the city was seized by Antiochus III in 198 B.C., virtually all of Palestine went from Ptolemaic to Seleucid control. Antiochus Epiphanes IV, in 168 B.C., reduced Jerusalem to the lowest point of its history when he destroyed the city's walls and desecrated the temple by sacrificing a pig to Zeus on the holy altar, as part of his program of Hellenization. This was the incident

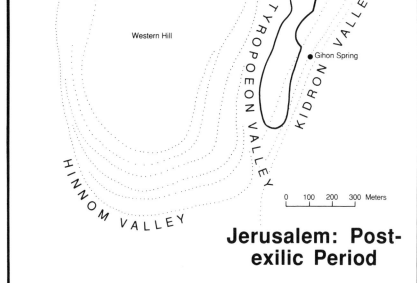

Mount Moriah

Temple

Western Hill

TYROPOEON VALLEY

KIDRON VALLEY

● Gihon Spring

HINNOM VALLEY

0   100   200   300 Meters

Jerusalem: Post-exilic Period

that precipitated the Maccabean revolt, led by Mattathias, a Jewish priest, and his five sons.

After a succession of other military victories by Judas Maccabaeus, most of the Holy City was captured and worship restored in the temple (164 B.C.). Previous to this, the Hellenizers and their one-time Syrian-Seleucid allies had divided the city, with the Jews occupying the Lower

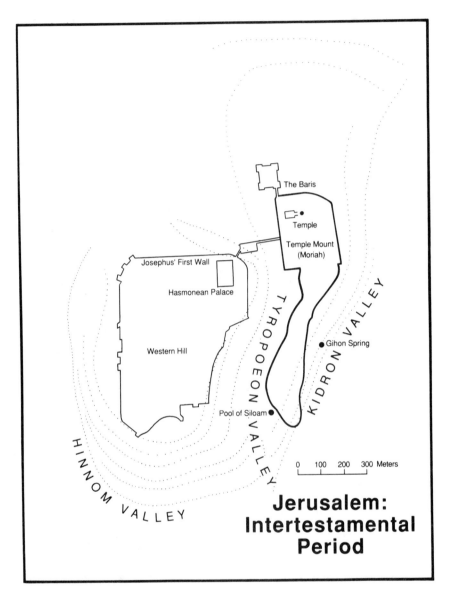

Jerusalem: Intertestamental Period

The Baris

Temple

Temple Mount (Moriah)

Josephus' First Wall

Hasmonean Palace

Western Hill

TYROPOEON VALLEY

KIDRON VALLEY

Gihon Spring

Pool of Siloam

HINNOM VALLEY

0   100   200   300 Meters

City (Mount Zion and the temple mount) and the conquerors established in the Upper City (the Western Hill), protected by a fortress, the Acra (Akra). This Seleucid citadel defied capture by the Maccabees until 141 B.C., when Simon Maccabaeus demolished the Acra and lowered the hill on which it stood, in hopes of preventing future domination of Jerusalem by foreign invaders. Protective walls were erected to safeguard the Upper City, and a palace was built on Acra's ruins, with a bridge across the Tyropoeon Valley (linking the Upper City with the temple area.

During the land's nearly hundred years as a "nation" following the Maccabean revolt, Jerusalem regained its importance as a Judean administrative and religious center. Eventually political divisiveness under the Hasmonean rulers weakened their control and paved the way for yet another period of foreign domination—this time under the growing power of the Romans. Pompey besieged and captured Jerusalem in 63 B.C., and another Roman, Crassus, plundered the temple ten years later. Next would come the administration of Herod the Great.

5. *Herodian Period* (40 B.C.–A.D.70) (See chapter 13 for historical details.) In 40 B.C., the Roman senate appointed Herod, an Idumean, king of the Jews, his domain to include Galilee, Perea, Judea, and Idumea. With the aid of Roman forces, Herod fought to take possession of this territory and did not secure his throne in Jerusalem until three years later. Herod immediately set about fortifying and embellishing the Holy City. Revenues from trade and taxes enabled him to construct a magnificent palace in the Upper City (the Western Hill). The palace was guarded by three strong towers named after Phasael (his brother), Mariamne (his Hasmonean wife), and Hippicus (his friend). Herod doubled the temple area and surrounded it with walls and covered porches. The sanctuary itself was refurbished and beautified. In honor of Mark Antony, Herod built the Antonia Fortress at the northwest corner of the temple area. He also constructed a theater to entertain the wealthy Hellenistic Jews. A hippodrome, or race track, was built, probably in the Tyropoeon Valley.

This was the city of Jerusalem that Jesus and his apostles knew. Jesus visited this city on many occasions and was crucified there in A.D. 33. There are many sites in today's Jerusalem that are traditionally considered to mark significant events in the life of Jesus, including the Church of the Holy Sepulchre (the site of Jesus' burial), the Via Dolorosa (the route of the cross), and the Grotto of Gethsamane.

It was probably during Herod's day that the walls of Jerusalem were extended northeast from the Gennath Gate (near Herod's palace and towers) to the Antonia Fortress. Just how far north this "second" wall extended is a matter of debate among archaeologists. A third wall, built by Herod Agrippa (A.D. 40–44), enclosed the residential area north of the second wall and the temple area, including the Pool of Bethesda. The present walls of the Old City of Jerusalem follow the lines of this "third" wall of the first century A.D.

Herod the Great built in a manner designed to immortalize his

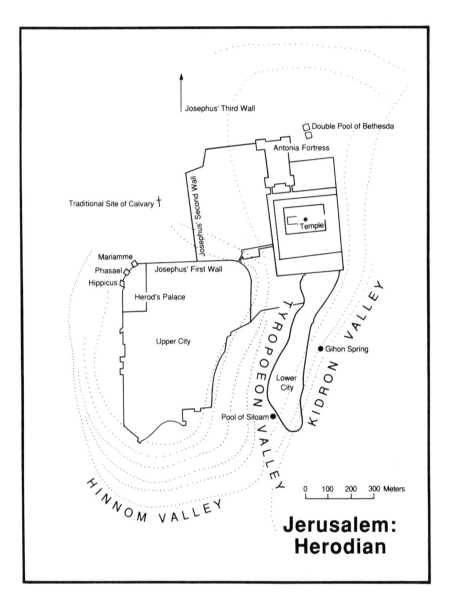

Josephus' Third Wall

Double Pool of Bethesda

Antonia Fortress

Josephus' Second Wall

Traditional Site of Calvary †

Temple

Mariamme

Phasael

Josephus' First Wall

Hippicus

Herod's Palace

TYROPOEON VALLEY

KIDRON VALLEY

Upper City

Gihon Spring

Lower City

Pool of Siloam

HINNOM VALLEY

0   100   200   300 Meters

Jerusalem: Herodian

name and perpetuate his memory. He used very large stones (up to thirty-six feet in length), prepared with a two-to-four inch margin for embellishment. Herodian stones can still be seen at the base of the walls around the temple area and at the lower portion of what was once the tower of Phasael.

6. *Post-Biblical Period* (A.D. 70–present). (For general historical

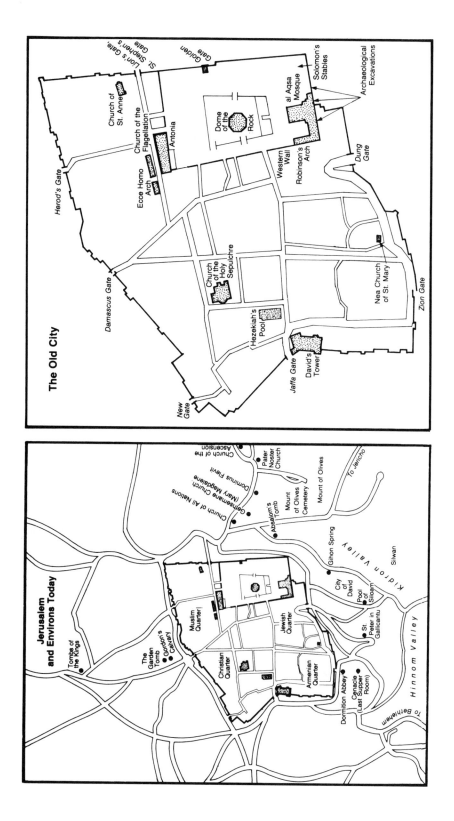

The Old City

Jerusalem and Environs Today

Herod's Gate

Church of St. Anne

Lion's Gate, St. Stephen's Gate

Golden Gate

Church of the Flagellation

Ecce Homo Arch

Antonia

Dome of the Rock

al Aqsa Mosque

Solomon's Stables

Archaeological Excavations

Western Wall

Robinson's Arch

Dung Gate

Damascus Gate

Church of the Holy Sepulchre

Hezekiah's Pool

Nea Church of St. Mary

Zion Gate

New Gate

Jaffa Gate

David's Tower

Tombs of the Kings

The Garden Tomb

Gordon's Calvary

Muslim Quarter

Christian Quarter

Jewish Quarter

Armenian Quarter

Dormition Abbey

Cenacle (Last Supper Room)

St. Peter in Gallicantu

City of David

Pool of Siloam

Gihon Spring

Silwan

Kidron Valley

Church of the Ascension

Pater Noster Church

Dominus Flevit

Gethsemane Church, (Mary Magdalene)

Church of All Nations

Absalom's Tomb

Mount of Olives Cemetery

Mount of Olives

To Jericho

Hinnom Valley

To Bethlehem

background, see succeeding chapters, especially chapter 16.) During the last decade before Jerusalem's destruction, Rome faced an increasing breakdown in law and order in Judea as the Jews begin to assert themselves against foreign rule. After a clash at Caesarea, the Jews were forced to leave that city. When news of this reached Jerusalem, the citizens broke out in revolt (A.D. 66). Nero sent his best general, Titus Flavius Vespasianus (Vespasian) along with three Roman legions, to Judea. After subduing Galilee, Vespasian marched on Judea. In the spring of A.D. 69, Vespasian left Judea to ascend the throne in Rome and sent his eldest son, Titus, to continue the campaign in Judea. Jerusalem was surrounded and besieged. The Romans entered and burned the temple on August 28, B.C. 70. It was another month before the Upper City was captured and Jewish resistance ceased. By order of Titus, the Jews were taken captive and many buildings of the city were leveled. The partially ruined city was placed under surveillance by the Tenth Roman Legion. (See "Rome's Destruction of Jerusalem" in chapter 15.)

In the years following the destruction of Jerusalem, it was gradually resettled, but news of the Emperor Hadrian's plan to found a Roman colony there sparked anew the Jewish struggle against Rome. After the Second Jewish Revolt (A.D. 131–135), Hadrian destroyed the city and rebuilt it in Roman style, naming it *Aelia Capitolina* after himself (Aelius) and the "Capitolina triad" (Jupiter, Juno, and Minerva). Today's Jerusalem roughly follows the plan of Hadrian's city, with intersecting north-south and east-west streets dividing it into four quarters.

Little is known of Jerusalem during two centuries from the end of the Hadrianic period until Constantine, who—as part of his Christianization of the land—ordered recovery of the sites of Jesus' crucifixion and burial (A.D. 326). One of the churches built during that time was the original Church of the Holy Sepulchre. In A.D. 469, Empress Eudocia commissioned the repair of the city walls and their extension to include the Pool of Siloam and added many churches, including one at Siloam and another above the reputed tomb of Stephen. Justinian (A.D. 527–565) likewise sponsored many building operations there, including the Golden Gate of the temple area and part of the church that later became the el-Aksa mosque under Moslem rule.

For the roughly three hundred years of the Byzantine era (A.D. 330–634), there was relative peace and prosperity in Palestine and the Holy City, which gradually became a destination for religious pilgrimages. This tranquility was broken at intervals by persecution of the Jews, which partially explains their loose alliance with Chosroes II of Persia when he swept through the land and eventually captured Jerusalem in A.D. 614. Although the Byzantines briefly regained control under Heraclius, a new threat to peace arrived with Caliph Omar, who brought the rising power of Islam to bear on the entire area. His capture of Jerusalem in A.D. 638 marked the beginning of Moslem domination of the city. Except for brief periods thereafter, especially during the Crusades, Jerusalem remained essentially in the control of various factions of the Islamic nations until its capture by General Allenby in 1917.

The present walls of Jerusalem were built during the years A.D. 1538–1540 by the Turkish ruler Suleiman the Magnificent. These walls cut across the Western Hill in the south, omitting David's city, Zion, from the walled city. The contours of the enclosure follow the Hinnom Valley to the northern wall, which appears to be built over the wall of Herod Agrippa. The east wall follows and joins the eastern wall of the Herodian temple mount. Suleiman also commissioned a number of fountains, many of which still beautify the city.

After World War I, Jerusalem was the center of the British-mandated territory of Palestine, and its modern era began. A new water system was engineered, electric power was introduced, and macadamized roads were laid. Despite the ever-present conflict between the Jewish and Arab adversaries, many public buildings and institutions of learning were erected. The end of the British mandate in 1948 and the establishment of the independent state of Israel brought

Note the Turkish influence at the top of the walls above the Damascus Gate. *John McRay.*

little immediate relief from the violence, but an armistice established Jerusalem as an "international" city and divided it between the rival states of Israel and Jordan.

Jerusalem today is the seat of ecclesiastical authorities of many faiths. It is the third holy city of Islam, the residence of the chief rabbis of the Jewish community, and the seat of many Christian dignitaries, including Roman Catholic and Greek Orthodox patriarchs and an Anglican bishop. The number of synagogues, churches, and mosques attest to the universal importance of Jerusalem, as does the variety of races and creeds crowding its thoroughfares.

13

Between the Testaments
430 to 5/4 B.C.

$\mathbf{T}$he four hundred years between the Testaments is often thought of as the silent age of Israel's history. This is especially true for Protestant Christians, whose Bibles do not include the two apocryphal books of the Maccabees that record many of the events of this period. Nevertheless, it is surprising how much of the history of the intertestamental period can be found tucked away in the Book of Daniel. Although one might be tempted to skip over this era and move directly into the New Testament period, a knowledge of these years is essential as a background for New Testament studies. We may rightly regard the period between the Testaments as an age of transition in the Bible lands—a time when predominantly Jewish ways were gradually eclipsed by Greek culture, language, and philosophy. This period of wide and drastic change sets the stage for the New Testament period.

Persian Decline (424–331 B.C.)

Following the death of Artaxerxes I (464–424 B.C.), who had appointed Nehemiah as governor of Judah, the Persian Empire was ruled by less able men and entered a period of decline. Darius II (424–404 B.C.) faced revolt in the more remote districts of his empire—Syria, Lydia, Media and Egypt. Artaxerxes II (404-358 B.C.) made two unsuccessful attempts to reassert Persian sovereignty over Egypt. His successor, Artaxerxes III (358–338 B.C.), marched on Egypt and reconquered it, but the king was poisoned by a member of his court.

In addition to these internal revolts, Persia faced an outside threat from the Greeks who were settled on the shores of the Aegean Sea. Persia, anticipating this threat, had made two attempts to conquer Greece (490 and 480 B.C.) and failed. By the middle of the next century, Philip of Macedon had united the Greek cities under his rule as a prelude to his goal of bringing the entire Mediterranean world under Greek control. When Philip was murdered in 336 B.C., his twenty-year-old son, Alexander, was elevated to leadership. A student of Aristotle and convinced of the superiority of the Greek way of life, Alexander shared his father's dream—the Hellenization of the world.

Envisioned by Daniel as the "large horn" of the male goat coming from the west (Dan. 8:5, 21), Alexander and an army of 35,000 crossed the Dardanelles from Macedonia into Asia in 334 B.C.. He engaged the Persian satraps who governed Asia Minor and defeated them soundly on the banks of the Granicus River. Advertising himself as their liberator from Pro-Persian rule, Alexander gained possession of the Greek cities on the coast of Asia Minor and then met Darius III and his army in 333 B.C. at Issus, the strategic pass at the northeast corner of the Mediterranean Sea. Darius was defeated but escaped with his life and fled east.

Instead of pursuing the defeated Persian ruler, Alexander marched southward to attack Phoenicia, Palestine, and Egypt. By 332 B.C., he had besieged and conquered Tyre and Gaza, two of the cities that offered resistance. According to Josephus, Alexander visited Jerusalem, where the high priest showed him from Daniel's prophecy (cf. Daniel 8:5–7, 20–21) that he was destined to conquer Persia. Alexander advanced to Egypt, which he took with little difficulty. After wintering there, he marched northward through Palestine, crossed the Tigris, and met the last of Darius' troops at Gaugamela. Once again Darius was defeated and fled east. Alexander next proceeded to occupy Persia's royal cities—Babylon, Susa, Persepolis, Pasargadae, and Ecbatana. Darius III was killed by his own men, marking the end of his Persian dynasty and the beginning of Greek rule in Asia Minor, although Alexander was to endure skirmishes with other Persian satraps and dissension among his own generals.

Greek Rule (330-167 B.C.)

After the death of Darius III, Alexander continued his march through eastern Persia and prepared to invade India. He reached the

Indus River and turned south, expecting to be met by supply ships on the coast of the Indian Ocean. None appeared. After much suffering, Alexander and his bedraggled troops returned to Babylon in 323 B.C. Having conquered the known world, Alexander the Great died in Babylon in June of that year. He was thirty-two years old.

Alexander's premature death left his vast empire without a leader. He had two heirs—his brother, Philip, and his child by Roxana, a Bactrian princess. Since the real power resided in the hands of the generals, the heirs were thrust aside. A struggle ensued between those who desired to keep the empire intact and those who wanted to divide it. After much internal fighting, the empire was divided among Alexander's four generals (cf. Daniel 8:24; 11:4). When the dust settled, Ptolemy held Egypt and Palestine, and Seleucus controlled the vast region from Phrygia to the Indus River, including Syria. Lysimachus ruled the regions of Thrace and Bithynia, and Cassander held Macedonia. Palestine fell first to control by the Ptolemies to the south, and then by the Seleucids to the North.

Ptolemaic Rule (301–198 B.C.)

Ptolemy ruled Egypt and Palestine from Alexandria, a Hellenic-style city in northern Egypt, founded in 332 B.C. by Alexander the Great. During the early period of Ptolemaic rule, the Jews in Palestine lived in relative peace. Though poor, the Judeans were well treated by the Ptolemies, and the Jewish high priest was allowed to serve as governing officer and legal administrator. It was in Egypt during this period that the Jewish Scriptures were translated into Greek (Septuagint) for the benefit of those Jews who no longer spoke or read Hebrew. Seleucus, who ruled Syria to the north, refrained from fighting his old comrade, Ptolemy. Later Seleucid rulers, however, were more aggressive in their desires to control Palestine, that much-coveted land bridge between the continents. Four Syrian wars resulted (cf. Daniel 11:5–16). The bloody contest was brought to an end in 198 B.C., when Antiochus III met and defeated the Ptolemaic forces at Panias (the site of Caesarea Philippi). The Seleucid army drove the Ptolemaic forces back to Egypt, and Palestine was brought under Seleucid control.

Seleucid Rule (198–167 B.C.)

The Seleucid rule of Palestine was directed from Antioch, the capital founded by Seleucus on the Orontes River. With the southern border of Syria secured by his victories over the Ptolemies, Antiochus III turned his attention westward. In 196 B.C., Antiochus invaded Greece, but the controlling Romans retaliated and defeated him in 190

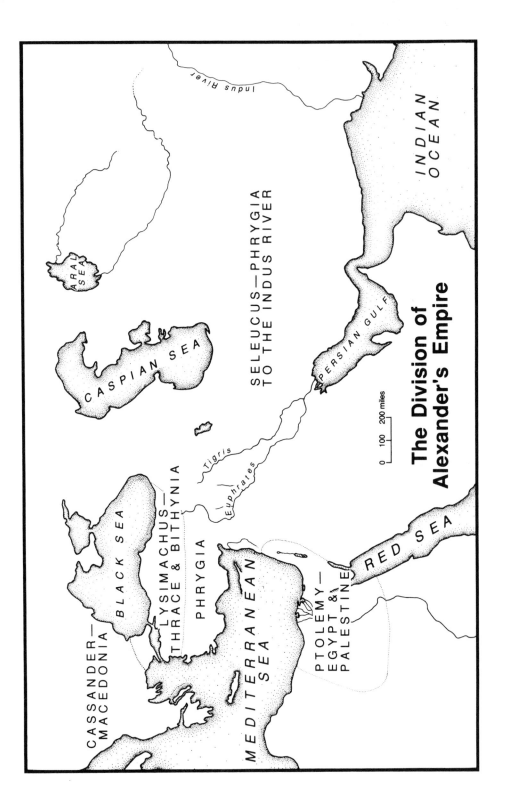

INDIAN OCEAN

Indus River

ARAL SEA

CASPIAN SEA

SELEUCUS—PHRYGIA TO THE INDUS RIVER

PERSIAN GULF

Tigris

Euphrates

LYSIMACHUS— THRACE & BITHYNIA

PHRYGIA

BLACK SEA

CASSANDER— MACEDONIA

MEDITERRANEAN SEA

PTOLEMY— EGYPT & PALESTINE

RED SEA

0 100 200 miles

The Division of Alexander's Empire

B.C. Antiochus signed a treaty requiring him to give up all of Asia Minor and most of his military forces. This defeat caused Antiochus III and the sons who succeeded him, Seleucus IV and Antiochus IV, to recognize the necessity of strengthening themselves in anticipation of future confrontation with Rome.

Antiochus IV (175–163 B.C.) is recognized as one of the most infamous characters affecting Jewish history. His character and activities are related in the Book of Daniel (Daniel 8:9–12, 23–25; 11:21–31). When Antiochus took power, he sought to unify the people under his rule through Hellenization. From the word Hellas ("Greece"), Hellenism involved adoption of the Greek language, philosophy, and religion. Laying claim to divine kingship, Antiochus began to encourage that he be worshiped as the incarnation of Zeus. He took the name *Epiphanes,* meaning "God manifest," which his enemies perverted to *Epimanes,* meaning "madman." He believed that the majority of the Jewish people living in Palestine were ready to accept Hellenism. For a money gift and pledge to support the Hellenization of Jerusalem, Antiochus deposed Onias III and installed his brother Jason (Joshua) as high priest. But Jason soon lost his position to another contender, Menelaus, who outbid Jason in bribes to Antiochus for the high priesthood.

In 170 B.C. Antiochus invaded Egypt (Dan. 11:25 ff.) defeated Ptolemy VI, and proclaimed himself king at Memphis. He was besieging Alexandria in 169 B.C. when he learned that Jason had tried to capture Jerusalem, forcing Menelaus to take refuge in the Acra fortress. Antiochus marched to Jerusalem, where he rescued Menelaus and appropriated the temple treasure.

Returning to Egypt in 168 B.C., Antiochus was confronted by a Roman commander near Alexandria and compelled to withdraw. Bitter about this humiliating turn of events, Antiochus returned to Jerusalem where he took out his bitterness on the Jews by indiscriminate slaughtering. (Daniel 11 describes these events.) Antiochus subjugated the city in 167 B.C. and dedicated the Jerusalem temple to the worship of Zeus by sacrificing a sow on the holy altar. These were dark days for God's people as the order went out from Antiochus that the Jews must henceforth sacrifice to Zeus.

Maccabean Revolt (167–143 B.C.)

Daniel predicted that "the people who know their God will stand firm and take action" (Dan. 11:32). When Antiochus ordered the villages in Palestine to set up altars and sacrifice to Zeus, Mattathias, a priest at Modin, refused. An apostate Jew stepped forward to sacrifice,

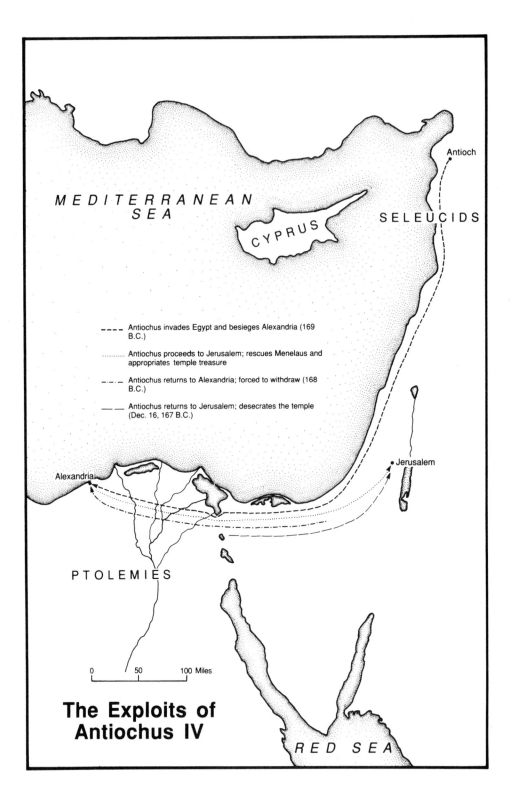

MEDITERRANEAN
SEA

CYPRUS

SELEUCIDS

• Antioch

- - - Antiochus invades Egypt and besieges Alexandria (169 B.C.)

.... Antiochus proceeds to Jerusalem; rescues Menelaus and appropriates temple treasure

- . - . - Antiochus returns to Alexandria; forced to withdraw (168 B.C.)

— — Antiochus returns to Jerusalem; desecrates the temple (Dec. 16, 167 B.C.)

Alexandria

• Jerusalem

PTOLEMIES

0   50   100 Miles

The Exploits of Antiochus IV

RED SEA

and Mattathias killed him, as well as Antiochus' representative. Mattathias and his sons—John, Simon, Judas, Eleazar, and Jonathan—took to the mountains and began their struggle against Antiochus and the Greek ways of the Seleucids, in what is known as the Maccabean revolt. They were joined by pious Jews who sought to defend the law of Moses against Hellenism. Mattathias died soon after the rebellion began and was succeeded by his son Judas, whose military successes won him the surname *Maccabaeus*, "the Hammerer." Using the surprise tactics of guerilla warfare, the followers of Judas "hammered" at the troops of Antiochus and soon had the enemy fleeing before them.

After defeating the Seleucid general Lysias at Beth-zur in 164 B.C., Judas marched to Jerusalem and purified and rededicated the Jewish temple making possible the reinstatement of worship rituals there. The Jewish feast of Hanukkah or Dedication (John 10:22) commemorates this event. The celebration is also called the "feast of lights," based on the legend that one small vessel of undefiled oil miraculously kept burning for eight days the lamps of the menorah, or ceremonial candelabrum.

Though highly significant, the rededication of the Jerusalem temple did not end the war for Jewish independence. Judas continued his military efforts, carrying on raids in Transjordan, the coastal plain, and Idumea, while brother Simon led an expedition into Galilee. Wherever there were complaints of mistreatment of Jews, the Maccabees (a name applied to all champions of Judaism in that period) would carry out their exploits. Having gained religious freedom in Jerusalem, Judas sought political freedom for all of Judea and he lost his life in this valiant effort. Killed in the Battle of Eleasa (161 B.C.), Judas was succeeded by his brother Jonathan and the struggle continued. Jonathan became a pawn in the political intrigues of the Seleucids and was eventually captured and put to death. Simon assumed leadership then and was able to secure political independence for Judah (142 B.C.).

Hasmonean Rule (142–63 B.C.)

After twenty-five years of fighting to maintain their control, the Seleucids finally granted the Judeans their independence, and Demetrius II exempted the land from further taxation and tribute. Simon Maccabeus was confirmed as ethnarch and high priest, with the right of succession granted to his heirs. Religious and political power now resided in one leader. The priestly descendants from the time of Simon until 63 B.C. were the Hasmoneans, derived from the family name of Hasmon.

The country enjoyed several years of prosperity and peace under Simon's administration, but after he and two of his sons were assassinated in 135 B.C. by the power-seeking Ptolemy, Simon was succeeded by his second son, John Hyrcanus. During the realm of Hyrcanus I (135–104 B.C.), the Seleucid ruler, Antiochus VII, reasserted Syrian authority, and Hyrcanus was compelled by famine to surrender Jerusalem and much of his power. When Antiochus VII was slain, Syria was plunged into civil war, and Hyrcanus was able to reestablish Jewish independence. In addition, he carved out an empire from surrounding territory by conquering Idumea on the south, Samaria on the north, and Medaba in Transjordan.

Sectarian controversy soon began to create internal dissension, as the rival Pharisee and Sadducee factions maneuvered for dominance in the realm. The Pharisees had emerged as a distinct group shortly after the Maccabean revolt and had as ancestors the pious Hasidim, who joined the rebel forces because they refused to compromise their dedication to the law by adopting the ways of Hellenism. However, the Pharisees' dedication to "the law" was twofold, in that they recognized both the written law of the Torah and its supplementation by the teachings of the prophets and unwritten tradition (the oral law). In contrast, the Sadducees, who based their authority on their supposed decendancy from David's faithful high priest Zadok (cf. 1 Kings 1:8; 2:35), recognized only the written law, although they managed to accommodate their ways to the Hellenists. These priests and wealthy aristocrats essentially controlled the workings of the Sanhedrin, the supreme Jewish council and tribunal, and their interests lay mainly in the political and secular realm. The Pharisees were generally laymen, middle-class Jews who centered their teaching and activities around the synagogues. They were branded "separatists" by the priestly Sadducees, and the differences between the two groups became crystallized when Hyrcanus aligned himself with the Sadducees, sparking a long struggle during which the Pharisees attempted to democratize the Jewish religion and remove it from the rigid control of the temple priesthood. A number of theological issues divided the two groups (cf. Acts 23:6-8).

Aristobulus I (104–103 B.C.), son and successor of John Hyrcanus, was able to conquer Galilee, extending the Hasmonean dominion yet further north. After his death, his widow, Salome Alexandra, married the next surviving brother, the warlike Alexander Jannaeus (103–76 B.C.), who expanded the kingdom to include most of the present land of Israel. He was not nearly as successful as Aristobulus in maintaining a stable administration and good public relations, managing to alienate both the Sadducees and the Pharisees and suppress any opposition with savage measures. Many Jews fled the country during his reign. One significant result of his rule was the appointment of Antipater, Herod's father, as governor of Idumea.

Salome Alexandra (76–67 B.C.) had been designated by Alexander Jannaeus as his successor. She selected her elder son, Hyrcanus II, as high priest and made peace with the Pharisees, since they influenced the majority of the people. When Alexandra died, Hyrcanus assumed the position as king as well as that of high priest. Somewhat a pliable weakling, he was challenged by his brother, Aristobulus II (67–63 B.C.), who quickly took power and captured Jerusalem. As the political situation in Jerusalem was deteriorating, the Roman general Pompey was marching east across Asia Minor. After annexing the Seleucid kingdom, which became the Roman province of Syria, Pompey turned his attention toward Judea. Though rivals, both Aristobulus and Hyrcanus appealed to him for support. When Pompey arrived at Jerusalem in 63 B.C., the supporters of Hyrcanus threw open the gates of the city to him. Suspecting that Pompey would not favor him, Aristobulus fled, but was later taken prisoner, released, and eventually slain. Hyrcanus was reinstated as high priest and given the title *ethnarch* ("ruler of a nation"). But the "nation" he ruled was only a fragment of what had been previously controlled by his people. Much of the country was placed under the authority of the Roman proconsul of Syria. Palestine was under the dominion of Rome.

Roman Rule (63–4 B.C.)

Although Hyrcanus II was high priest and ethnarch of Judea, his friend and supporter Antipater (father of Herod the Great) was the power behind the throne. When Pompey and Julius Caesar engaged in civil war, Antipater threw in his lot with Caesar. He was rewarded with Roman citizenship and appointed procurator of Judea, a position that actually gave him more power than that of Hyrcanus. Antipater used this authority to appoint his elder son, Phasael, as governor of Jerusalem and his younger son, Herod, as governor of Galilee.

The assassination of Julius Caesar in 44 B.C. resulted in renewed civil war in Rome, but Antipater and his sons managed to stay in favor with the ruling party. When Antipater was murdered in 43 B.C., Herod and Phasael were appointed co-rulers of Judea.

In 40 B.C., the Parthians invaded Syria from their territory southeast of the Caspian Sea and soon swept into Palestine. They were joined by Antigonus, surviving son of Aristobulus II, who wanted to regain the position of high priest for his lineage. Under his direction, Phasael and Hyrcanus were captured by the Parthians, but Herod managed to escape to Masada, then to Petra, and finally to Rome. Antigonus was appointed ruler by the Parthians, and Hyrcanus carried away and mutilated, making him unfit for the high priesthood.

When Herod arrived in Rome, he was recognized as a hero and received with honor. Octavian (the future Emperor Augustus) and Mark Antony persuaded the Roman senate to appoint Herod "king of the Jews." Although it was an empty title at the time, because Antigonus was still in power in Jerusalem, Herod was determined to make the most of this opportunity.

He returned to Palestine and began his campaign for Galilee in the winter of 39 B.C. with the support of Roman soldiers. During the next two years, Herod secured the territories appointed to him by Rome. Jerusalem fell to Herod's forces in the summer of 37 B.C., Antigonus was executed, and Herod the Idumean became the undisputed King of Judea.

After securing his power, Herod solidified his position by punishing those who had opposed him and rewarding his supporters. Herod executed forty-five former supporters of Antigonus and confiscated their properties. He was never really liked, even by the Jews, whom he attempted to conciliate. They loathed his Idumean heritage, although he encouraged the Pharisees and conformed to Judaic law, at least publicly. Herod's Edomite ancestors had been forced to convert to Judaism by John Hyrcanus. He was not a true Jew and could claim no hereditary right to the throne, despite his marriage to the Hasmonean princess, Mariamne.

Herod was a great builder and taxed the people heavily to support his many projects. To protect his domain, he built fortresses at Masada, Herodium, and Machaerus. He established Caesarea, a lovely port city on the Mediterranean coast, and Sebaste, in the hills of Samaria. At Jericho, Herod built a winter villa, complete with a large swimming pool. As already noted, in Jerusalem he commissioned a palace, a theater, towers, and Antonia Fortress. His magnificent restoration of the Jerusalem temple was his crowning work. Herod enlarged the temple mount by adding retaining walls and a platform supported by subterranean arches and surrounded by colonnaded porches. In the center of this great courtyard was erected the sanctuary where the priests ministered. Although Herod spared no expense in embellishing the great temple, it failed to win him the support of the Jews, for they knew this work stemmed from his vanity, not out of love for the God of Israel.

During the last ten years of his life, Herod the Great was plagued by domestic problems. His multiple wives had given him several heirs, each of whom wanted a part of the father's dominion. In a fit of jeal-

This unique construction occurs only in Herodian structures. It is called *opus reticulatum* (diamond-shaped stone) and *opus quadratum* (rectangular-shaped stone). *John McRay.*

ousy, Herod had Mariamne put to death in 29 B.C. and later—suspecting their two sons, Alexander and Aristobolus, of plotting against him—the king approved their assassination at Sebaste. On his deathbed, Herod discovered that his eldest son, Antipater, was also disloyal, and he, too, was put to death. Herod himself died five days later in Jericho (4 B.C.). Octavian, who had assumed the name Augustus, divided Herod's kingdom between his three surviving sons: Archelaus and Antipas (the son of Herod's marriage with Malthace, a Samaritan) and Philip (son of "Cleopatra of Jerusalem," of whom little is known). Archelaus (4 B.C.–A.D. 6) was appointed tetrarch of Judea, Idumea, and Samaria.

Large pool in the Herodium. *John McRay.*

Antipas (4 B.C.–A.D. 39) was granted the territories of Galilee and Perea. Except for the mention of "Herod" (the Great) and his "slaughter of innocents" around the time of Jesus' birth in Matthew 2, Antipas was the "Herod" figuring in the Gospels. Described as "that fox" (Luke 13:31–32), Herod Antipas was the ruler who ordered the execution of John the Baptist and before whom Jesus was brought shortly before his crucifixion.

Philip received the tetrarchate of the regions northeast of the Sea of Galilee. His subjects were mainly Greeks and Syrians, and he earned a reputation as an excellent ruler who loved peace.

Shortly before his death, Herod the Great learned of some strange visitors from the east who were inquiring, "Where is he who has been born king of the Jews?" (Matt. 2:2). That question, though it troubled Herod and some others in Jerusalem, brings us out of the transitional period between the Book of Malachi and the Gospel of Matthew—and into the New Testament era.

14

The Life of Christ
5/4 B.C. to A.D. 33

$\mathbf{B}$ut when the time had fully come, God sent forth his Son . . ." (Gal. 4:4). The birth of Christ is without doubt one of the most significant events of human history. Indeed, history is commonly divided into two eras—"before Christ" (B.C.) and "in the year of the Lord" (A.D., for the Latin *anno Domini*). Many comprehensive books have been written on the life and ministry of Christ on earth. Our purpose here is limited to presenting a brief chronological overview and then exploring the region of Galilee, the major geographical center of Christ's earthly ministry. The dates used here are those set forth so convincingly by Harold W. Hoehner's *Chronological Aspects of the Life of Christ*.

Chronology of Events

The Birth of Christ

Christ was born in Bethlehem (cf. Mic. 5:2) in the winter of 5/4 B.C. This date needs a bit of explanation. The dating system of the present Christian era was invented by a monk in Italy, Dionysius Exiguus (c. 496–540 A.D.) at the request of the pope. He placed Christ's birth at 753 A.U.C. (from the founding of Rome), failing to take into account that Christ was born during the rule of Herod the Great, who died in 750

The star in the altar of the Church of the Nativity marks the traditional spot of the birth of Christ. *Levant.*

A.U.C. The error was recognized in the ninth century, but the dating system has continued to the present day. Thus, Christ was actually born "before Christ" according to the errant dating system that we still follow.

After the visit by the Magi (Matt. 2:1–12), Joseph took his family to Egypt to escape Herod the Great's bloodletting in the Bethlehem region. Josephus reports that Herod died in March or April of 4 B.C. No longer fearing the maddened king, Joseph prepared to take his family back home. When it was discovered that Archelaus, who shared his father's ugly temperament, was ruling Judea, Joseph "was afraid to go there" (Matt. 2:22). Warned by God through a dream, Joseph departed instead for Galilee and settled his family in Nazareth, where Jesus lived and grew until he began his public ministry. Except for the Luke 2 account of Jesus in the temple at age twelve, and that he "increased in wisdom and stature, and in favor with God and man" (Luke 2:51), the Gospels shed no light on his early life.

The Inauguration of Christ's Ministry

It was probably in A.D. 28 or 29 that John the Baptist began preaching: "Repent, for the kingdom of heaven is at hand" (Matt. 3:2). As the messianic forerunner (Mal. 3:1; 4:5), John announced Christ's imminent coming and sought to prepare a people who would welcome him. Those who repented in preparation for the Messiah's work were baptized by John in the Jordan River. In the summer or autumn of A.D. 29, Jesus was introduced as "the Lamb of God" and baptized by John at

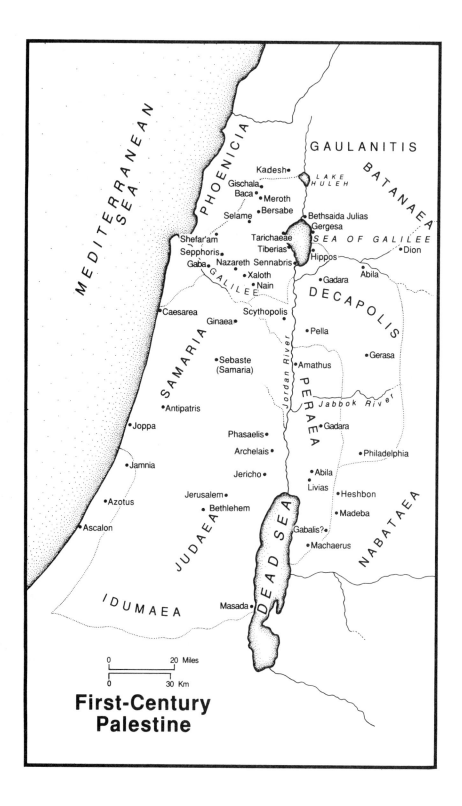

MEDITERRANEAN SEA

PHOENICIA

GAULANITIS

BATANAEA

Kadesh●

LAKE HULEH

Gischala●
Baca● ●Meroth
  ●Bersabe
Selame●

Bethsaida Julias
Gergesa
SEA OF GALILEE

Shefar'am●
Sepphoris●
Taricheaeae●
Tiberias●
Hippos●
●Dion

Gaba● Nazareth Sennabris●
GALILEE
●Xaloth
  ●Nain
Gadara●
Abila●

DECAPOLIS

Caesarea●
Ginaea●
Scythopolis●
●Pella
●Gerasa

Sebaste
(Samaria)●
Amathus●
Jabbok River
PERAEA

SAMARIA

Antipatris●
Gadara●

Joppa●
Phasaelis●
Archelais●
●Philadelphia

Jamnia●
Jericho●
●Abila
Livias●

Azotus●
Jerusalem●
●Bethlehem
●Heshbon
●Madeba

Ascalon●
JUDAEA
DEAD SEA
Gabalis?●
●Machaerus

NABATAEA

IDUMAEA
Masada●

0   20 Miles
0   30 Km

First-Century
Palestine

Bethany beyond the Jordan, about eight miles southeast of Jericho (John 1:28–29; Matt. 3:13–17). Following his forty-day temptation in the Wilderness of Judah (Matt. 4:1–11), Jesus and his first disciples journeyed three days to Cana of Galilee. There Jesus gave his disciples a foretaste of kingdom blessings by turning spring water into wedding wine (John 2:1–11; cf. Joel 3:18).

The Early Judean Ministry

After a visit to Capernaum (John 2:12), a city Jesus would later call home, Jesus journeyed to Jerusalem, where he attended the first Passover of his public ministry (April 7, A.D. 30). Finding the temple precincts mobbed by merchants and money changers, Jesus overthrew their tables and drove them out (John 2:13–22). This act had messianic significance, since Jesus was thereby claiming authority over his Father's house. Although the Jews did not challenge the legitimacy of the temple cleansing, they did question Jesus' authority to carry it out. "What sign have you to show us for doing this?" (John 2:18).

After the Passover, Jesus continued his ministry in Judea until early A.D. 31. He spent time there with his disciples who "baptized" (John 3:22; 4:1–2). John's ministry, having fulfilled its purpose, was on the decline (John 3:26–36).

The Baptist's arrest by Herod Antipas led Jesus to withdraw to the north. John had been arrested for speaking out publicly against the incestuous marriage of Herod Antipas with Herodias, the wife of his brother Philip (Matt. 14:3–4). According to Josephus, John was imprisoned and later put to death at the Transjordan site of Machaerus, which had originally been fortified as a desert retreat by Herod the Great. The arrest and imprisonment of John led Jesus to withdraw to the quieter districts of Galilee (Matt. 4:12–13).

The Samaritan Ministry

On his way to Galilee, probably in January or February of A.D. 31 (cf. John 4:35), Jesus passed through Samaria and met the woman at "Jacob's well" (John 4:1–42). The village of "Sychar" is identified with Askar, one-half mile north of the well, where tombs from the Roman period have been found. Sitting by the well between Mount Ebal and Mount Gerizim, Jesus offered the Samaritan woman "living water" and instructed her concerning the nature of true worship. His ministry to the Samaritans, regarded as outcasts by the Jews, was very significant theologically. Jesus was not just the Savior of the Jews, but of all mankind, including the "unclean" Samaritans. The Samaritans themselves acknowledged that "this is indeed the Savior of the world" (John 4:42).

Traditional site of Jacob's Well at Sychar. *Matson.*

The Galilean Ministry

After ministering in Samaria, Jesus journeyed north to Cana of Galilee, where he healed the nobleman's son (John 4:46–54) before returning to Nazareth, the city of his childhood. After Jesus preached in the synagogue from Isaiah 61:1–2, the people turned against him. Jesus departed for Capernaum, which he adopted as his hometown in Galilee (Matt. 4:13–16). From that time on, Jesus began to proclaim the same message John the Baptist had preached: "Repent, for the kingdom of heaven is at hand" (Matt. 4:17). Jesus journeyed with his disciples about Galilee, teaching in the synagogues (Luke 4:31–37), proclaiming the gospel of the kingdom (Matt. 5–7), authenticating his message by a ministry of healing (Matt. 8–10).

A turning point in the ministry of Jesus is recorded in Matthew 12, where Jesus is accused by the religious leaders of doing his miracles by

Satan's power rather than God's. "It is only by Beelzebul, the prince of demons, that this man casts out demons," the Pharisees declared (Matt. 24:12). Jesus refuted their accusation, charged them with blaspheming the Holy Spirit's work in his life, and denied them any further signs, "except the sign of the prophet Jonah"—his own resurrection (Matt. 12:39). Sensing his rejection by both the religious leaders and the multitude, Jesus began to speak "the secrets of the kingdom of heaven" to his disciples through parables (Matt. 13). This method of instruction was a means of revealing truth to the responsive and concealing it from those who were rejecting him (Matt. 13:10–17). Jesus continued to minister to the multitudes but gave priority time to training the Twelve, who would carry on his ministry after his death (Mark 6:6–13).

The Training of the Twelve in Districts Around Galilee

During the spring Passover season of A.D. 32, the year before his death, Jesus was ministering to his disciples at a deserted place in the vicinity of Bethsaida-Julias (Luke 9:10; Mark 6:31). Even in such a remote area, the multitude sought him out. The feeding of the hungry five thousand gave the disciples a lesson regarding the sufficiency they would have in their ministries as they depended upon him (John 6:1–14). The miracle was followed by Jesus' discourse at Capernaum, where he declared, "I am the bread of life" (John 6:22–59).

At this period of his ministry, Jesus frequently withdrew from the district of Galilee. Three reasons seem apparent. First, he wanted to spend time with his disciples (cf. Mark 3:14). Second, he wanted to avoid Herod Antipas, the ruler of Galilee and Perea who had put John the Baptist to death (Matt. 14:1–13). Third, he wanted to expand the disciples' concept of ministry to include the Gentiles (Matt. 15:21–28, Mark 7:24–30).

The disciples experienced some high points in the development of their faith during this period. Near Caesarea Philippi, Peter made his great confession: "You are the Christ, the Son of the living God" (Matt. 16:16). This faith was enhanced as Jesus was transfigured in the presence of Peter, James, and John, probably on 9,100-foot Mount Hermon (Matt. 17:1–8).

The Later Judean and Perean Ministry

In the fall of A.D. 32, Jesus traveled from Galilee to Jerusalem to attend the feast of Tabernacles. The major discussion among those attending the feast was the nature of this Galilean rabbi. Opinion was divided as to whether he was "a good man" or a deceiver (John 7:12). Jesus took the opportunity to clarify the issue by speaking to the people in the temple. Although the religious leaders sent officers to arrest Jesus and silence his ministry, none laid a hand on him. They simply reported, "No man ever spoke like this man" (John 7:46). It was after the feast—when the ceremonial candelabra had been darkened—that Jesus claimed to be "the light of the world" and then proved his claim by giving sight to the man born blind (John 9).

Several months later (December 18, A.D. 32), Jesus was back in Jerusalem for the feast of Dedication. After he claimed oneness with God the Father, Jesus was charged with blasphemy and barely escaped being stoned (John 10:22–39). After a brief ministry in Perea, he returned to Bethany near Jerusalem and raised Lazarus from the dead (John 11:1–44). This event and the publicity it generated prompted the religious leaders' decision that Jesus be put to death: "So from that day on they took counsel how to put him to death" (John 11:53). Jesus withdrew to the borders of Samaria and the village of Ephraim for a time with his disciples (John 11:54), before returning to Galilee and later beginning His final journey to Jerusalem.

The Final Journey from Galilee to Jerusalem

In the spring of A.D. 33, Jesus left Galilee for the last time and joined the pilgrims traveling to Jerusalem for Passover (Matt. 19:1–20:34). His route took him through Perea, and he taught the people as they journeyed along. Near Jericho, Jesus came upon two blind men and healed them (Matt. 20:29–34). Jesus next visited the home of a repentant tax gatherer, Zacchaeus (Luke 19:1–10). From the Herodian city of Jericho, Jesus ascended the hill country through Wadi Qilt to Jerusalem.

The Passion Week in Jerusalem

Jesus' royal entry into Jerusalem probably took place on a Monday, rather than on the traditional "Palm Sunday". It was March 30, A.D. 33. He came on the very day prophesied by Daniel (Dan. 9:24–26; cf. Luke 19:40–42) and in the manner announced by Zechariah on the foal of a donkey (Zech. 9:9). The multitude welcomed him crying out "Hosanna" ("Save!"), thus appealing for deliverance in the name of his messianic office ("Son of David"). Jesus knew there could be no crown without the cross. Later that week many in the fickle multitude, under the influence of their Jewish leaders, were to cry out for his crucifixion.

During his last week in Jerusalem, Jesus cleansed the temple a second time, engaged in controversy with the religious leaders, and delivered his Olivet discourse. On Thursday evening, Jesus met in the upper room with his disciples for the Passover supper. He was betrayed later that night by Judas, arrested in the Garden of Gethsemane, and

The Upper Room, used by Jesus and his disciples (traditional site). *Israel Tourist Bureau.*

examined by Annas, Caiaphas, the Sanhedrin, Pilate, Herod Antipas, and by Pilate again. Although Pilate found Jesus innocent (Luke 23:4, 14–15; John 19:4; Matt. 27:24), he yielded to the demands of the populace and turned Jesus over to the Roman soldiers for crucifixion. About 9:00 A.M. on Friday, April 3, A.D. 33, Jesus was nailed to a rough cross. After his death, Joseph of Arimathea and Nicodemus secured the body of Jesus and arranged for its burial. But Jesus broke the bonds of death and, on Sunday morning, visitors at the tomb found it empty. Instead, they met an angel who announced, "He is not here, for he has risen, just as he said!"

That evening, Jesus appeared to ten disciples in the upper room (John 20:19–25) and a week later to the eleven (John 20:24–29). During his forty-day post-resurrection ministry, Jesus appeared to many of his disciples (1 Cor. 15:5–7) and spent time teaching them concerning the kingdom of God (Acts 1:3). Then, from the Mount of Olives, he ascended into heaven.

The District of Galilee

Since Galilee served as the locale for most of Jesus' ministry, a survey of this region is necessary for a thorough background of Christ's life and ministry.

The mountains of Syria in the distance form a backdrop for this fertile plain along the shores of the Sea of Galilee.

The name *Galilee* means "circle" or "district," the fuller expression of which is "district of the Gentiles" (Isa. 9:1; Matt. 4:15). The term was applied to the northern district of Palestine, which was surrounded on three sides by foreign (Gentile) nations.

The saddle-shaped Horns of Hittin guard this valley in lower Galilee. *Israel Tourist Bureau.*

"Galilee" is geographically bounded on the north by the Litani River, on the west by the Mediterranean Sea, on the east by the Sea of Galilee and Upper Jordan (Huleh) Valley, and on the south by the Valley of Jezreel. There is some debate as to whether, under Roman administration, the political district included any part of the Valley of Jezreel, since it has been regarded as neutral ground or possibly royal domain. Although it may have been administered by Herod Antipas in the time of Jesus, the Jezreel is not in geographical continuity with the region of Galilee and has been considered elsewhere (see chapter 7).

Regions of Galilee

According to Josephus, Galilee is divided naturally into two regions: upper and lower. The border between the two regions is marked by a steep slope that rises 1,500 to 2,000 feet. This fault, known as Esh-Shaghur, cuts across the country between Acco/Ptolemais/Acre on the Mediterranean Sea and the Northern end of the Sea of Galilee. Galilee is a mountainous plateau between the fault of Esh-Shaghur and the Litani River. The elevations in the northern region, so isolated by mountains and narrow valleys, average about three thousand feet above sea level. Upper Galilee's highest peak (Jebel Jermuk) rises to 3,962 feet along the eastern slopes of the fault of Esh-Shaghur. The terrain slopes northward to between 1,500 and 1,800 feet before dropping into the Litani River gorge. The region is composed primarily of hard ridges of Cenomanian limestone and plateaus of softer Senonian chalk. This windswept mountainous area was densely forested in antiquity. Though in Roman times there were some small villages and fortresses, upper Galilee was sparsely populated and enters little into biblical history. Its rugged terrain and isolation made it a "region of escape" for Israelites resisting political domination by foreign powers.

Lower Galilee is less uniformly mountainous than the region to the north. The average elevation is around two thousand feet above sea level. The mountains are bisected by a series of small east-west valleys, resulting from faulting and cross-folding. This gives the region the structure and general form of a staircase as it descends from upper to lower Galilee. From south to north, the valleys include the Tur'an Basin (just north of the Nazareth Ridge), the Beth Netufa Valley, the Halazun Basin, and the Beth Ha-Keram Valley (bordered on the north by the fault of Esh-Shaghur). These basins and valleys provided a number of easy routes across lower Galilee to the Sea of Galilee, where they tend to converge on the northwest shore, the Plain of Gennesaret. Because of inadequate drainage and the steepness of the valleys, travelers often followed the mountain ridges rather than the valleys, especially during the wet winter months.

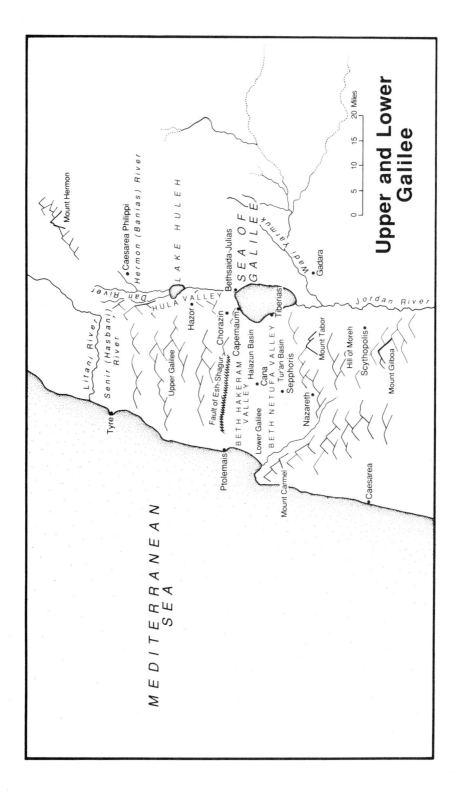

Upper and Lower Galilee

MEDITERRANEAN SEA

Mount Hermon

Caesarea Philippi

Hermon (Banias) River

LAKE HULEH

Bethsaida-Julias

SEA OF GALILEE

Litani River

Senir (Hasbani) River

Dan River

HULA VALLEY

Hazor

Chorazin

Capernaum

Tiberias

Jordan River

Wadiyarmuk

Gadara

Upper Galilee

Fault of Esh-Shagur

BETH HAKERAM VALLEY

Cana

Halazun Basin

Turan Basin

BETH NETUFA VALLEY

Sepphoris

Mount Tabor

Hill of Moreh

Scythopolis

Mount Gilboa

Lower Galilee

Nazareth

Tyre

Ptolemais

Mount Carmel

Caesarea

20 Miles

0 5 10 15 20

Galilee was allotted to the tribes of Asher, Zebulun, Naphtali, and Issachar (Josh. 19:10–39). Asher occupied western Galilee in the vicinity of the coastal plain, and Zebulun received central Galilee. Northeastern Galilee fell to Naphtali, and Issachar received the eastern part of the Jezreel and the regions directly north.

Climate of Galilee

Since precipitation in Palestine tends to increase as one goes north, it is not surprising that Galilee has a relative abundance of rainfall. In fact, because of its elevation and proximity to the sea, Galilee has the coldest and wettest winter of any region in Palestine. Lower Galilee receives between twenty and thirty inches of rain annually; upper Galilee may receive as much as forty inches.

Galilee is also known for its copious dew (cf. Ps. 133:3), which forms when the moisture-laden Mediterranean air settles on the cool Galilean hills and valleys. The western portion of lower Galilee receives at least two hundred dew nights annually, a climatic feature of considerable benefit to the agricultural endeavors of the Galileans during the rainless summer months.

Temperatures in Galilee vary considerably, depending on elevation and distance from the sea. During the summer months, the temperature range is 65–85° F. Winter temperatures average between 40 and 50° F., with frequent freezes occurring.

Galilee is affected considerably by the Mediterranean sea breezes. Afternoon winds are known to sweep through the valleys of lower Galilee, funneling down to the Sea of Galilee and causing violent gales (cf. Matt. 8:24–25). In the hills of Galilee, winter storm winds with a velocity of seventy-five miles per hour have been measured.

Economy of Galilee

The fertility of Galilee was highly praised by Josephus, who stated that no part of the land was left uncultivated. The abundant rains, gentle terrain, wide valleys, and deep, rich soil contributed significantly to the agricultural prosperity of the Galileans. Other natural resources included its fine forests and plentiful fish from the Sea of Galilee.

The fishing industry was a primary source of income near the Sea of Galilee and fishermen from Capernaum were among the first followers of Jesus (Matt. 4:18–22; Mark 1:16–20). Galilee's salted or pickled fish was sold all over Palestine. The Galileans also profited from the linen that they manufactured from flax grown in the region.

Galilee was also well known in ancient times as a wheat-producing region. Olive oil, too, was produced in abundance. Olive groves were planted on the lower slopes of the hills, while grain grew mainly in the fields of the fertile basins. (According to the Midrash, it was easier to bring up a legion of olives in Galilee than one infant in Judea.) The Galileans cultivated a variety of vegetables, and Josephus reported that Galilee was Palestine's largest wine-producing region.

One of its most important commercial assets was Galilee's location on the most important trade route of the ancient Near East. The Via Maris descended from Damascus, crossed the Jordan, and brushed the Sea of Galilee as it cut through lower Galilee toward Mount Carmel and the coastal plain. The early Galileans profited from the trade and the customs they levied on the caravans that passed through their region. (Matthew Levi was a customs collector for Herod Antipas in Capernaum, an important toll station on the Via Maris, when he was called to become Christ's disciple [Mark 2:14]).

Physical Features of Galilee

Several topographic features of Galilee are worthy of special note. The Jordan River has its origin near the foot of 9,100-foot Mount Hermon in the upper reaches of northern Galilee in the form of three streams that eventually unite to form the Jordan River. From west to east, they are the Senir (Hasbani), the Dan, and the Hermon (Banias). In ancient times, these rivers discharged independently into a swampy region known as Lake Huleh. They became one river only after their exit from the swamp, about ten miles north of the Sea of Galilee. More recently, the swamp has been drained and the three streams unite into one river, the Jordan, not more than a few miles from their place of origin.

The Huleh Valley is part of the Great Rift Valley that cleaves the whole of Palestine from the mountains of Lebanon to the Gulf of Eilat (Aqaba). The valley, which lies north of the Sea of Galilee, extends about fifteen miles from the foot of Mount Hermon to a basalt dam ("Bridge of Jacob's Daughters"), which constricts the Jordan just east of Hazor. Situated about three hundred feet below sea level, the valley became a vast swamp sometime in antiquity, when a basalt flow from the Golan Heights dammed the flow of the Jordan. The water rose quickly and began to overflow, allowing erosion to cut through the basalt. Today, most of Lake Huleh has been drained, except for a small nature preserve.

The Sea of Galilee is a freshwater body located 685 feet below sea level. It is twelve miles long, more than seven miles across at its widest point, and covers an area of about seventy square miles, with a maximum depth of about two hundred feet. In the Old Testament, the sea was known as Chinnereth meaning "harp," apparently due to its shape

(Num. 34:11; Josh. 13:27). It is referred to in the New Testament as the Lake of Gennesaret (Luke 5:1) or Tiberias (John 6:1, 21:1), after prominent cities on its western shore. It is known today as either Lake Kinneret or the Sea of Galilee. On its shores were located such biblical cities as Capernaum, Bethsaida, Magdala, and Tiberias.

Cities of Galilee

Jesus traveled and ministered in many cities and villages in Galilee. A brief survey of some of the major sites will shed further light on the life of Jesus.

Capernaum. Located on the northwest shore of the Sea of Galilee, Capernaum ("Village of Nahum") became the center for Christ's ministry in Galilee after his rejection at Nazareth (Matt. 4:12–14). Jesus performed some of his greatest miracles there (Mark 2:1–12; Luke 4:23, John 4: 46–54) and taught in its synagogue (Mark 1:21–22). Capernaum is noted for a well-preserved synagogue that dates from the late second or early third century A.D. Recent excavations have uncovered the floor of an earlier synagogue under the one presently standing. This may have been the synagogue in which Jesus preached. A Byzantine church of octagonal shape has also been excavated. It stands over a first-century house, believed to be the home of Peter (Matt. 8:14).

Chorazin. In the hills of Galilee, just three miles north of Caper-

Palm tree carved into a section of the synagogue in Capernaum. *John McRay.*

Ruins of the synagogue prayer room in Chorazin. *John McRay.*

naum, is Chorazin. Jesus performed many miracles there, but the people did not respond with repentance and were rebuked for their unbelief (Matt. 11:20–21). Chorazin has a well-preserved synagogue made of the black basalt that is natural to the region. Among the finds in the synagogue was a basalt seat, the Throne of Moses, which was used during the reading of the Torah.

Bethsaida. The home of Philip, Andrew, and Peter (John 1:44; 12:21), was Bethsaida, a small fishing village on the northeast shore of the Sea of Galilee. In New Testament times, it was linked closely with Julias (a site located abut two miles from the shore), which Philip the Tetrarch elevated to the status of *polis* ("city") and named after the daughter of Augustus. A Roman road linked the double site of Bethsaida (el-'Araj) and Julias. Jesus healed a blind man in this vicinity (Mark 8:22) and later reproached the city for its unbelief (Matt. 11:21). It was at a deserted site southeast of Bethsaida-Julias that Jesus fed the five thousand. (Luke 9:10–17)

Tiberias. Located on the western shore of the Sea of Galilee and named in honor of the emperor, Tiberias was established by Herod Antipas between 18 and 22 A.D. to serve as the capital of Galilee and Perea. The site was selected partly because of its hot sulphur springs, which served as a health spa for the Roman officials assigned to the city. Josephus relates that the city was built on an old Jewish cemetery, rendering the place unclean according to Jewish law. Herod Antipas

The city of Tiberias. *Israel Tourist Bureau.*

eventually managed to populate the city with the poor and landless, freed slaves, and retired soldiers. (There is no record in the Gospels of Jesus having visited this city.)

Nazareth. Important as the early home of Jesus, Nazareth is located in the hills that form the northern boundary of the Valley of Jezreel. Joseph and Mary settled there when they returned from Egypt after the death of Herod the Great (Matt. 2:19–23). Here Jesus lived and grew to adulthood. That this city was not highly esteemed by Jews in the Roman period is reflected in the words of Nathanael: "Can anything good come out of Nazareth?" (John 1:46). Two factors probably

One of the main streets in Nazareth. *Guy P. Duffield.*

contributed to the unfavorable reputation of the city. First, it was apparently not "worthy" to be mentioned even once in the Old Testament.) Second, it was located just four miles south of Sepphoris, the Roman capital of Galilee until Herod Antipas built Tiberias. The people of Nazareth were servants and workers for the Roman oppressors who ruled Galilee from their neighboring city. For this reason, Nazarenes were lightly esteemed by other Jews in the Galilean region.

Cana of Galilee. The home of Nathanael (John 21:2), Cana was where Jesus performed his first miracle (John 2:1–11) and later healed the nobleman's son (John 4:46–54). Cana has been traditionally identified with the site of Kefr Kenna, located about four miles northeast of Nazareth. There, in a Greek Orthodox church, tourists are shown two stone basins purported to be among the six waterpots used in the miracle. However, the more likely site for Cana is Khirbet Kana, located nine miles north of Nazareth in the Beth Netufa Valley and still known to the natives of the region as "Cana of Galilee." The site fits better with the description given by Josephus, who used Cana as his headquarters when preparing Galilee for the war against the Romans. Although Khirbet Kana has not been excavated, a survey has reported the presence of pottery that indicates Roman occupation during the time of Christ.

The village of Caesarea Philippi. *Matson.*

Caesarea Philippi. Located on the southern slopes of Mount Hermon at the headwaters of the Hermon (Banias) River (one of the main sources of the Jordan) is Caesarea Philippi, near which Peter made his great confession to Jesus, "You are the Christ, the Son of the living God" (Matt. 16:16). The city is first cited in history as Panion (Panias), where Antiochus III achieved victory over the Ptolemies (198 B.C.). Herod the Great's son Philip made it the capital of his tetrarchy and renamed it Caesarea in honor of either Augustus or Tiberius. To distinguish it from Caesarea on the Mediterranean, it was called Caesarea Philippi.

Hazor. Although it did not figure during the period of Jesus, we cannot leave our discussion of Galilee without mention of the Old Testament city of Hazor, located ten miles north of the Sea of Galilee and four miles west of the Jordan. Hazor, with an upper city of twenty-five acres and a lower city of nearly two hundred acres, was the largest city ever built in Palestine during the early biblical period. The strategic importance of the city was due to its location just west of the main ford of the Jordan ("Bridge of Jacob's Daughters") north of the Sea of Galilee. Thus Hazor was able to control the Via Maris as it angled through Galilee. Hazor, the political and military hub of Palestine in the second millennium B.C., entered into biblical history at the time of the conquest of Canaan. Joshua fought against Jabin, ruler of Hazor, and his coalition of kings and was victorious at the waters of Merom (Josh. 11:1–11). The city was later fortified by Solomon to protect the northern entrance into Palestine (1 Kings 9:15). As did the other Solomonic fortress cities of Megiddo and Gezer, Hazor had an intricate water system and a multiple gate. The last biblical reference to Hazor records its conquest by Tiglath-pileser III in 732 B.C. (2 Kings 15:29).

15

The Early Apostolic Period
A.D. 33 to 70

The biblical Apostolic Period—much of which was chronicled so carefully by Luke, the physician and friend of Paul, in the Book of Acts—takes us from the ascension of Christ to the destruction of Jerusalem by the Romans in A.D. 70. Jesus commissioned the disciples to be his witnesses "in Jerusalem and in all Judea and Samaria and to the end of the earth" (Acts 1:8). Yet, he instructed them not to leave Jerusalem until they received "the promise of the Father"—the gift of the Holy Spirit—to empower them for ministry (Acts 1:4; cf. Luke 2:33; Luke 24:49). Ten days after Christ's ascension, the promise was fulfilled and the Holy Spirit descended upon the believers gathered in prayer (Acts 2:1–4). Peter explained the phenomenon as a precursor of the messianic age (cf. Joel 2:28–32) and called on those in Jerusalem to repent of their rejection of Jesus. His sermon on the day of Pentecost (Acts 2:14–41) resulted in three thousand baptisms. Although the preliminary period of church expansion was off to a good start, there was much hardship ahead for those who would bring the gospel to the world.

Preliminary Expansion of the Church (Acts 1–8)

The first target area for apostolic witness was Jerusalem. Luke records three sermons that Peter preached there—to the Jerusalem visitors (Acts 2:14–40), to those who observed the miraculous healing of the lame man in the temple area (Acts 3:12–26), and to the Jewish religious leaders (Acts 4:8–12). Acts 4:33 summarizes the thrust of this early ministry: "And with great power the apostles gave their testimony to the resurrection of the Lord Jesus. . . ."

Early efforts of Peter and John and other members of the Twelve met with opposition from many of the Hebrew priests and elders and the Roman-appointed civil rulers in Jerusalem. This did little to diminish the apostles' evangelistic zeal, especially after the appointment of a special body of seven deacons, including Stephen and Philip (the Evangelist). We learn that "the word of God increased; and the number of the disciples multiplied greatly . . . (Acts 6:7). Stephen's "wonders and signs" and preaching further enraged the religious establishment, and he was brought before the council and accused of blasphemy against the God of Moses. After his impassioned disputation, Stephen was stoned to death by order of the officials, who saw his message as a threat to their power (Acts 7).

Stephen's martyrdom was the first incident in a series of persecutions against the new Christians in Jerusalem, and many of them fled and "scattered throughout the region of Judea and Samaria, except the apostles" (Acts 8:1). There then ensued an expanded witness, as "those who were scattered went about preaching the word" (Acts 8:4). One of these evangelists was Philip, who was the key figure in bringing the gospel to Samaria (Acts 8:5–24) and later to the cities of the Judean coastal plain, from Azotus (Old Testament "Ashdod") to Caesarea (Acts 8:40).

Expansion of the Church (Acts 9–27)

Peter and Philip were the initiators of the preliminary expansion of the church throughout Jerusalem, Judea, and Samaria, but God soon raised up a new powerful witness through Saul of Tarsus, later known as the apostle Paul, who would proclaim the message of the resurrected Christ throughout the entire Mediterranean region.

The Preparation of Paul (Acts 9–12)

After Stephen's martyrdom, Saul of Tarsus became fiercely involved in the persecution of the new church in Jerusalem. Not content with this local reign of terror, he obtained authority from the Sanhedrin to travel to Damascus to arrest the Christians there and bring them back to Jerusalem for prosecution.

Damascus, the oldest continuously occupied city in the ancient Near East, is located at the foot of the Anti-Lebanon Mountains, about sixty miles northeast of the Sea of Galilee. The city was an oasis on a barren stretch of the Via Maris as it passed from eastern Syria to Galilee. Damascus was a very strategic site. Geographer Denis Baly has acknowledged, "He who would command the Levant must always control Damascus, which is the hub of the entire area."

Paul (Saul) was on his way to Damascus when he was blinded by his confrontation with the risen Lord. Three days later—through the ministering of Ananias—Paul was formally converted and took up his new role as missionary. After preaching in Damascus, Paul spent time in Arabia and then went back to Damascus before returning once again to Jerusalem for the first time since his conversion (Gal. 1:17–18). There he reported to the apostles how he had seen Jesus on the road to Damascus and demonstrated the genuineness of his conversion by speaking out boldly in the name of the Lord throughout Jerusalem (Acts 9:27–28). A death plot against his life forced Paul to retire to Tarsus, his hometown in Cilicia, where he remained until his call to teach the church at Antioch (Acts 11:25–26).

Antioch, founded in 300 B.C. as the capital of Seleucid Syria, was the most prominent of all Syrian cities during the Roman period. The third largest city in the Roman Empire (after Rome and Alexandria), Antioch served as capital of the Roman province of Syria. Located on the Orontes River about fifteen miles from the Mediterranean Sea,

St. Paul's window in the wall of Damascus, Syria. *Guy P. Duffield.*

Nestled between Mount Silius and the Orontes River is the city of Antioch. *Matson.*

Antioch was a center of trade and commerce, with Seleucia serving as its seaport (Acts 13:4). The church at Antioch had a strong heart for missions and soon became the center for evangelizing the Roman world. Paul's three missionary journeys began at Antioch, a city where "the disciples were for the first time called Christians" (Acts 11:26).

Paul's First Missionary Journey (Acts 13–15)

In the spring of A.D. 48, Paul, Barnabas, and John Mark were sent out by the church in Antioch on the first of a series of missionary expeditions. The trio set sail from Seleucia for Cyprus, the island homeland of Barnabas, where they spent several months traveling about and preaching the word of God in the synagogues.

Cyprus, measuring 60 by 140 miles, is the third largest island in the Mediterranean, exceeded in size only by Sicily and Sardinia. The island has two mountain ranges—one extending along the northern coast (2,000 to 3,000 feet in elevation) and another extending along the southern coast (4,500 to 6,400 feet). The broad and fertile plain between these two ranges serves as the granary of the island. Forests were once one of the main natural resources of Cyprus, and the timber was used mainly for shipbuilding. Copper and silver smelting were also important industries. (The word *copper* is derived from "Cyprus.") The Cypriots enjoy a mild Mediterranean climate, and it is reported that the sun shines for at least a part of every day.

Salamis, where the missionary team landed, was the main port and commercial center of the island. Roman influence had brought to the city a splendid forum (place of public assembly), gymnasium, public baths, a large theater, and a temple dedicated to Zeus. Salamis was noted for having the largest *agora* (marketplace) in the Roman colonial empire.

After ministering in Salamis, the missionary team journeyed from the east to the west end of the island and preached in the Jewish synagogues along the way. They finally reached Paphos, the western port and seat of the Roman government at the time. Paphos was the worship center for Aphrodite (Venus), the Greek goddess of love, beauty, and fertility. According to legend, the goddess was born from the foam of the sea, floated in a shell on the waves, and landed on Cyprus near Paphos. Thousands of pilgrims came annually to visit her temple at that ancient city. It was there at Paphos that the Roman proconsul, Sergius Paulus, "believed" (Acts 13:6–12).

Leaving Paphos, Paul and his companions sailed to Asia Minor (modern Turkey). This massive land area is equal to the combined territories of northeastern United States from New England through West Virginia. Asia Minor is a three-to-five-thousand foot plateau

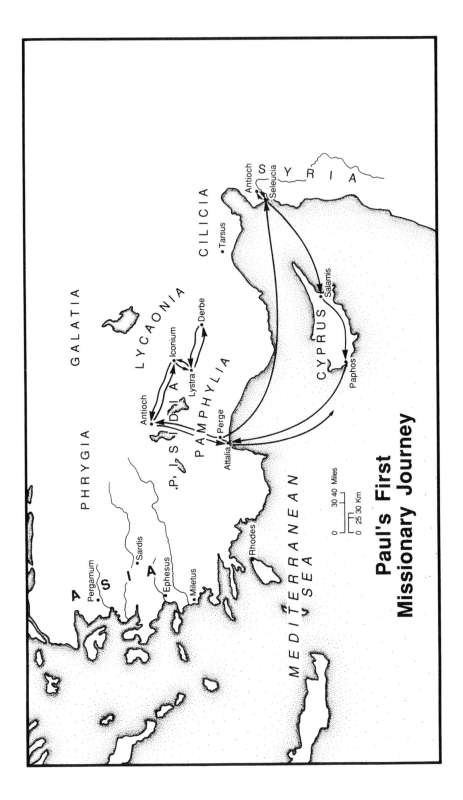

Paul's First
Missionary Journey

SYRIA • Antioch • Seleucia

CILICIA • Tarsus

GALATIA

LYCAONIA • Derbe • Iconium • Lystra

• Antioch

D I **A**

P I **S**

PAMPHYLIA • Perge • Attalia

PHRYGIA

A S I A

• Pergamum • Sardis • Ephesus • Miletus

Rhodes

CYPRUS • Salamis • Paphos

MEDITERRANEAN SEA

0   30 40 Miles

0 25 30 Km

fringed on all sides by higher mountain ranges. Since the area has few natural resources and is somewhat arid, it was used mainly for grazing and grain. The surrounding mountains, although a hindrance to communication and transportation, are a great source of wealth. In addition to timber on their slopes, the mountains house deposits of gold, silver, copper, lead, iron, zinc, and marble. The coastal areas have plenty of rainfall and produce the traditional Mediterranean crops of grapes and olives. The main trade route that spanned Asia Minor in Paul's day went from Ephesus on the coast to Antioch of Pisidia and then split. The northern route continued through Cappadocia to the Euphrates. The southern route continued through Cilicia to Tarsus and then to Syrian Antioch.

Having landed on Asia Minor, Paul and his associates journeyed eight miles inland to Perga, where John Mark left the missionary party and returned to Jerusalem (Acts 13:13). From Perga, Paul and Barnabas continued north about a hundred miles, to "Antioch of Pisidia" in the central plateau area of Asia Minor (Acts 13:14). There they began evangelizing the southern region of the province of Galatia.

Antioch of Pisidia was actually "near" rather than "in" Pisidia. It became the chief administrative and military center for southern Galatia after Emperor Augustus had made it a Roman colony. This city was an important commercial center on the great trade route linking coastal Ephesus with Syria and the cities of Mesopotamia. It was also a place of pagan worship and contained a great temple dedicated to Men Ascaenus, the chief deity of the city. Antioch of Pisidia was a highly strategic place from which to propogate the gospel. Paul and Barnabas preached there and enjoyed a generally positive response. As a result of their witness, "the word of the Lord spread throughout all the whole region" (Acts 13:49).

After being driven from Antioch of Pisidia by the mob action incited by certain Jews, Paul and Barnabas traveled eighty miles in a southeasterly direction to Iconium (Acts 13:51). This settlement was located in the central plateau region at the foot of the Taurus Mountains, which tower five to six thousand feet in this region. Iconium had a good water supply and was well situated for defense. As a garden spot in an arid region, Iconium has been called "the Damascus of Asia." Although a great multitude believed the gospel at Iconium, the city was divided in opinion about the message preached by the evangelists. When a threat was made on their lives, Paul and Barnabas fled to Lystra.

Lystra, located about eighteen miles southwest of Iconium, was not positively identified until the discovery of an inscription at the site in 1885. The town—now a litter of fallen ruins—lay in a small valley watered by a stream flowing to the east. Lystra had once been a mili-

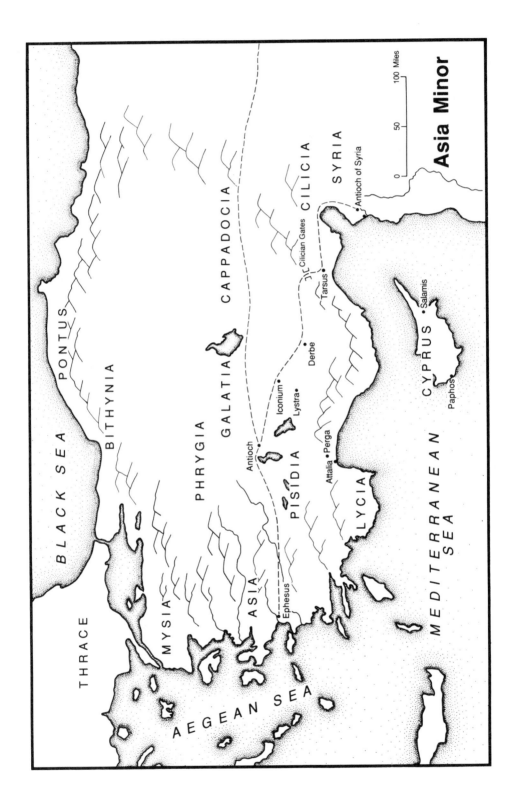

A corner of the Roman forum, dating back to the time of Barnabas and Paul. *Levant.*

tary outpost of Rome but declined in population and importance after the area was subdued. It was off the main roads, and its inhabitants spoke their native Lycaonian language rather than the Greek used by most citizens of the Roman Empire in Paul's day (Acts 14:11). To Paul and Barnabas, Lystra seemed to be a good place to wait out the storm of opposition stirred up in Iconium. But Jews from Iconium and Antioch of Pisidia came to Lystra and turned its citizens against the missionaries. Paul was stoned, dragged out of the city, and left for dead.

The day following Paul's stoning at Lystra, the missionary team journeyed to another rather secluded city, Derbe, located about seventy miles southeast of Lystra. Only recently has it been identified with certainty, and we have little information about the site. Paul preached in Derbe and "made many disciples" (Acts 14:21), one of whom (Gaius) later accompanied Paul on his later journey through Greece (Acts 20:4).

Rather than taking the most direct return route to Antioch of Syria, Paul and Barnabas retraced their steps through Lystra, Iconium, and Antioch of Pisidia, encouraging the disciples and appointing elders (Acts 14:21–23). They also returned to Perga and preached the gospel there before proceeding to coastal Attalia, which lay southwest of Perga and was an important harbor and commercial center in Paul's day. From there, Paul and Barnabas sailed for Syrian Antioch, arriving in the autumn of A.D. 49. They had been gone for a year and a half and had traveled an estimated 1,250 miles.

Paul's Second Missionary Journey (Acts 15:41–18:22)

Paul was busily engaged in ministry following his return from Asia Minor. He wrote the Epistle of Galatians (A.D. 49) to the recently established churches to emphasize the faith principle over and against legalistic Judaism. Later that winter, he participated in the Jerusalem Council (Acts 15) regarding the issue of whether a Gentile had to become a Jew to be a Christian. After a time, Paul suggested that he and Barnabas visit once again the churches they had so recently planted in Asia Minor. A disagreement rose between them as to whether to take John Mark, who had prematurely left the previous expedition. In the end, Barnabas took Mark and sailed for Cyprus, while Paul selected Silas to accompany him on his next journey. They set out traveling north from Antioch in the spring of A.D. 50.

Passing through his hometown, Tarsus, Paul ascended the Taurus Mountains via the Cilician Gates, the main pass through the mountains to the Asian plateau. Paul came once again to Derbe and then Lystra, where he was joined by Timothy, a convert from his earlier journey. Passing through Phrygia and Galatia, they came finally to

Paul's Second Missionary Journey

Troas, (Alexandria Troas). This city had an excellent harbor and received a large number of ships carrying cargo across the Aegean Sea between Asia Minor and Macedonia. Where was Paul to go from Troas? The answer came through a dream in which he was summoned to Greece: "Come over to Macedonia and help us" (Acts 16:9).

Joined by the narrator, Luke (note the "we" in Acts 16:11), Paul and his companions sailed across the Aegean and arrived in Macedonia, the northern province of Greece (then a Roman colony). Including Achaia to the south, the territory of Greece covered about fifty thousand square miles, the approximate land size of Wisconsin. The topography of Greece is dominated by rugged mountains, covering seventy-five percent of the land area. This mountainous terrain made travel difficult and discouraged the unification of the Greek people in ancient times. Independent city-states developed instead. Unable to negotiate snow-buried mountain passes in winter, the early Greeks

ILLYRICUM

THRACE

MOESIA

Apollonia •
Ignatian Way

Philippi
Amphipolis   • Neapolis
Thessalonica
Berea •   Apollonia
                                            SAMOTHRACE

MACEDONIA
△
Mount Olympus

AEGEAN SEA

Nicopolis

Athens
Corinth •
Cenchreae

ACHAIA

MEDITERRANEAN SEA

0   50   100 Miles

CRETE

Greece

Phoenix   Fair Havens

took to the sea and spread their culture throughout the Mediterranean world. The sea has been very important in the life and cultural development of Greece, and there are many splendid seaports along its 2,600-mile coastline.

Greece partakes generously of the pleasant Mediterranean climate, which includes plenty of sunshine. The annual rainfall is heaviest in the west (about forty inches), decreasing to about twenty inches in the east along the Aegean coast. Since the soil is poor, the Greek people depended to a large degree on trade and shipping to maintain their economy. The main highway through Greece was the Via Egnatia, which went from Byzantium, through northern Macedonia, and on to

Apollonia. Ships linked the route with the Appian Way in "the heel of the boot" in southern Italy.

Disembarking at Neapolis, the colorful port for Philippi, Paul took to the road and walked about eight miles along the Via Egnatia to Philippi, described by Luke as "the leading city of the district of Macedonia" (Acts 16:12). Philip of Macedon, father of Alexander the Great, had founded the city to control the nearby gold deposits. Philippi was of strategic importance because of its command of the plain through which passed the Egnatian Way. Augustus honored the city in 42 B.C. by making it a foreign colony. Since there was a famous school of medicine there, Philippi is thought by some to be the original home of Luke the Physician, or perhaps where he studied medicine. Luke's description of the city seems to express a fondness for the place, and he appears to have remained at Philippi after Paul's departure (note the "they" in Acts 17:1).

Paul met on the Sabbath with a small group of Jews who gathered for prayer on the banks of a rapid stream (the Gangites) (Acts 16:13). There, Lydia—a Jewish proselyte and merchant from Thyatira—believed and was baptized, and a church was established at Philippi in her home. Acts 16:16–34 records Paul's healing of "a slave girl who had a spirit of divination" and the subsequent brief imprisonment of Paul and Silas. When their songs and prayers were followed by a "great earthquake" that opened the cell doors and unbound the prisoners' fetters, so impressed was the jailor that he and his family became converts to the new faith.

Leaving Philippi, Paul and his associates traveled along the Via Egnatia about a hundred miles to Thessalonica, located at the head of the Thermaic Gulf west of the Chalcidice, the three "fingers" reaching into the Aegean. In 315 B.C., Cassander, one of Alexander's generals, had reconstructed Therma and named it Thessalonica after his wife, daughter of Philip of Macedon. The city had an excellent harbor and was very important commercially. It was the capital of the province and the largest and most prosperous of the Macedonian cities of Paul's day. Because of its strategic importance, Thessalonica has been called the key of the whole of Macedonia.

Paul's ministry in Thessalonica undoubtedly extended beyond the three weeks (Sabbaths) mentioned in Acts 17:2. Indeed, Paul seems to have taken a job there (1 Thess. 2:9; 2 Thess. 3:8) and received more than one gift from the Philippians while ministering at Thessalonica. Although a church was established at Thessalonica, some of the city's Jews, jealous of the positive response to Paul's preaching, incited mob action against the missionary team. To avoid further trouble, the brethren sent Paul and Silas by night to Berea (Acts 17:10).

Berea was located about forty miles west of Thessalonica, a few

The old and the new blend in this view of the Thessalonican water front. *Greek Tourist Bureau.*

miles south of the Via Egnatia. It was a pleasant little city of no great political or historical importance, but its significance in Luke's narrative lies in its secluded nature. Cicero describes how an unpopular Roman governor once used Berea as a place of retreat when besieged with complaints, and this isolated location briefly protected Paul and Silas, too. There they found a responsive group of fair-minded Jews, who carefully examined the Scriptures as Paul preached the gospel. But when the opposing Jews of Thessalonica learned of Paul's ministry in Berea, they came and stirred up the crowds against him. Leaving Silas and Timothy to finish the evangelism in Berea, Paul was escorted to the sea, where he took a ship to Athens, about two hundred miles to the south.

Athens is five miles inland from the Aegean seaport, Piraeus. Its original site was selected because of its good water supply and mass of limestone that rises 230 feet above the surrounding area. This "Acropolis" was a natural fortress against attack and also served as a lofty worship center in times of peace. Crowning its heights was the Parthenon, completed in 438 B.C. and dedicated to Athena, goddess of wisdom. This magnificent temple (228 feet long, 100 feet wide, and 60 feet high) housed a forty-foot gold and ivory statue of "the Virgin" (Greek, *parthenon*). In classical Greece, the city was well known for its exports of olive oil and wine. More importantly, Athens was a vibrant

Ruins of the Parthenon, Athens. *Greek Tourist Bureau.*

cultural and intellectual community and the birthplace of democracy—"rule by the people."

Paul seems not to have been greatly impressed by either Athenian intellectualism or the city's architecture, for he was grieved by the idolatry he saw (Acts 17:16). While waiting to be rejoined by Timothy and Silas, he preached Jesus and the resurrection in the Jewish synagogue and in the public market. Stirring interest, he was invited to speak before the council of Aeropagus, which met on Mars Hill (just below the entrance to the Acropolis). Although a few people believed Paul's message, including "Dionysius the Areopagite" (Acts 17:34), it does not appear that a church was established at Athens. Paul then left Athens and journeyed sixty miles west to Corinth.

Corinth is regarded as one of the most vitally located cities of the ancient world, for it was situated on the isthmus that links the Peloponnesus peninsula to the mainland of Greece. The city could control any trade or travel passing through the narrow isthmus. With its 1,886-foot Acrocorinth, the city could be easily defended in case of enemy attack. Lying between two seas, Corinth became an important

View of Mars Hill, Athens. *John McRay.*

trade center. The city controlled two fine ports—Cenchreae on the Aegean to the east and Lechaeum on the Gulf of Corinth, an inlet leading to the Ionian Sea, to the west. In ancient times, smaller ships avoided the treacherous two-hundred-mile journey around the Peloponnesus by being dragged on rollers across the isthmus. Emperor Nero attempted to build a canal across the four-mile–wide isthmus, but such a project was not realized until 1893.

A thriving commercial center, Corinth was also noted for its wealth, indulgence, and immorality. Its worship center on the Acrocorinth was dedicated to Aphrodite, the goddess of love. Strabo (64 B.C.–A.D. 21) reports that there were once a thousand temple prostitutes serving there, but it is not certain that this was the case in Paul's day.

Paul spent a year and a half teaching the word of God in Corinth during his second missionary journey (Acts 18:11). With the assistance

Shops in the marketplace (agora) of Corinth. *John McRay.*

of Silas and Timothy and a tent-making couple, Aquila and Priscilla, an important church was established there. From Corinth, in A.D. 51, Paul wrote two Epistles—First and Second Thessalonians—in which he corrected some misunderstandings concerning Christian conduct and prophetic events.

After the church at Corinth was firmly established, Paul left the city, accompanied by Priscilla and Aquila, and crossed the Aegean (from Cenchreae) to Ephesus, where his tent-making associates remained. Acts 18:22 records that Paul returned to Antioch after landing at Caesarea, concluding his second missionary journey (late autumn of A.D. 52). He had been gone for two and a half years and had traveled approximately two thousand miles.

Paul's Third Missionary Journey (Acts 18:23–21:16)

Paul embarked on his third journey from Antioch in the spring of A.D. 53. Once again he headed north through the Cilician Gates to visit the churches of southern Galatia and Phrygia that he had established on his first journey. But Paul's ultimate destination appears to have been Ephesus, which he had visited briefly while homeward bound on his second journey (Acts 18:19).

Ephesus, the foremost city of Asia Minor in Paul's day, is situated on the mouth of the Cayster River, which empties into the Aegean Sea. The importance of the city was threefold—commercial, religious, and political. Ephesus was the terminus of the great trade route that passed through Asia Minor from Mesopotamia. The harbor, which was maintained against silting by regular dredging, was also ideally situated on the north-south route along Asia Minor's coast, but neglect of the harbor eventually led to the demise of the city. As a religious center, Ephesus was the guardian of the temple of Artemis (Diana), the mother goddess of the region. Her image, according to legend, fell from heaven and was maintained in a splendid temple (Acts 19:35). An annual spring festival devoted to the worship of Artemis included athletic, dramatic, and musical contests. Ephesus was politically important as the capital of the Roman province of Asia, and there the Roman governor resided. The theater at Ephesus (Acts 19:29) seated 25,000. From the theater, the marble-paved Arcadian Way led westward to the harbor.

Paul spent approximately three years ministering in Ephesus (Acts 20:31), longer than in any other city. He obviously recognized the strategic importance of Ephesus for reaching all of the province with the gospel. Indeed, during his two years of teaching in the school of Tyrannus, "all the residents of Asia heard the word of the Lord, both Jews and Greeks" (Acts 19:10). Paul was assisted in this outreach by such

Paul's Third Missionary Journey

able disciples as Timothy, Erastus, Gaius, and Aristarchus. It was probably during this period that the churches of the Lycus Valley—Hierapolis, Laodicea, and Colossae (Col. 1:2; 4:13)—were founded. During his ministry at Ephesus (probably in the spring of A.D. 56), Paul responded to some troubling reports he had received concerning the church at Corinth. In the Epistle known as First Corinthians, Paul rebuked the church divisions and disorders and replied to a number of inquiries the Corinthians had raised (1 Cor. 7:1; 8:1; 12:1; 16:1).

A riot staged by Ephesian silversmiths, whose business had been hurt by Paul's preaching (Acts 19:23–25), led to Paul's departure from the city. He then went to Macedonia (Acts 20:1) where he undoubtedly visited the churches at Philippi and Thessalonica that had been estab-

Ruins of the Fountain of Memnius, Ephesus. *Guy P. Duffield.*

lished on his second journey. While ministering in Macedonia in the autumn of A.D. 56, Paul wrote his second letter to the church at Corinth, both correcting some misunderstandings regarding his authority and ministry and encouraging the collection for the Jerusalem saints. Paul then journeyed south to Corinth, from which he wrote his Epistle to the Romans some time during the winter of A.D. 56/57. His purpose in writing this letter was to set forth a thorough statement of the gospel message and to prepare the church for his intended visit.

Heading north again from Corinth to Macedonia, Paul next sailed from Philippi to Troas, where he spent a week ministering (Acts 20:3–12) before continuing south by ship along the coast. Paul's eventual destination was Jerusalem, and he wanted to arrive by the feast of Pentecost (Acts 20:16), but he paused long enough at Miletus to summon and bid farewell to the elders of the church at Ephesus (Acts 20:17–38). Departing from Miletus, Paul continued by sea to Caesarea and ministered there for several days before ascending the hill country to Jerusalem. The apostle arrived in the Holy City late in May, A.D. 57. His third journey, from Antioch to Jerusalem, had taken four years and involved approximately 2,700 miles of travel.

Paul's Return to Jerusalem and Internment in Caesarea

On his return to Jerusalem, Paul was welcomed by the brethren as he shared the results of his missionary travels. The church leaders, however, were concerned about reports that Paul had encouraged believing Jews to forsake the laws and customs of Judaism. The apostle was urged to go with four of the converts to the temple to be purified, thus demonstrating that he had not abandoned his ancestral faith. Paul agreed, but his conduct was misinterpreted. Recognized there by some of the Jews who had opposed him in the province of Asia, Paul was accused of "teaching men against the people" and of defiling the temple by bringing Gentiles into the inner courts (Acts 21:28), a charge that was apparently untrue.

The ensuing riot in the temple area resulted in the intervention of the Roman tribune and Paul's arrest. Although the tribune honored Paul's request to "speak to the people" (Acts 21:39), the apostle's words were unheeded by the restless crowd. Paul was taken into custody and next allowed to plead his case before the high priests and the Sanhedrin. When it became obvious that the Sadducees and Pharisees were bitterly divided in their opinion about Paul, the tribune once again placed him under custody, pending further examination. Learning of a plot to assassinate Paul, the official secretly sent him by night via Antipatris to Caesarea, which had become the seat of the Roman procurator after the death of Herod Agrippa I. There Paul was tried by Felix, the governor, and imprisoned for two years, during which time he was allowed a few privileges (Acts 24). Festus, Felix's successor, also examined Paul, but he then decided to lay the case before King Agrippa II, honoring the apostle's request that—as a Roman citizen (Acts 22:27–28)—his fate should be determined by "Caesar's tribunal" (Acts 25:10). After hearing Paul's defense, the king could make no other decision but to order that Paul be escorted to Rome for final resolution of his case (Acts 26).

Paul's Journey to Rome (Acts 27:1–28:16)

Under guard, Paul set sail from Caesarea with Luke (note "we" in Acts 27:1), Aristarchus (cf. Col. 4:10), and some other prisoners, in the late summer or early autumn of A.D. 59. Luke's account of the voyage and shipwreck is truly unique among biblical materials. Containing an abundance of geographical and navigational terms, it is regarded as one of the most instructive documents of ancient seamanship. The ship on which Paul embarked from Caesarea had its home port at Adramyttium, southeast of Troas, and would be stopping at the various ports of Asia Minor. Julius, the centurion, knew that he would find a ship bound for Rome at one of those ports. They traveled north to Sidon and then along the southern coast of Asia Minor to Myra, one of the chief ports of the grain fleet that carried wheat from Alexandria to

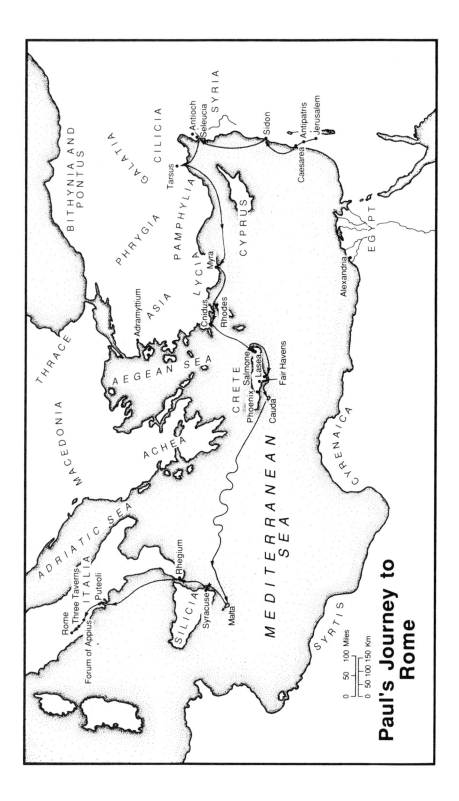

Paul's Journey to Rome

Rome. Julius then secured passage for Paul and his companions on one of those ships and they set off for Rome (Acts 27:6).

Sailing on the Mediterranean in ancient times was seasonal, being considered safe mainly during the spring and summer months. Transitional seasons, subject to sudden winds and storms, existed during the months of September through mid-November and February through March. Mid-November through January was regarded as "off season" for Mediterranean travel, since small sailing vessels could easily be dashed to pieces by the sea's sudden winter storms.

By the time Paul and his companions arrived at Fair Havens on Crete, "the fast" (Day of Atonement, October 5) had already passed, and the dangerous transitional season was upon them (Acts 27:9). Dismissing Paul's experienced counsel (cf. 2 Cor. 11:25), they set out to winter in Phoenix, which had a harbor offering better protection against the winter winds.

En route to Phoenix, the wind changed and the ship was caught by a northeasterly gale ("Euraquilo") that pushed them from the safety of Crete's shores to the storm-tossed waters of the central Mediterranean Sea (Sea of Adria). After fourteen days adrift, the ship approached the island of Malta. As the crew attempted to beach the stricken vessel in a small bay, the ship ran aground on a reef and was soon being broken up by the pounding waves and crashing surf. Providentially, all 276 passengers and crew arrived safely on land.

After spending the winter (November through January) on Malta, where the travelers were hospitably treated, Julius secured passage for his prisoners on an Alexandrian ship headed for Rome. Stopping along the way at Syracuse (on Sicily) and Rhegium (at the toe of Italy's "boot"), the party finally disembarked at Puteoli (modern Pozzuoli), the great emporium for the Alexandrian wheat fleet in the Bay of Naples. (Just across the bay was Pompeii, which was later buried under twenty feet of volcanic debris when Mount Vesuvius erupted in A.D. 79.) Paul visited with some believers in Puteoli and was then taken by land along the famous Appian Way toward Rome. Christians who had heard of his arrival came out to escort him. Some met him at Appii Forum (forty-three miles south of Rome) and others at Three Inns (thirty-three miles south of Rome). Thus, late in February of A.D. 60, Paul realized his wish to come to that all-powerful city on the Tiber— Rome—which served as the very hub of the Mediterranean world.

The city of Rome developed on the Tiber River at a ford that was indispensable for traveling between northern and southern Italy. An important east-west route from the sea to the mountains ran through the same general area. The ridges surrounding the Tiber Valley (Rome's famous seven hills) provided hilltop fortifications and places of refuge in times of attack. The community that clustered around these significant topographical features eventually developed into the city of Rome, capital of the Roman Empire.

When Paul entered Rome through the Porta Capena, over which ran an aqueduct, he received his first view of the Circus Maximus. This enormous area, designed for chariot races, had a seating capacity of an estimated 200,000. To the right of the Circus Maximus, Paul would have gazed up at the palaces of the Caesars that crowned Palatine Hill. On the other side of the hill was the Roman forum and its magnificent temples and senate, where Paul may have appeared before the emperor. At the west end of the forum was the Mamertinum Prison where, according to tradition, Paul and Peter were later imprisoned before their execution. Half a mile farther west were the Baths of Nero, built by the reigning emperor (A.D. 54–68). The Colosseum, so impressive to visitors today, was not dedicated until A.D. 80 and thus was not contemporary with Paul's visit.

Rather than being confined in prison, Paul was placed under house arrest and remained in his own rented quarters under the supervision of the Praetorian guard (cf. Acts 28:16, 23, 30). This arrangement gave him a great deal of freedom for ministry and interaction with visitors. Luke records that for two full years Paul continued to preach the kingdom of God and teach concerning the Lord Jesus "quite openly and unhindered" (Acts 28:31). The apostle wrote at least four Epistles during this period—Ephesians, Philippians, Colossians, and Philemon. Paul rejoices in his letter to the Philippians that the circumstance of his imprisonment "has really served to advance the gospel," for his witness penetrated the Praetorian guard and even Caesar's household (Phil. 1:12–13; 4:22).

Paul's Life After the Events in Acts

It appears that Paul's accusers never showed up in Rome and—without an indictment and witnesses—a trial failed to materialize (cf. Acts 28:21). After two years of confinement in Rome (Acts 28:30), Paul was released from prison and was able to continue his ministry throughout the Mediterranean world. Exactly what happened in Paul's life and ministry after Acts 28 is somewhat of a puzzle. Yet, many clues are provided in his letters, especially his Pastoral Epistles (1 and 2 Timothy, and Titus), which were written during the period after this first Roman imprisonment.

Since Paul had written to Philemon requesting that he prepare him a lodging (Philem. 22), he probably first headed for Asia Minor after leaving Rome. The logical route to Philemon's home in Colossae would

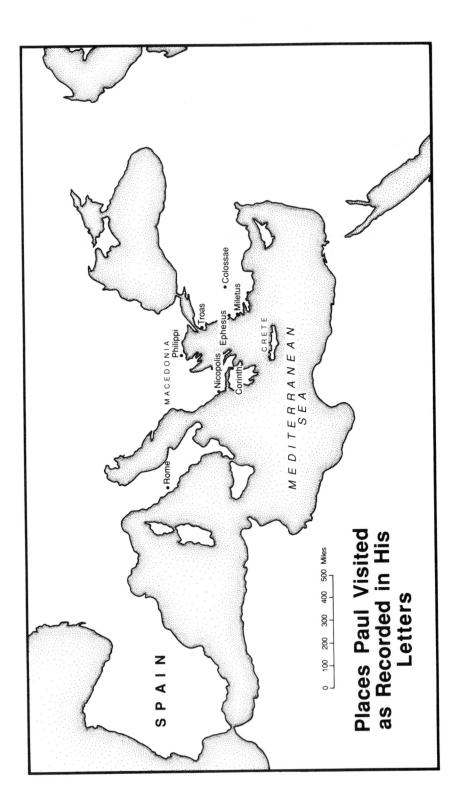

Places Paul Visited
as Recorded in His
Letters

be to sail to Ephesus and then follow the Meander River to the Lycus Valley. Visiting believers in both Colossae and Ephesus, Paul departed for Macedonia, leaving Timothy in Ephesus to continue the work (1 Tim. 1:3). While in Macedonia, Paul undoubtedly fulfilled his desire to visit Philippi (Phil. 1:25; 2:24). During this stay in Macedonia, Paul wrote Timothy with the hope of joining him in Ephesus soon. But, in case of delay, Paul set forth instructions concerning church policy and practice (1 Tim. 3:14). Paul may have actually revisited Ephesus and remained there for some time, ministering to the believers.

At this point, Paul's itinerary becomes more speculative. It is believed that sometime during this later period of Paul's ministry, he realized his desire to journey to Spain (Rom. 15:28). Clement of Rome wrote in his Epistle to the Corinthians that Paul journeyed to "the extreme limit of the west," a phrase understood to refer to the Spanish peninsula (1 Clement 5:7). Since the Muratorian Canon (A.D. 170) also mentions Paul's journey to Spain we can assume that a trip to Spain by Paul was accepted by the early church as historical fact.

Next, it would be logical for Paul to have visited Crete on his return voyage from Spain. After a successful ministry on the island, he departed, leaving Titus to complete the follow-up and appoint elders in every city (Titus 1:5). The details of Paul's life are even less certain at this point, but references indicate that he was in Asia Minor (2 Tim. 4:13, 20) and Greece (Titus 3:12; 2 Tim. 4:20). Perhaps he traveled to Asia Minor first, visiting Miletus—where he left the ailing Trophimus (2 Tim. 4:20)—and then journeying on to Troas. It appears that at this time Paul was being pursued by the Roman authorities. It may have been because of an arrest or a quick escape from the authorities that Paul left his cloak, books, and parchments in Troas (2 Tim. 4:13). The apostle may have written Titus from Asia Minor at this time, requesting that he join him in Nicopolis for the winter (Titus 3:12). Paul was apparently on his way to Nicopolis when he wrote the Epistle to Titus that instructed him regarding his ministry to the Cretans. When Paul wrote to Timothy from Rome during his final imprisonment, he mentioned that "Erastus remained at Corinth" (2 Tim. 4:20). This may indicate that Paul was also at Corinth again sometime before his arrest.

Paul was arrested a second time and brought once again to Rome (2 Tim. 1:8, 16–17). During this imprisonment, he was treated more harshly (2 Tim. 2:9) and anticipated death as the ultimate outcome (2 Tim. 4:6–8). From the Mamertinum Prison, adjacent to the Roman forum, he wrote to Timothy and requested that he join him before winter (2 Tim. 4:21).

Paul's martyrdom is placed by Eusebius in the thirteenth year of

Mamertinum Prison. According to tradition, Paul and Peter were held here before their deaths. *John McRay.*

Nero (the year 2083, commencing October, A.D. 67), although Jerome places it in A.D. 68. Paul's death probably occurred in the spring of A.D. 68, for he had hoped Timothy could join him before winter. According to tradition, Paul was beheaded with a sword outside the gates of Rome on the Ostian Way and buried in the catacombs south of the city. What seems reasonably certain is that he suffered a martyr's death. More importantly, the interpretation of the Christian faith and its spread throughout the world are so interwoven with the apostolic ministry and theology of Paul that neither can be considered apart from this man and his work. Few figures stand so high in the esteem of the church through the centuries.

Rome's Destruction of Jerusalem

The fall of Jerusalem to the Roman legions in A.D. 70 brought the early apostolic age to a close. Peter had been martyred under the Neronian persecution of A.D. 64. Paul, too, was gone. There were some apostles, including John, whose ministries extended beyond the date of Jerusalem's destruction, but—in a very real sense—A.D. 70 marked the end of an era.

Upon the death of Agrippa I in A.D. 44 (Acts 12:23), Emperor

Claudius had decided to return Judea to the rule of Roman procurators, whose subsequent corruption and cruelty helped ignite a revolt by the Jews. In A.D. 66, tensions between the Jews and Greeks at Caesarea led to a clash that resulted in the Jews being forced to leave the city. When reports of this expulsion reached Jerusalem, rioting broke out among the Jews. It was late summer of that year before Cestius Gallus, governor of Syria, was able to start south from Antioch with forty thousand soldiers to quell the rebellion. He marched to Jerusalem and attacked the fortified city, but it was not to be vanquished. The Jews resisted valiantly and Gallus was forced into a humiliating retreat. When word of his failure reached Rome, the current emperor, Nero, appointed his best general, Titus Flavius Vespasian, to bring the area to its knees with three legions of soldiers.

Vespasian amassed his troops at Ptolemais and was able to subjugate Galilee by the end of A.D. 67. He then turned his attention to crushing opposition in Samaria, Perea, and Idumea. By the next summer, Vespasian's position in Palestine was sufficiently secure for him to lay siege to Jerusalem. He was about to do so when word arrived from Rome of Nero's death. After an accession crisis in Rome—during which three new emperors were overthrown (Galba, Otho, and Vitellius)—the army proclaimed Vespasian emperor. In the spring of A.D. 70, Vespasian ascended the throne in Rome. After a nearly two-year lull, Vespasian sent his son Titus with four legions and auxiliary troops (approximately eighty thousand soldiers) to bring Jerusalem to submission. Although Titus offered the offenders a chance to surrender, the refusal of the Jews brought on a Roman siege. After breaking through the two outer walls, the Romans launched an attack on the Antonia Fortress and Herod's palace. The fortress was captured and razed. On August 6, temple activities ceased, after which it was entered and burned on the 9th of Ab (about August 28). The Upper City was overthrown and Herod's palace captured about a month later. Only then did Jewish resistance cease. According to Josephus, over a million Jews perished in the assault on the city of Jerusalem. The survivors were taken captive to work as slaves and the city was leveled. The ruined city was placed under occupation by the Tenth Legion, while Titus returned to Rome in triumph, displaying slaves and temple treasure as fruits of his victory. The Arch of Titus near Rome's Forum commemorates this triumphal return.

Resistance by the Jews to Roman rule did not end with the fall of Jerusalem. The fighting dragged on another three years, until the Romans captured the remote mountain fortress of Masada. But Silva's victory there was an empty one, as the over nine hundred defenders took their own lives rather than subject themselves to the slavery of

Romans carrying away the menorah from the temple in Jerusalem in 70 A.D., as depicted on the Arch of Titus in Rome. *John McRay.*

Rome. Following Rome's victory over the Jews in Palestine, Vespasian decreed the termination of Jewish religion and worship. Although the priesthood and Sanhedrin were abolished, even the world's most powerful political and military force could not quench the flame of Judaism. The faith of Abraham's people endures to this day—in both the independent country of Israel and other national states around the world.

Epilogue to the Period: The Revelation of John

The life and ministry of the apostle John continued after the destruction of Jerusalem and is worthy of special mention. Irenaeus wrote that John resided at Ephesus, where he served as bishop and wrote his Gospel, probably around A.D. 85 (although some have argued well for a pre-A.D. 70 date of authorship). John wrote his three Epistles from Ephesus around A.D. 90. Later, in the fifteenth year of Domitian (A.D. 81–96), he was exiled to the island of Patmos where, at the close of Domitian's reign, he wrote Revelation. Victorinus records in his third-century commentary on Revelation 10:11 that John wrote Revelation on Patmos and was liberated when Domitian was assassinated in A.D. 96.

After his Patmos exile, John resided again in Ephesus and spent the closing years of his life visiting the Asian churches, ordaining elders, and ministering. Irenaeus recorded that John lived in Ephesus until the time of Emperor Trajan (A.D. 98–117). Polycrates, Bishop of Ephesus (A.D. 189–198), states that John was buried in Ephesus.

John's Revelation contains letters to seven churches of Asia Minor. A study of New Testament geography would be incomplete without some attention to the historical and geographical background of these churches.

Ephesus

Ephesus, capital of the Roman province of Asia, was a thriving commercial and religious center. Paul had viewed his mission at Ephesus as crucial to the evangelization of Asia Minor. Indeed, the city's central location and influence earned it an important place in biblical and ecclesiastical history. At the time of John's writing, the church of Ephesus was troubled by false teachers and lacked its former high level of devotion. The city declined after the fifth century A.D. and

The Churches of Revelation

is now uninhabited ruins. For further information on Ephesus, refer to "Paul's Third Missionary Journey."

Smyrna

Smyrna was located about thirty-five miles north of Ephesus at the head of a gulf that provided a fine port and made the city an important trade center. One of the main inland trade routes went from Smyrna through the Hermus Valley to the interior of Asia Minor. The city was also an educational center and boasted fine schools of science and medicine. Of religious significance as well, Smyrna, from A.D. 23 on, was the center of the imperial cult (emperor worship), symbolized by its temple to Tiberius. The city was also noted for its temples to Zeus and Sybele. The gospel probably reached Smyrna at an early date, presumably as a result of Paul's ministry at Ephesus (cf. Acts 19:10). Polycarp served as bishop of Smyrna and was martyred there around A.D. 156 when he refused to recant his faith. As today's Izmir, Smyrna continues to be one of the most important cities in Asia Minor (Turkey).

Pergamum

Pergamum (modern Bergama) was located about fifty miles north of Smyrna and fifteen miles from the sea. To reach the city from the Aegean coast, one could travel up the Caicus River, which was navigable for small craft. Pergamum had a fine library and was the place where parchment was first used. The city was chiefly known as the religious center of the province of Asia. Here, four beautiful temples

Pergamos (Pergamum), now Bergama, Turkey. *Guy P. Duffield.*

were erected for the great cults honoring Zeus, Athena, Dionysus, and Asclerius. The first temple dedicated to the imperial cult (in honor of Augustus) was built at Pergamum in 29 B.C. Pergamum's many pagan temples and idolatry prompted John to refer to the city as the place "where Satan's throne is" (Rev. 2:13). Under Roman rule, Pergamum ranked with Ephesus and Smyrna as one of the three great cities in the Roman province of Asia and it, too, was an early seat of Christianity.

Thyatira

Thyatira (modern Akhisar) was an important manufacturing center approximately forty miles southeast of Pergamum. The city lay in a valley on the road from Pergamum to Laodicea. Thyatira was especially noted for its trade guilds, which were more completely organized here than in any other ancient city of the time. (Their meetings were generally bound up with acts of pagan worship and immorality.) Dye manufacturing was an important industry in Thyatira, and its brilliant pigments are still highly prized. Garment making, pottery, and brass working have been important to the city's economy for centuries. In its early days, Thyatira had a temple dedicated to Tyrimnos, an ancient sun god. The gospel may have been brought to the city by Lydia of Thyatira, who was converted under Paul's ministry in Philippi (Acts 16:14). The city is commended in Revelation for its deeds, love, faith, service, and perseverance, but rebuked for tolerating the false prophetess "Jezebel" (Rev. 2:19–29).

Sardis

Sardis, in the western part of the Roman province of Asia, lay about thirty miles southeast of Thyatira. The ancient city stood on the northern slope of a mountain with a river flowing at its base. This setting rendered the city almost impregnable, and Sardis was once the capital of the kingdom of Lydia. In A.D. 17, the city was destroyed by a great earthquake. Although rebuilt by Tiberius, its former glory and importance were never completely recovered. The ancient city was noted for its fruits and wool. The making and dyeing of woolen garments was the chief industry of Sardis (cf. Rev. 3:4–5). Pagan worship at Sardis had a sexual emphasis focused on Sybele, a goddess similar to Diana in Ephesus. Its Christian church was probably founded during Paul's ministry at Ephesus (Acts 19:10). John's message to the church in Revelation 3:1–6 implies that its members were notoriously soft and fainthearted.

Philadelphia

Philadelphia, twenty-eight miles southeast of Sardis, was a wealthy trade center in the wine-producing district of Asia Minor. The city was situated on a 650-foot terrace above the banks of the Cogamus River at the threshold of a fertile plateau from which its agricultural prosperity was derived. Philadelphia was called "Little Athens" because of its magnificent temples and public buildings. Dionysus, the god of wine, was the chief deity of the city. The Christian believers at Philadelphia were commended by John for their deeds and their obedience and loyalty to Christ (Rev. 3:8). Of the seven churches of Revelation, only Philadelphia was exempted from John's condemnation or criticism.

Ruins of the North Theater, Laodicea. Hierapolis is in the distance. *Levant.*

Laodicea

Laodicea was located in the Lycus Valley on an important crossroads forty-five miles southeast of Philadelphia and about ninety miles east of Ephesus. Besides being a prosperous banking and commercial center, Laodicea was the manufacturing center for clothing made from the glossy black wool of the sheep raised in the area. It was also a center for medical studies and was noted for its production of a salve used to cure eye diseases (cf. Rev. 3:18). Because Laodicea had no local water supply, water was brought by conduit from a hot springs some distance away. The water no doubt arrived lukewarm, like the spiritual condition of the Laodiceans (Rev. 3:16). Laodicea, with the other Lycus Valley churches (Hierapolis and Colossae), was probably established during Paul's ministry at Ephesus (Acts 19:10), perhaps through the work of Epaphras (Col. 4:12, 13).

16

Israel Since the Biblical Period
A.D. 70 to Present Times

Because the Palestinian lands have a special place in the history and development of three great world religions—Judaism, Christianity, and Islam—interest in this region extends beyond that of the biblical period. A brief survey of the history of "the land of the Bible" from A.D. 70 will serve as a fitting conclusion to our study. (For the purposes of simplicity, all dates hereafter will refer to the *anno Domini* era.)

The Roman Period (70–330)

Although the fall of Jerusalem in the year 70 to the Roman legions under Titus brought an end to the second-temple period, it did not completely snuff out Jewish resistance to Roman rule. Reports that Emperor Hadrian (76–138) was planning to found a Roman colony in Jerusalem resulted in an uprising known as the Second Jewish Revolt. This rebellion, which broke out in 131, was led by Bar Kokhba (Bar Kosiba), who was regarded by many Jews to be the Messiah. The rebels managed to force the Roman soldiers and citizens from Jerusalem. Temple sacrifices were resumed and new coins were issued by the Jewish administration.

In the end, however, Roman might prevailed over the Jewish insurgents. In the fourth year of the revolt, the Jews were once again forced to abandon Jerusalem and were driven into the fortress of Bethther. The Jews resisted courageously, but by the end of the summer of 135, the fortress walls were breached and its defenders slaughtered.

With Jewish opposition subdued, Hadrian proceeded with his plans for Jerusalem. The city was razed and rebuilt in Roman style. This is still reflected in the divisions of the Old City today. Hadrian built a temple dedicated to Venus (Aphrodite) over the site of Calvary. Where the Jewish temple once stood, he erected a temple to Jupiter and a statue of himself. Jerusalem was renamed *Aelia Capitolina* after Hadrian's middle name (Aelius) and the god Jupiter Capitolinus. By the decree of Hadrian, Jews were prohibited from living in what was once their Holy City.

During the five hundred years that followed the Second Jewish Revolt, the land enjoyed a good measure of security from invasion or conquest. Judea became a consular province of Rome, garrisoned permanently by the Tenth and Sixth Legions. Though ruined and impoverished, "Syria Palestine," as the Romans called it, still had a population of 800,000 Jews.

Later Roman emperors, particularly Septimius Severus (193–211) and Alexander Severus (222–235), were more benevolent in their dealings with both Jews and Christians. When Constantine I came to power in 306, he showed tolerance for all religions in the empire. Even Judaism was regarded as a "permitted religion," although Jews were still banned from living in Jerusalem. Constantine, however, made two decisions that had a significant effect on the land of Israel. First, he chose Christianity for himself and his empire (313). Second, he moved his capital from pagan Rome to Byzantium, which he renamed Constantinople (330). Thus began what is regarded as the Byzantine period of Roman rule over Palestine.

The Byzantine Period (330–634)

The Byzantine era was marked by considerable building activity in Palestine, especially after the Council of Nicaea (325) decided to preserve the holy places in Jerusalem. Helena, Constantine's mother, traveled in the Holy Land soon afterward and initiated the construction of a number of basilicas, including the Church of the Holy Sepulchre in Jerusalem and the Church of the Nativity in Bethlehem. A century later, Eudoxia, wife of Theodosius II, commissioned the St. Stephen basilica, the restoration of the city walls and Golden Gate, and a shrine at the Pool of Siloam. Justinian (527–565) was also an enthusiastic builder of churches at holy sites. It has been said that Jerusalem never had so many churches as under Justinian. During these days, Palestine was becoming more and more a place of pilgrimage, and the land was becoming thoroughly Christianized.

Growth and prosperity in Palestine came to a quick conclusion in 614, when the land was conquered by the Persians under King Chosroes II. Many churches, shrines, and monasteries, including the Holy Sepulchre, were desecrated or ruined completely. In addition to prisoners, the Persians carried off the traditional "true cross," which had been discovered by Helena in the fourth century. Persian rule did not last long. The Byzantine emperor Heraclius invaded Persia and quickly regained control over Palestine. On March 30, 630, he passed through the Golden Gate and returned the "true cross" to the Church of the Holy Sepulchre. Byzantine rule had been reestablished over the land, but out of the desert was soon to appear the crescent of Islam.

The Early Arab Period (634–1099)

Although the Byzantine rulers continued to dominate remnants of the Roman Empire until the Ottoman conquest of Constantinople in 1453, the appearance of Islam and the Moslem conquest soon deprived the empire of the lands of Israel and Egypt.

This political transition began with the rise of the prophet Mohammed (570–632), who escaped assassination in Mecca and fled to Medina, where he was able to establish a theocratic state that soon engulfed all of Arabia and large parts of North Africa and Western Asia. Shortly after the death of Mohammed, Caliph Omar Ibn el-Khattab led an army into Palestine and conquered the entire area. In 638, he captured Jerusalem, cleared the debris from the temple site, and erected a simple structure for Moslem worship. Later, the Moslem ruler Abdul Malik Ibn-Marwan built the famous Dome of the Rock (691), now called Haram esh-Sharif, "the Noble Enclosure."

The Jews generally fared well under Islamic rule. Jerusalem was spared destruction when captured, and Jews were allowed to return to the land and live in Jerusalem, their sacred city. From about 700 to 1000, the Jewish people flourished in the region. Jewish communities and learning centers developed in such places as Tiberias, Haifa, Ashkelon, and Gaza.

Toward the end of this early period of Arab rule, the political situation became turbulent, as governing authorities were being challenged. After Egypt became an independent power and extended its

The Golden Gate, Jerusalem. *John McRay.*

influence over both Palestine and Syria, the rulers were less tolerant of Christian pilgrimages to the holy city, and travel by Europeans across Moslem territory became increasingly disrupted.

These difficulties culminated toward the end of the eleventh century, when the Turkish Seljuks advanced into much of the Byzantine territory and eventually captured the lands of Palestine. These Turkish "infidels" mistreated Christian pilgrims in Jerusalem and charged heavy fees for visits to the city's holy sites. Soon appeals were sent to the papacy in Rome, asking that the sacred places of Christianity be liberated. The eventual answer to these pleas was the bloody era of the Crusades.

The Crusader Period (1099–1291)

The Crusades (Spanish *crusada*, "marked with a cross") involved a series of ostensibly religious wars undertaken by the Christians of Western Europe for the immediate purpose of recovering the Holy Sepulchre and similar holy places in Jerusalem. In a broader sense, the Crusades were a papal-sanctioned campaign directed against anyone declared to be an enemy of Christ. Economic factors undoubtedly also motivated these "holy wars," since there was rich potential for trade and commerce in the Moslem countries and little protection available through the now-weakened Byzantine leaders. Also important were the plans of Pope Urban II, leader of a reform movement that sought to channel all mankind's activities into the service of the Christian God and establish the Roman Catholic pope—the "vicar of Christ"—as ecclesiastic ruler of the church universal. The latter aim would indirectly involve healing the breach that had developed between the papacy in Rome and the Byzantine (Greek Orthodox) patriarch and clergy.

Urban's appeal for holy warriors drew volunteers from many parts of Western Europe. Armies arose in northern and southern France and in southern Italy. These military units were joined by bands of common people and their popular leaders. At intervals in 1096 and 1097, the forces of European Crusaders (or "Franks," as they were called) assembled at Constantinople, where they were joined by their Byzantine counterparts.

In this First Crusade, the loosely allied armies advanced across Asia Minor and into Syria, en route to their ultimate goal—Jerusalem. Not all of these warriors reached the Holy City, since many died along the way from hunger, disease, and sorties against the Islamic bands they encountered. In June of 1099, a force of twelve thousand Crusaders reached Jerusalem, besieged its walls for several weeks, and eventually claimed the city for Christianity. It is estimated that about forty thousand of Jerusalem's inhabitants were slaughtered—both Moslems and Jews—with their blood mingling with that of the "liberators." A new basilica for the Holy Sepulchre was constructed, and the Dome of the Rock was promptly renamed *Templum Domini*, "temple of the Lord"—all part of the general aim of establishing a Latin Christian kingdom in Palestine, with Jerusalem as its capital. The city and its environs were classified as a feudal kingdom (not as an ecclesiastical state, as some desired), and three other sovereignties were named: Edessa, Antioch, and Tripoli.

The success of the First Crusade was followed by an all-too-brief period of relative peace and prosperity in the area, despite fragmented attempts by Moslem factions to regain control. But, by 1144, the Islamic forces had staged a comeback, as Edessa was recaptured and other Christian strongholds plagued by their attacks. The rising threat from the Moslems sparked the Second Crusade. New forces arrived from Europe to reinforce the waning Christian dominance over Asia Minor, Syria, and Palestine, but the Franks were relatively unsuccessful on all fronts. After abandoning the key city of Damascus, they suffered a loss of prestige among their Byzantine allies and the formerly submissive Islamics, who had not yet been able to unify their opposition to the Christian interlopers.

Newly combined forces of several Moslem leaders soon began to drive the Europeans from Palestine and Syria—a goal mainly accomplished through the efforts of Saladin (Sultan Salah-ed-Din), who had gradually been establishing a degree of religious and political harmony in the Islamic groups. Concurrently, Saladin had shrewdly avoided serious trouble with the Franks, built up his own army, and played on the reciprocal suspicions between the Franks and the Byzantines. By 1187, an internal power struggle had so weakened the Christian forces that Saladin was able to advance easily through much of Palestine and finally overwhelm the exhausted Frankish army at the Horns of Hattin, within sight of the Sea of Galilee. The brilliant military leader then proceeded to capture most of the now-defenseless cities, including Jerusalem.

Once again there was a cry for action from the papacy, which led to the Third Crusade, under the leadership of Richard I (the Lionhearted) of England, Philip II Augustus of France, and the German king and Holy Roman emperor, Frederick I Barbarossa. This Crusade (1189–1192) was basically a failure, although the Christian forces were able to maintain possession of the coastal plain and reestablish their supremacy in such cities as Caesarea, Athlit, and Acre (Ptolemais). Richard I was also able to gain permission for pilgrims to visit the Holy City, although Jerusalem itself remained under Moslem control.

When the port city of Acre fell to Sultan Qalawun in 1291, the major Crusade efforts essentially came to an end, although there were subsequent minor campaigns on behalf of Christianity in various parts of the Middle East, all of which were unsuccessful. The Fourth, Fifth, Sixth, Seventh, and Eighth Crusades likewise failed to unseat the Islamic powers, despite isolated and short-lived victories in a few locations. Although the ideal of the Crusades persisted for a few centuries thereafter, the economic and cultural developments of the European Renaissance, and the religious implications of the Protestant Reformation, were to turn the attention of Christians in other directions.

The ultimate results of the Crusades were far-reaching. One positive effect was the exchange between east and west of the many ideas, philosophical principles, material goods, and scientific discoveries that had taken place during the Crusader period. A second result was the decline of the Byzantine Empire, which never recovered from the disruption of the Fourth Crusade, during which the Franks had imposed Roman supremacy on their capital in Constantinople by installing a Latin emperor and Latin patriarch of the church. Perhaps the most important outcome of the Crusades was the military triumph of Islam in the Middle East, since only in Spain and the eastern Baltic coast did Christianity attain dominance.

One unfortunate result of the entire Crusades period was the rise of intolerance throughout the Mediterranean, Middle East, and European domains. In the Middle East, the firmly entrenched Moslems, who had originally been quite tolerant of their Christian and Jewish subjects, reacted to the violence of the Crusaders by persecution of any members of both groups who remained in the Islamic lands. Intolerance appeared in Europe, too, as the harassment of Jews and members of the Greek Orthodox church that had first surfaced during the First Crusade continued in many parts of the western world during the Renaissance period and beyond.

After that brief survey of the entire Crusades period—which actually lasted until the mid-fifteenth century—we will return to the events following the failure of the last major Crusade.

The Mamluk Period (1291–1516)

Mamluks (Mamelukes; literally "owned men") served as a major component of Muslim armies as early as the ninth century A.D. Often these slave armies exploited the power vested in them and seized control over the legitimate political authorities. By the thirteenth century, Mamluks had succeeded in establishing dynasties of their own.

The Mamluk dynasty which ruled Egypt and Syria was originally a slave army, primarily of Turkish origin, under the control of the Al-Malik as-Salih Ayyub (1240-49). This army, led by Baybars, was commissioned to run the Turks out of Jerusalem, a feat accomplished in 1244. Thus 250 years of Mamluk sovereignty in Palestine was inaugurated.

After the death of Ayyub, the Mamluk generals murdered his heir and established their own ruler, Aybek. Following a decisive battle with the Mongol invaders near Beth-shean, the able general Baybars I (1260-77) was elected sultan in Egypt and given the title, "The Ascendant King." Ruling Palestine from Cairo, Baybars is regarded as real founder of the Mamluk State.

The Mamluk period was characterized by almost continual conflict. Baybars halted the westward advance of the Mongols and drove the remaining Crusaders from their isolated strongholds in Palestine. From 1382 to 1516, almost the entire Middle East was governed by the Mamluks.

Culturally, the Mamluk period is known mainly for its achievements in historical writing and architecture. The Mamluk historians were prolific chroniclers and biographers. Their builders endowed the Middle East with some of its finest mosques, bridges, fountains, and tombs. Many of these structures can be recognized today by their massive stone domes offset by geometrical carvings. Baybar's symbol was the lion, which can still be seen on many monuments erected during his rule. Four lions can be seen on Jerusalem's St. Stephen's gate, also known as the "Lion's Gate."

The Ottoman Period (1517–1917)

By 1453, the Ottoman Turks had captured Constantinople, bringing the diminished and weakened Byzantine Empire to its knees. In its place arose Moslem Turkey and the beginnings of the Ottoman Empire. In 1517, as the Protestant Reformation was being sparked by Martin Luther in Germany, the city of Jerusalem was captured by the Turkish Sultan Selim on behalf of the Ottoman Empire. Jerusalem remained under Ottoman control for the next four hundred years.

The Jews enjoyed favorable treatment by the Ottomans. This was in marked contrast to the treatment they were then receiving in other regions, such as Spain and Portugal. Jews were invited to settle in Turkey and Palestine, and Jewish communities flourished in Tiberias, Acre, Gaza, Hebron, and Jerusalem. Safed, a city on a hill in Galilee,

St. Stephen's or Lions' Gate in the old wall of Jerusalem. *John McRay.*

became a significant center for Jewish spiritual life and scholarly studies.

Suleiman the Magnificent (1520–1566), who expanded the Ottoman Empire to its maximum extent and is regarded as its greatest ruler, spent great sums of money to restore and beautify Jerusalem. The walls and gates of the city were rebuilt. (These are the same walls seen by Jerusalem's visitors today.) Suleiman also provided the city with many lovely fountains and gave the Dome of the Rock a new glazed-tile exterior.

During the nineteenth century, the Ottoman Empire began to crumble. The government was plagued with corruption and threatened by external pressure from the stronger nations of Europe. The Crimean wars (1853–1856)—fought to halt Russia's expansion into the Balkans and end the dispute between the Greek Orthodox and Roman Catholics over guardianship of the holy places in Palestine—placed a severe financial drain on the Ottomans. During World War I (1914–1918), Turkey sided with Germany and Austria against the Allies. In 1917, General Allenby, commander of the British forces in the Middle East, led his troops against the Turks and their German allies in Palestine. Advancing from British-controlled Egypt, Allenby captured Beersheba in October, 1917. Several weeks later he led his men into Jerusalem, thus ending four hundred years of Ottoman Turkish rule.

The British military administration undertook measures to remedy the hardships created in Palestine during the war years, a task made more difficult by the rising level of hostilities between Arab nationals and the growing number of Zionist settlers who sought recognition and the homeland first proposed by Theodor Herzl in 1896. Both to secure their hold on the Palestinian lands and to recognize the rights of the Jewish people, the British government issued the Balfour Declaration on November 2, 1917, which formally recognized the Zionist principle. Although endorsed by the principal Allied powers, especially the United States, the terms of this document were so vague as to allow for many different interpretations. However, it did prepare the way for the ultimate establishment of the Jewish State of Israel.

The British Mandate (1917–1948)

On April 25, 1920, the Allied powers appointed Great Britain to govern Palestine and Transjordan, a decision approved two years later by the League of Nations. This led the way to increased Jewish immigration into Palestine, as Jews flocked to their homeland from eastern Europe and began to develop the country economically and intellectually. Early accomplishments included a medical center on Mount Scopus and Hebrew University. The Arab population continued to re-

The magnificent Dome of the Rock. The glazed-tile exterior was added by Suleiman in the sixteenth century. *Israel Tourist Bureau.*

sent the influx of Jews and hostilities became the "order of the day" for the duration of British rule.

In part to ease the growing concerns of the Arabs, the mandate was further interpreted in a 1922 statement of policy by Winston Churchill, then Britain's colonial secretary. The White Paper in effect rejected the earlier idea that Arab interests were to be subordinated to those of the Zionists, since it limited Jewish immigration and land purchase in Palestine. Although it pacified some in the Zionist organization, many Jews considered this paper a reversal of the Balfour Declaration. The Arabs, too, were divided in their opinion of the new policy, since some felt it did not go far enough in endorsing their rights and might eventually mean their extinction as a people.

Tensions continued to grow in Palestine until the outbreak of World War II. As widespread rioting erupted in 1939, the British issued another White Paper. Again, its principle satisfied neither side. The paper promised, after a period of ten years, the establishment of an independent Palestine in which Arabs and Jews would share authority. Meanwhile, Jewish immigration was to be severely limited, and the Arab farmer in certain parts of Palestine would be protected in his possession of the land. The Zionists, in particular, questioned the terms of the 1939 statement and appealed to the League of Nations for a determination as to whether it fulfilled the terms of the original mandate. A decision by the League was prevented by the outbreak of World War II.

The Palestinian Arabs maintained a relative neutrality during the second world war, but the Zionists generally cooperated fully with the Allies, because of their desire to gain political credibility and their hatred of Nazi Germany. Many Jewish units served with British military forces in the Middle East throughout the war years. Meanwhile, thousands of Jews sought to escape the death grip of Nazi Germany by seeking sanctuary in Palestine. Although many were turned away as "illegal" immigrants by British authorities, hundreds more arrived in leaky, overloaded vessels and established residency in what they considered their homeland. To protect themselves from ongoing Arab hostilities and prepare for what they predicted as a postwar struggle for survival, the Zionists equipped an underground defense unit, the Haganah.

When tensions and violence between Arab and Jew mounted in severity at the close of World War II, the British became virtually powerless to control the area, although several attempts to attain a peaceful compromise were made. In a final move to reach a solution, the British referred the Palestinian question to the newly formed United Nations, which voted on November 29, 1947, that Palestine should be partitioned into two independent countries—Jewish and

Arab. Jerusalem would be designated an "international enclave," accessible to all. Showing their immediate dissatisfaction with the terms of the proposal, Arab nationalists launched attacks on the Jewish section of the Holy City and other Jewish communities. A widespread war between Arab and Jew was well under way by May 15, 1948, when the British Mandate officially expired.

The State of Israel (from 1948)

On May 14, 1948, the day before the British mandate was to end, the Jews of Palestine announced the formation of a new, independent country—the State of Israel. The undeclared war between Arab and Israeli forces now became official. Bitter battles were fought as both sides tried to retain control of Jerusalem. The fighting continued until an armistice was worked out in 1949 that left Jerusalem a divided city. Jordan, the Arab state, controlled the Old City and lands to the east. Israel, the Jewish state, retained west Jerusalem and a narrow corridor of land that broadened at the coastal plain. The Hinnom Valley was part of a "no man's land" that divided the city. Once again, Jews were barred from visiting the temple area and their traditional place of lamentation and worship—the western wall.

Meanwhile, Israel's relationship with Egypt continued to be strained by Egypt's refusal to allow ships trading with Israel to use either the Suez Canal or the Gulf of Eilat, both of which the Egyptians controlled. This led to a second major conflict between Israel and her Arab neighbors. To deal with the economic boycott imposed on the nation by the Arab League, Israel invaded Egyptian-held Sinai in October of 1956 and quickly gained control of the region. The United States, however, pressed Israel for a prompt withdrawal, which was completed on March 8, 1957. A United Nations emergency force was established to help maintain peace along the Egyptian-Israeli border.

The Sinai campaign did not resolve the economic and international issues facing Israel. Egypt continued to interfere with Israeli shipping in the Suez Canal and Gulf of Eilat. This was brought to a crisis in late May of 1967, when Egypt's President Nasser closed the Tiron Straits to Israeli shipping and demanded a withdrawal of United Nations troops from the Egyptian-Israeli border. Anticipating unavoidable warfare, Israel initiated a preemptive strike. On the morning of June 5, Israeli warplanes bombed the airfields of their Arab neighbors—Egypt, Jordan, Syria, and Iraq. The fighting continued for six days (June 5–11), during which the Israelis gained control of Egypt's Sinai, Jordan's West Bank, and Syria's Golan Heights. The most significant result of the Six-Day war was that Jerusalem was brought under Israeli administration and the city was reunited.

The 1967 cease fire did little to bring Israel a lasting peace with her Arab neighbors. In 1973, Israeli-held Sinai was invaded by Egypt. Conflict with Syria and Arab-held southern Lebanon has continued in the north. As the psalmist exhorted, we must "pray for the peace of Jerusalem!" (Ps. 122:6), for while the city has been reunited, there is still conflict at Israel's borders. May the time soon come when "Shalom, my friend," will be more than just a daily greeting in the city of Jerusalem, when it will also characterize the spirit and condition of those who live there in peace and contentment with themselves and their neighbors.

Selected Bibliography

The following books and atlases will be helpful for further study of the Land of the Bible.

Books

Aharoni, Yohanan. *The Land of the Bible.* Revised and enlarged ed. Translated by A. F. Rainey. Philadelphia: The Westminster Press, 1979.

Avigad, Naham. *Discovering Jerusalem.* Nashville: Thomas Nelson, 1980.

Baly, Denis. *The Geography of the Bible.* New and revised ed. New York: Harper and Row, 1974.

Berrett, LaMar C. *Discovering the World of the Bible.* Nashville: Thomas Nelson, 1979.

Hoehner, Harold W. *Chronological Aspects of the Life of Christ.* Grand Rapids: Zondervan, 1977.

Orni, Efraim, and Efrat, Elisha. *Geography of Israel.* 3rd ed. Philadelphia: The Jewish Publication Society of America, 1971.

Owen, G. Fredrick. *Jerusalem.* Grand Rapids: Baker Book House, 1972.

———. *The Holy Land.* Grand Rapids: Baker Book House, 1977.

Pfeiffer, Charles F., ed. *The Biblical World.* Grand Rapids: Baker Book House, 1966.

Pfeiffer, Charles F., and Vos, Howard F. *The Wycliffe Historical Geography of the Bible Land*. Chicago: Moody Press, 1967.

Smith, George Adam. *The Historical Geography of the Holy Land*. London: Hodder & Stoughton, 1908.

Turner, George A. *Historical Geography of the Holy Land*. Washington, D.C.: Canon Press, 1973.

Vos, Howard F. *Beginnings in Bible Geography*. Chicago: Moody Press, 1973.

———. *Archaeology in Bible Lands*. Chicago: Moody Press, 1977.

Wilkinson, John. *The Jerusalem Jesus Knew*. Nashville: Thomas Nelson, 1978.

Wood, Leon. *A Survey of Israel's History*. Grand Rapids: Zondervan, 1970.

Atlases

Aharoni, Yohanan, and Avi-Yonah, Michael. *The Macmillan Bible Atlas*. New York: Macmillan, 1977.

Atlas of Israel. Jerusalem: Survey of Israel. Ministry of Labour. Amsterdam: Elsevier Publishing Company, 1970.

Baines, John, and Malek, Jaromir. *Atlas of Ancient Egypt*. Oxford: Phaidon Press, 1980.

Beitzel, Barry J. *The Moody Atlas of Bible Lands*. Chicago: Moody Press, 1985.

Baly, Denis, and Tushingham, A. D. *Atlas of the Biblical World*. New York: World Publishing, 1971.

Kraeling, Emil G., ed. *Rand McNally Bible Atlas*. New York: Rand McNally, 1956.

May, Herbert G., ed. *Oxford Bible Atlas*. 2nd ed. London: Oxford University Press, 1974.

Pfeiffer, Charles. *Baker's Bible Atlas*. Grand Rapids: Baker Book House, 1961.

Pritchard, James B., ed. *The Harper Atlas of the Bible*. New York: Harper and Row, 1987.

Vilnay, Zev. *The New Israel Atlas*. London: H. A. Humphrey, 1968.

Wright, George Ernest, and Flison, Floyd Vivian, eds. *The Westminster Historical Atlas to the Bible*. Philadelphia: Westminster Press, 1956.

Subject Index

Scripture Index